Copyright © M Publishing 2015

All rights reserved

No part of this publication may be reproduced, stored in or introduced into a retrieval system, or transmitted, in any form, or by any means (electronic, mechanical, photocopying, recording, or otherwise) without the prior written permission of the copyright owner.

Published by
M PUBLISHING

Printed by
Lightning Source, UK

A catalogue record for this book is available from the British Library

ISBN
978-1-909323-66-7

COLOURS
ON RICE PAPER

by
milena

M PUBLISHING

CONTENTS

FROM THE ARTIST

PAINTINGS ON RICE PAPER

flora
medieval saints
beyond thoughts
architecture
eros

WATERCOLOUR PAINTINGS

flora
architecture
portraits

PAINTINGS ON SILK

Note: The dimensions of each painting are shown in centimetres

FROM THE ARTIST

Unity – Harmony – Order are in the very foundation of the highest laws of Creation. Manifestation and beauty of this ever-present divine certainty are evident from micro to macro levels of life.

Light is one of the primordial creational forces. Each colour represents its specific vibrational aspect. Colours permeate and uniquely describe our environment – black being the source, or the total, of all of them. Forms around us are each a specific assemblage of energies. They are denser energy than the "empty" space of their surroundings.

After moving from watercolour to gauche, used in a manner of Chinese contemporary paintings on rice paper, I was able to paint the invisible with more technical tools in my hands. Hence, in my paintings, both realistic and abstract forms usually float in a field of vibrations not much different from their own colour. The relationship between an object and its background is therefore organic, and of an unbreakable unity. Forms seem to appear as if the viewer has just sharpened their focus in a blink of an eye, to recognise a particular ephemeral configuration within the ongoing colour (energy) interplay.

Colours convey information by appealing to the core of our being, which is built upon Divine Light – Sound – Fire elements, Love and the power of Thought.

Paintings on rice paper featured in this book are impregnated with the awareness of those primordial forces. Energy waves and titrations are often explicitly depicted throughout the composition of a given work. Hence, colour harmony and exceptional calmness are both a starting point and the resulting attributes of this artwork.

Since all harmonies and beauty speak directly to our divine essence, regardless of the field in which I express myself, my artistic interest has always been to create and offer these values to society.

I wish you enjoy my aesthetic findings about the objective world
summed up in "COLOURS on rice paper",

Milena

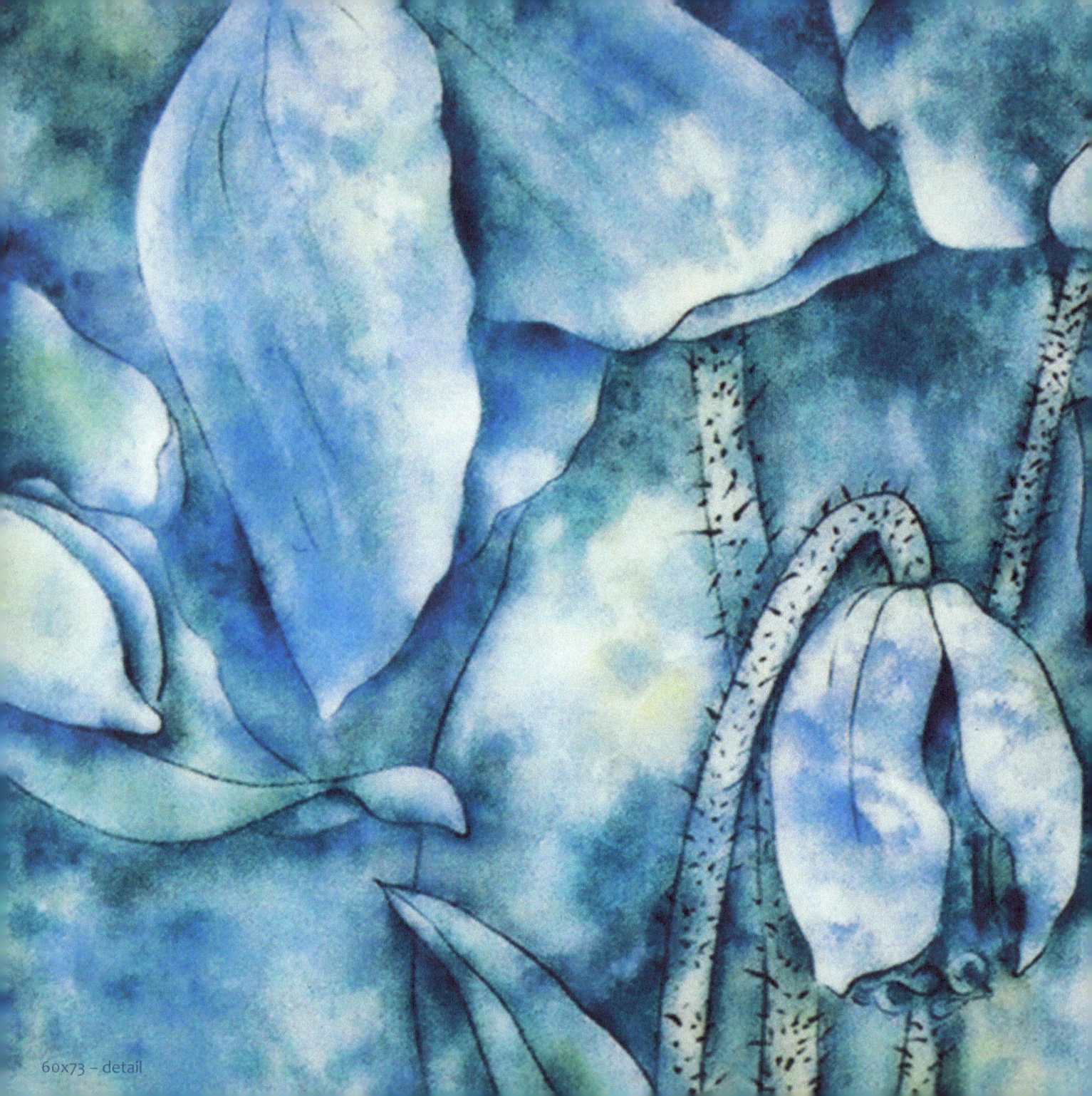
60x73 – detail

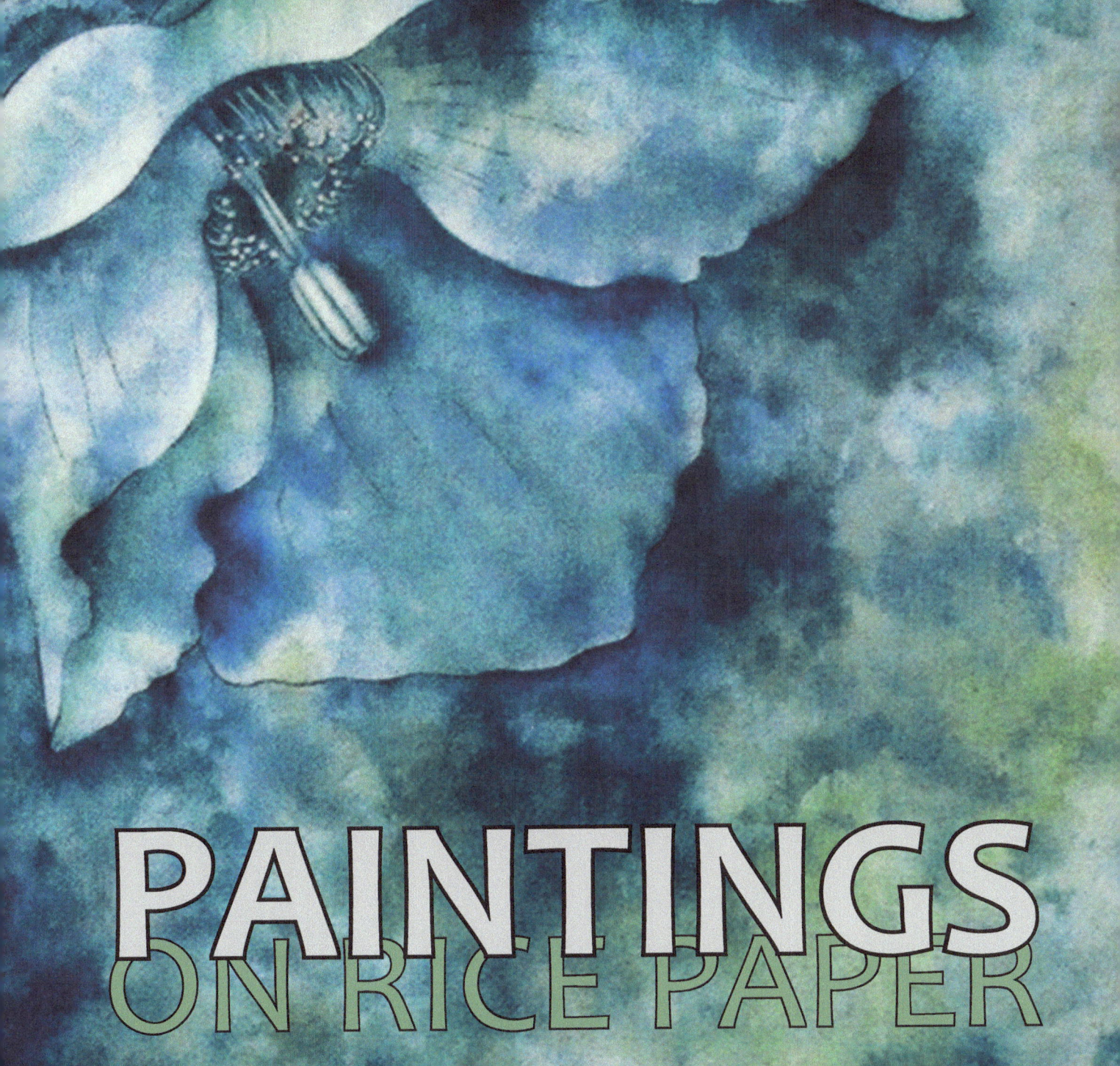

FLORA

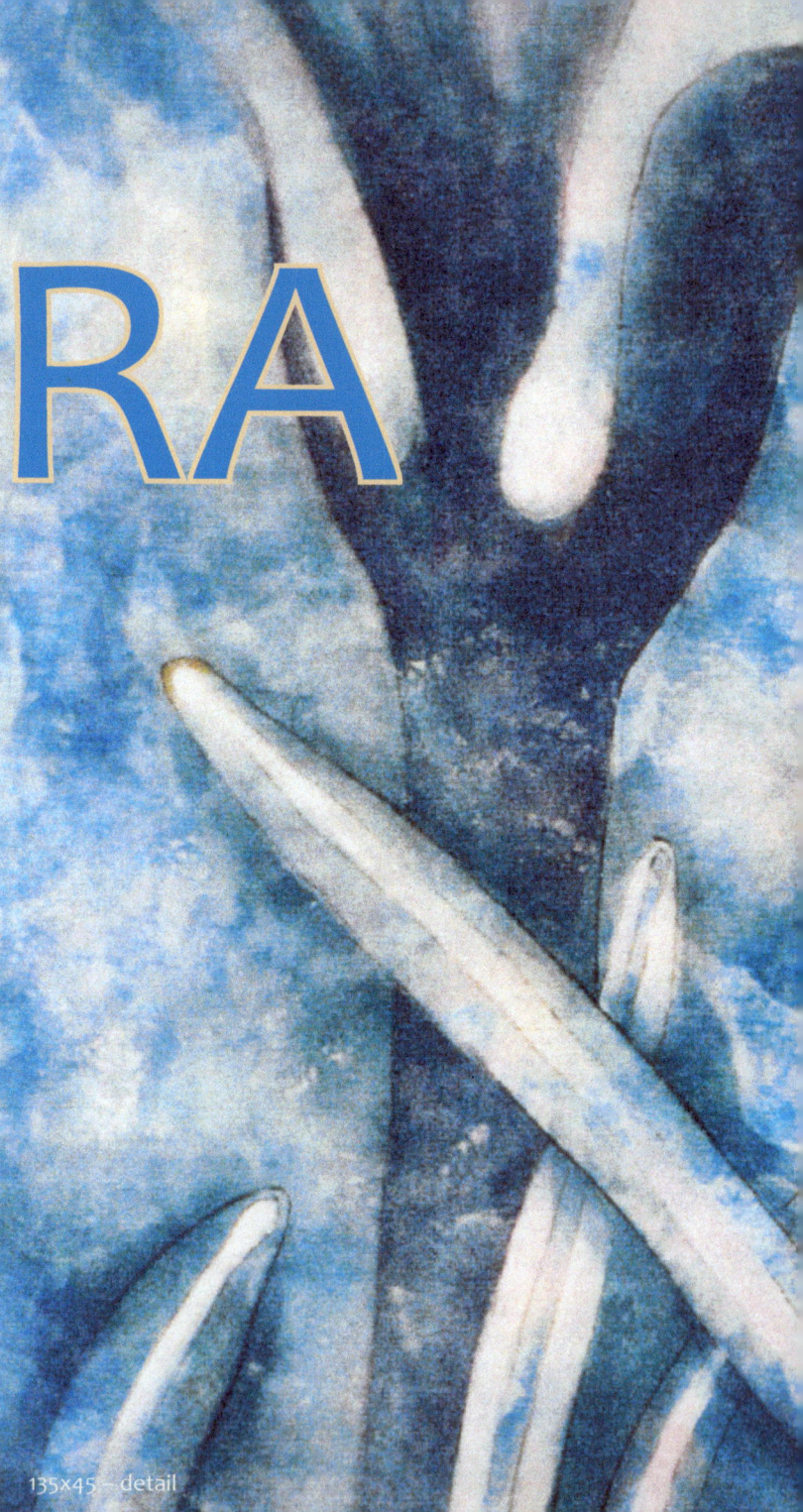

135x45 – detail

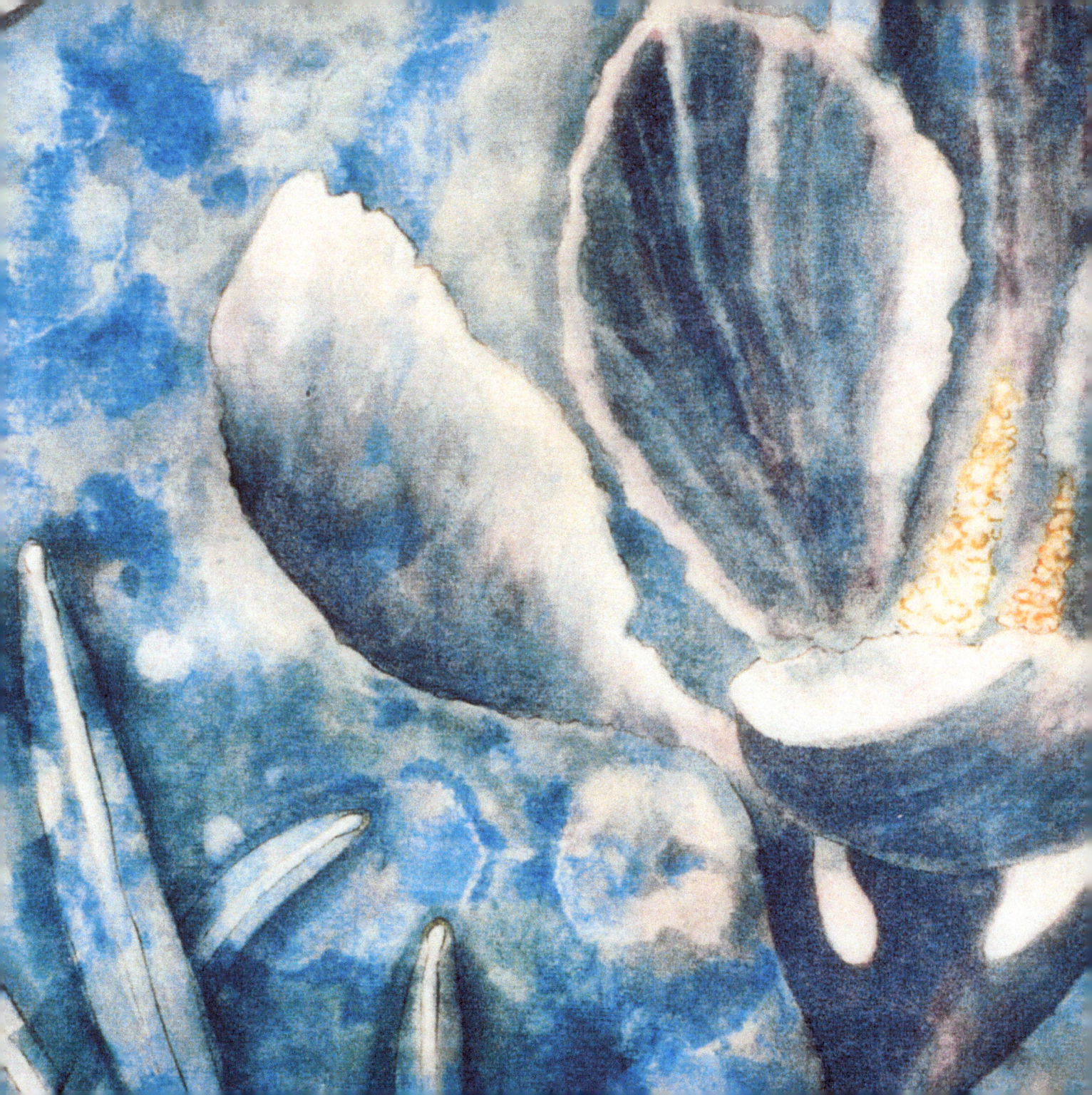

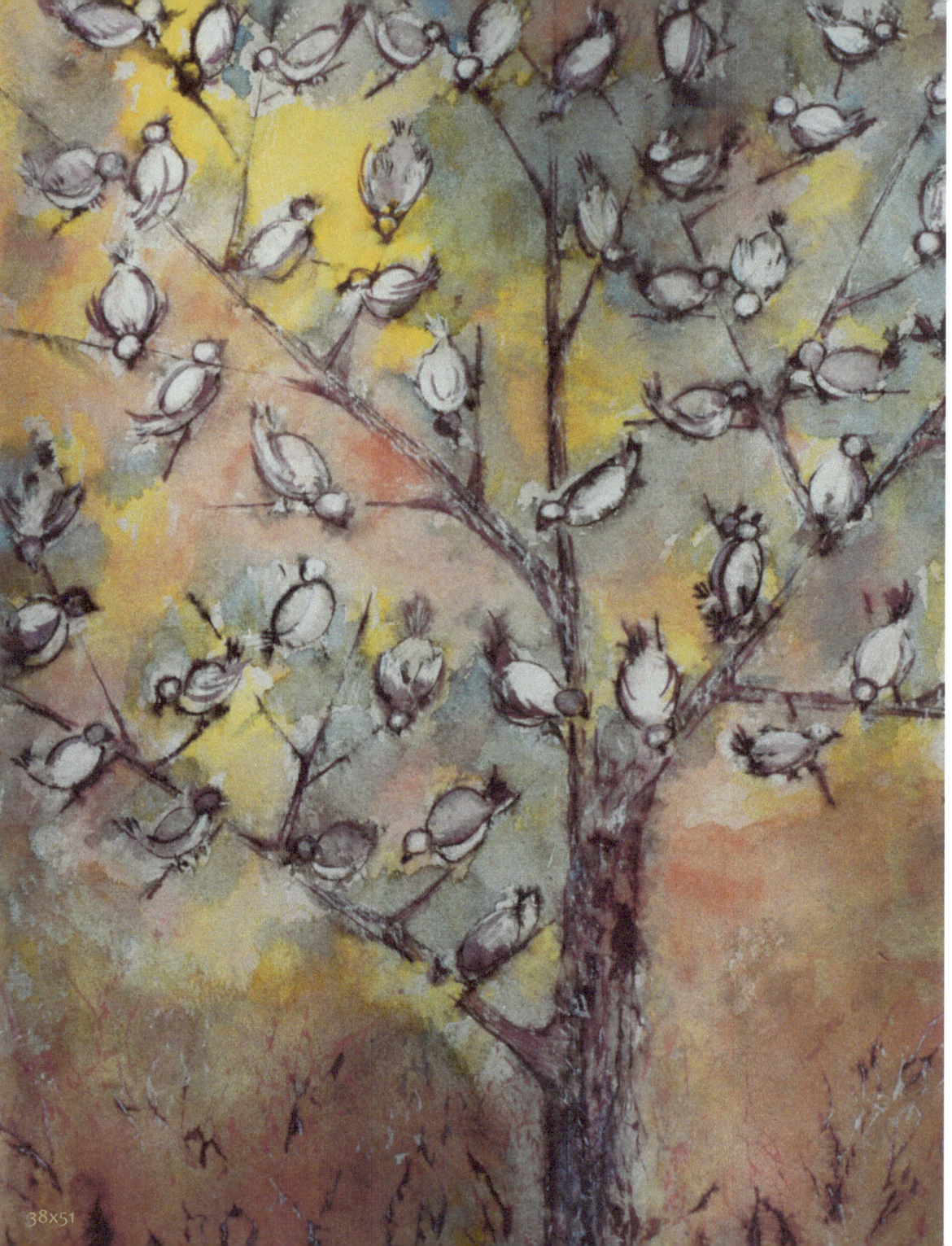

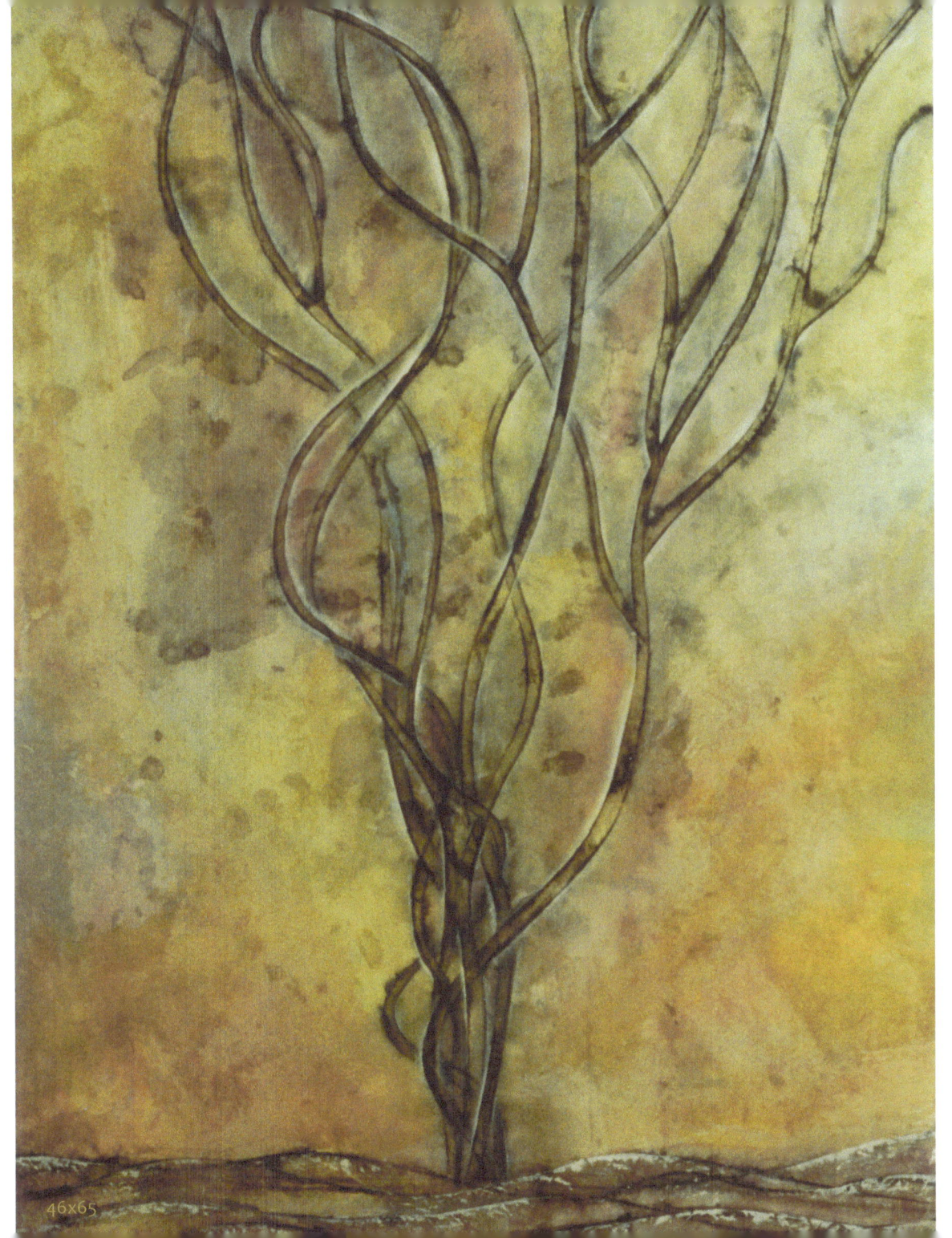

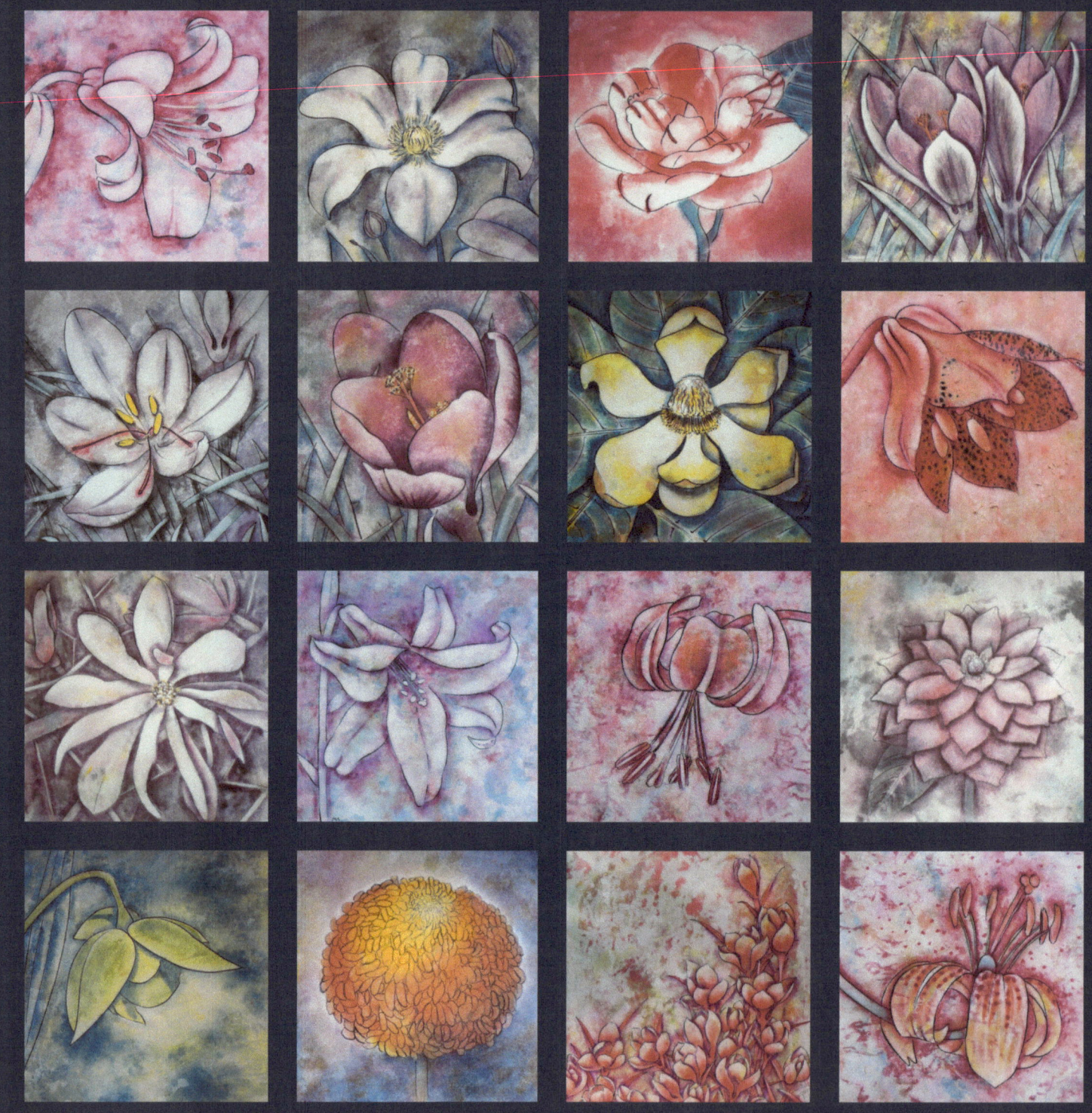

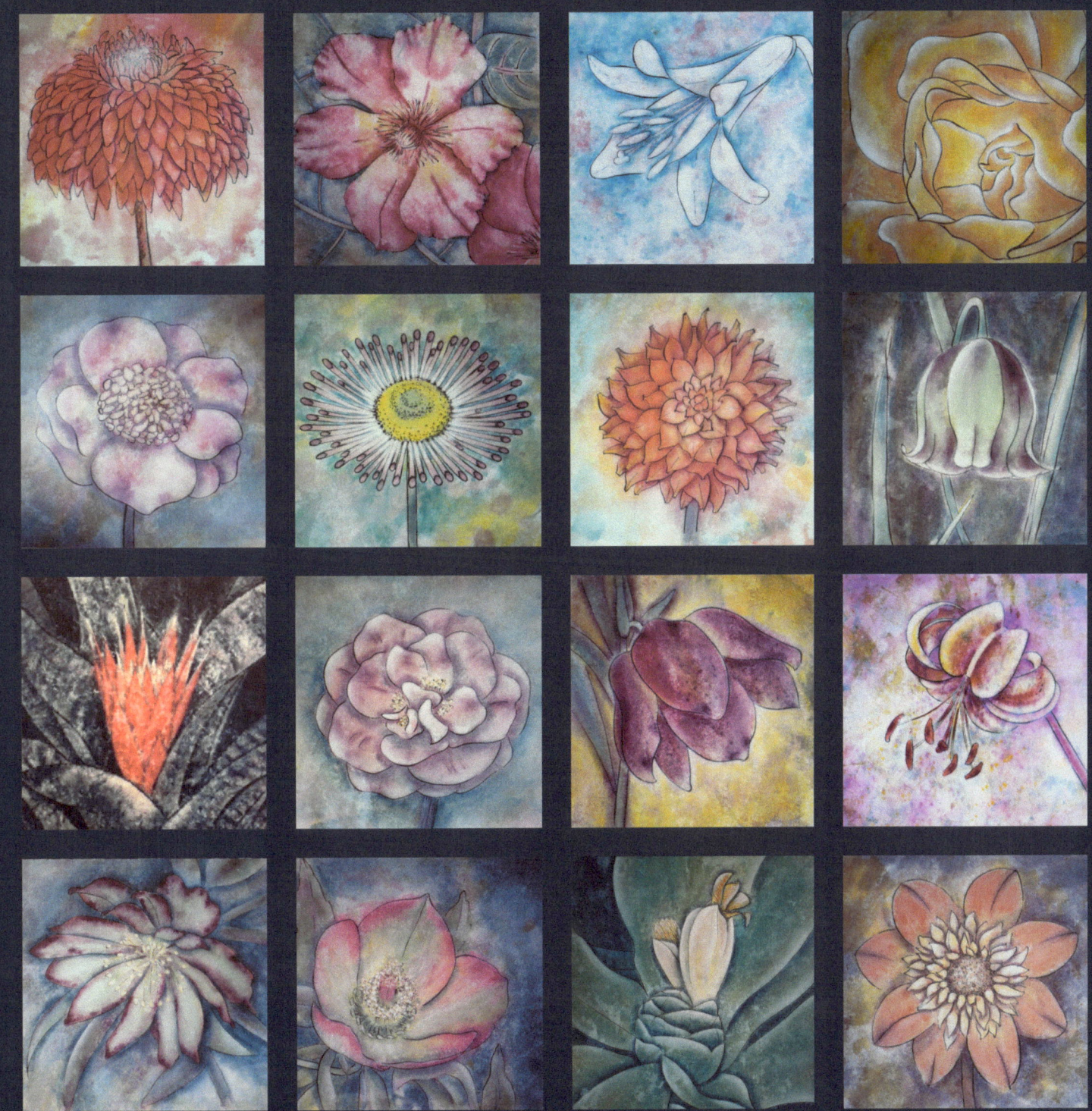

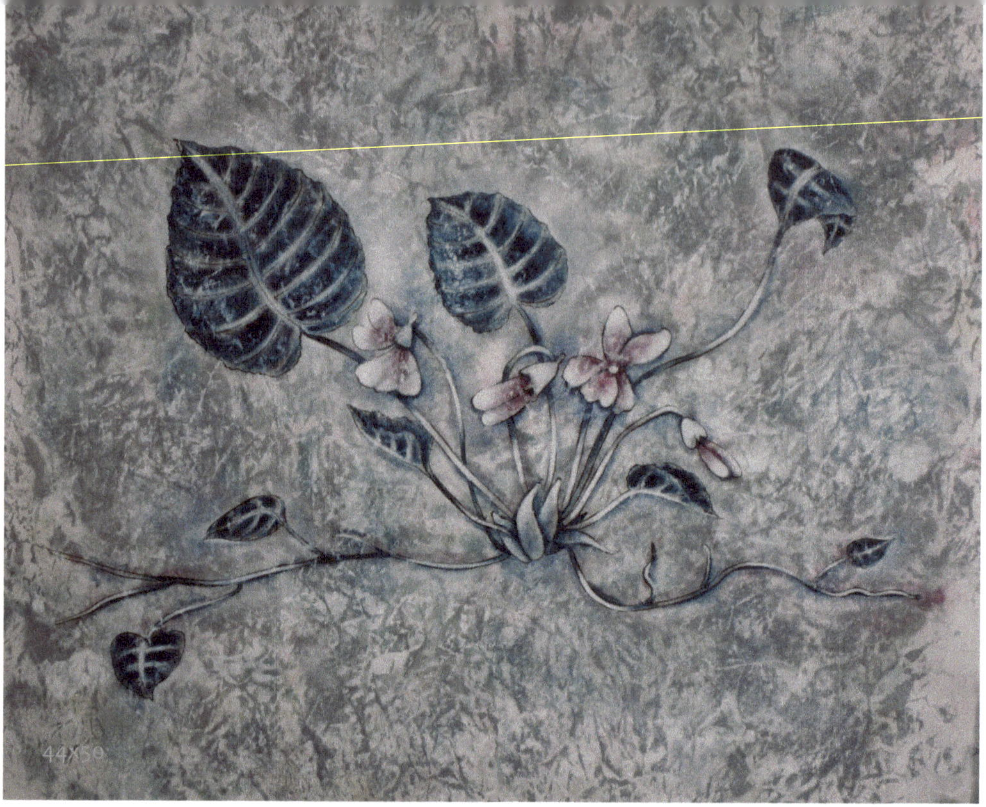

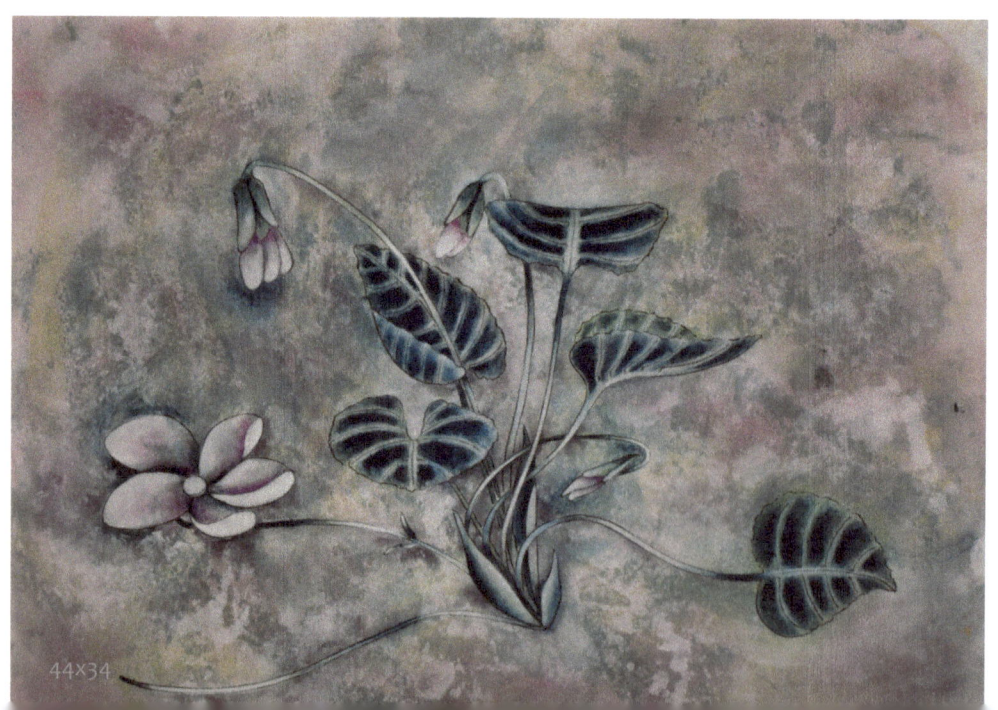

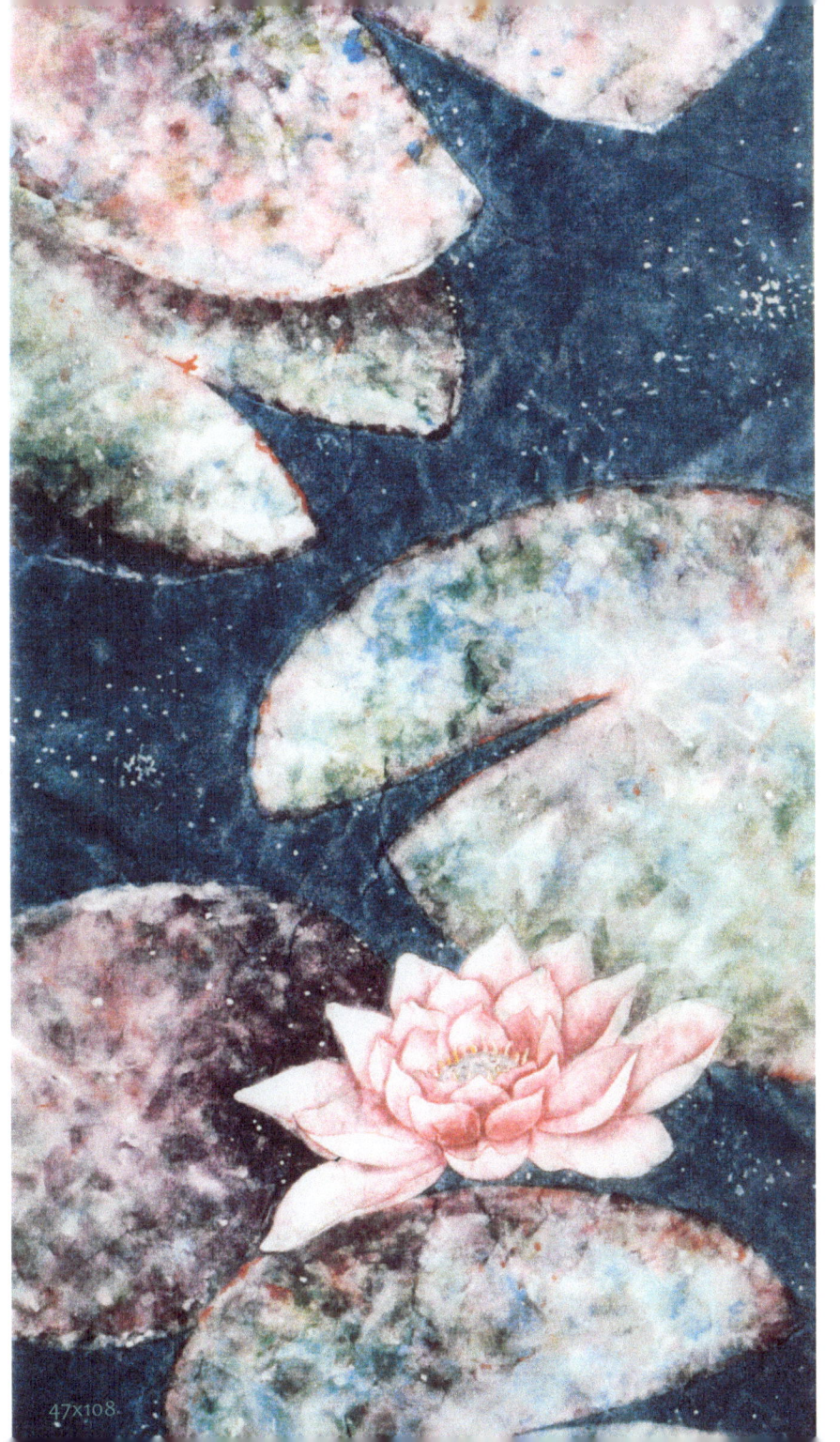

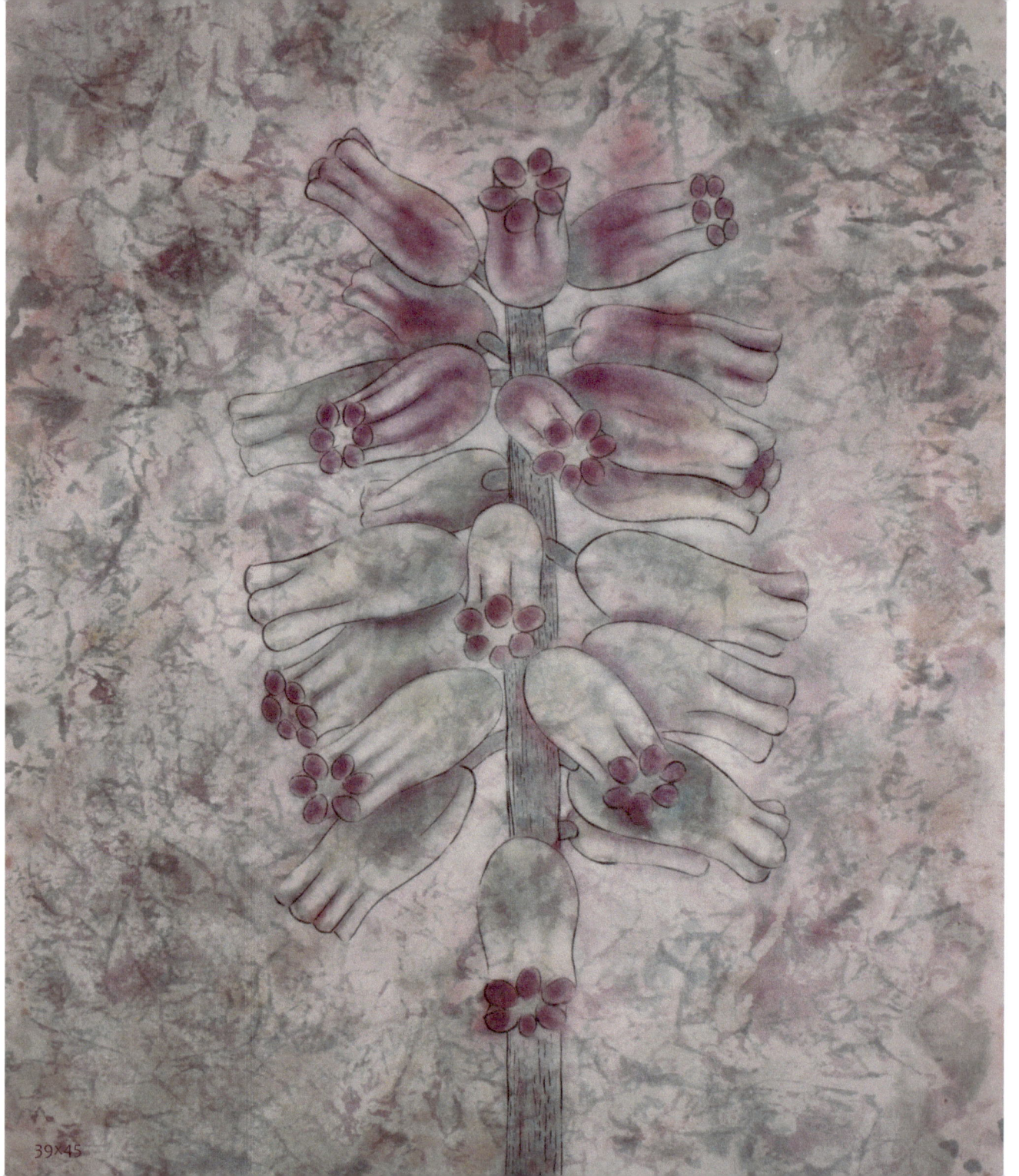

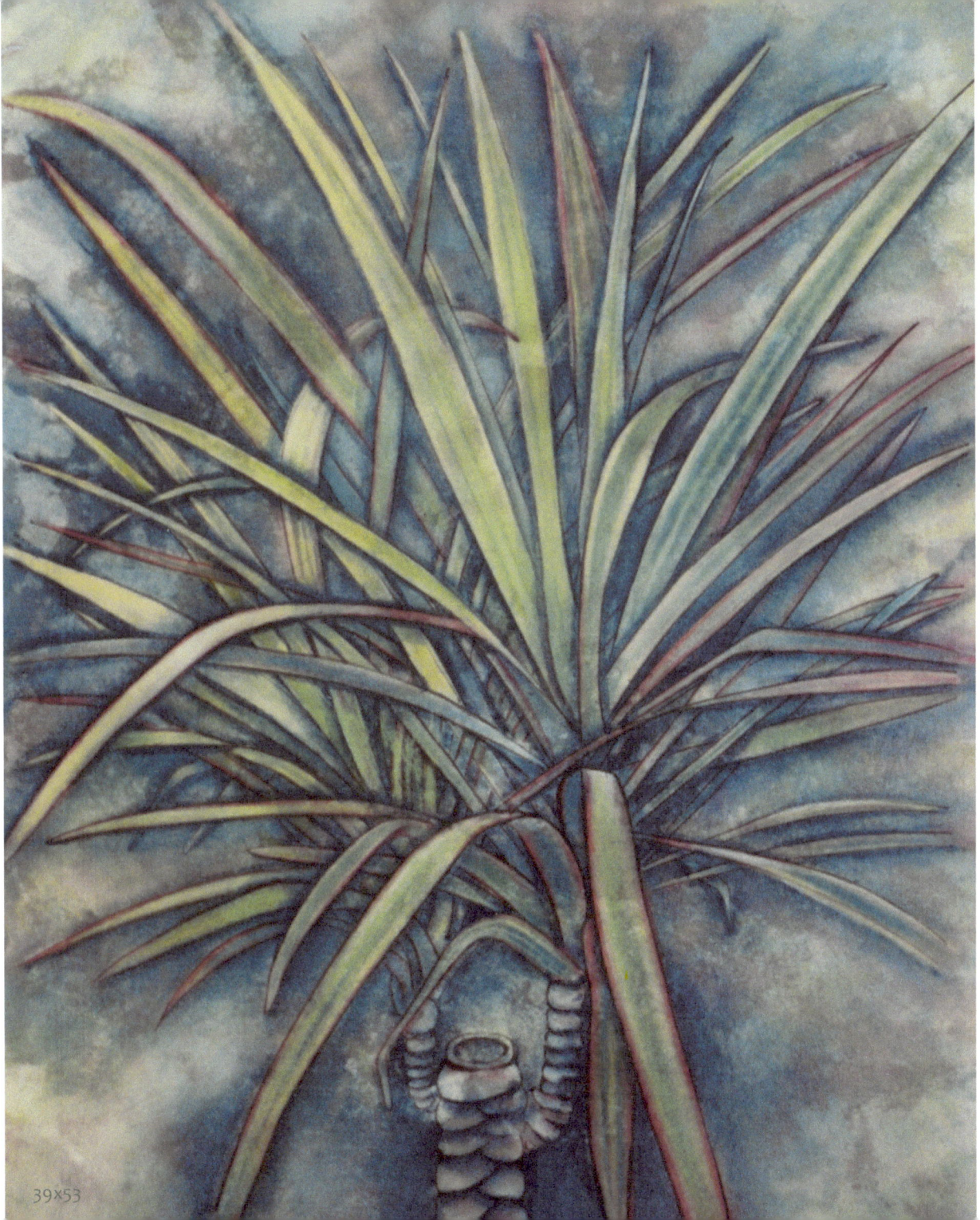

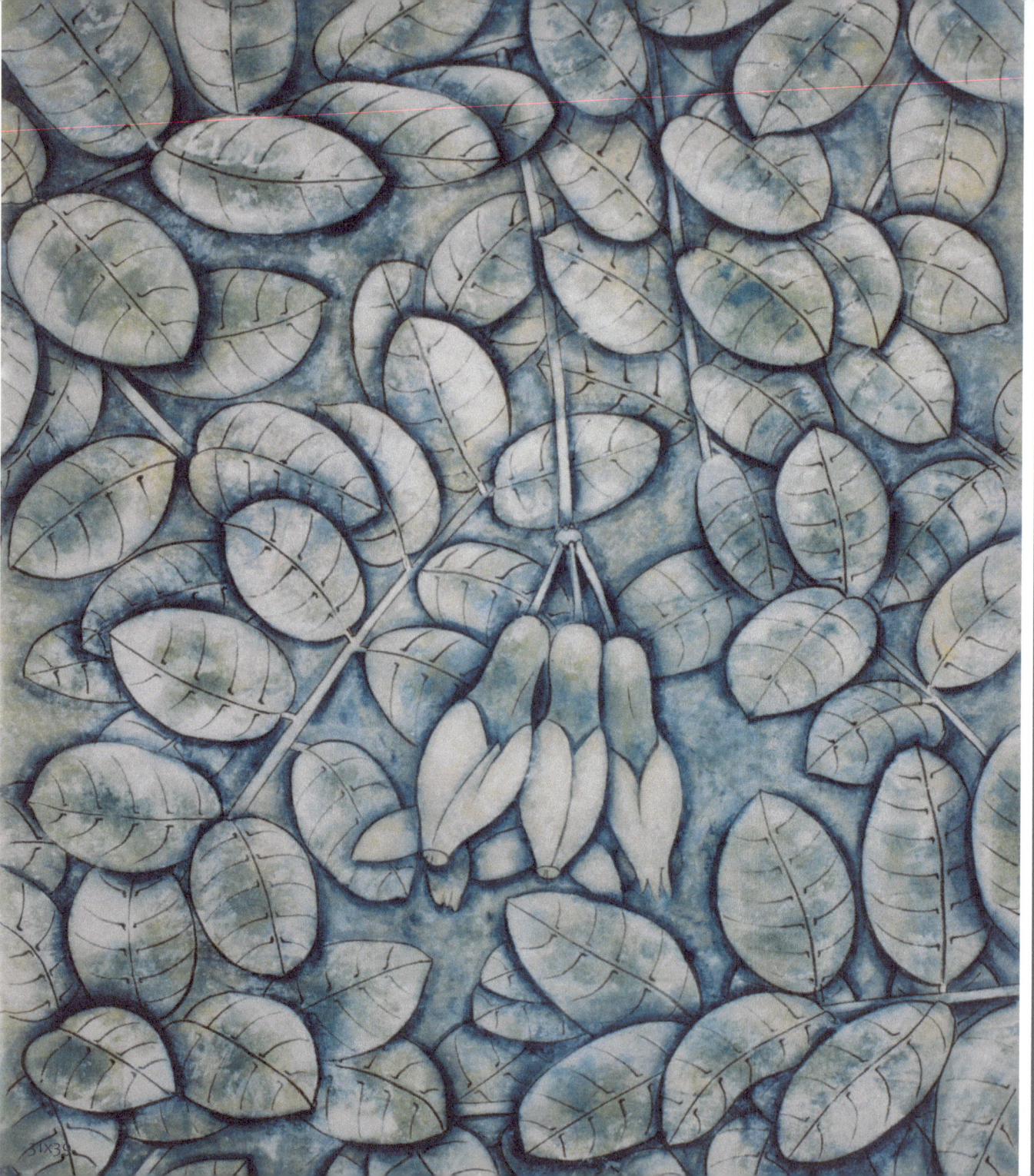

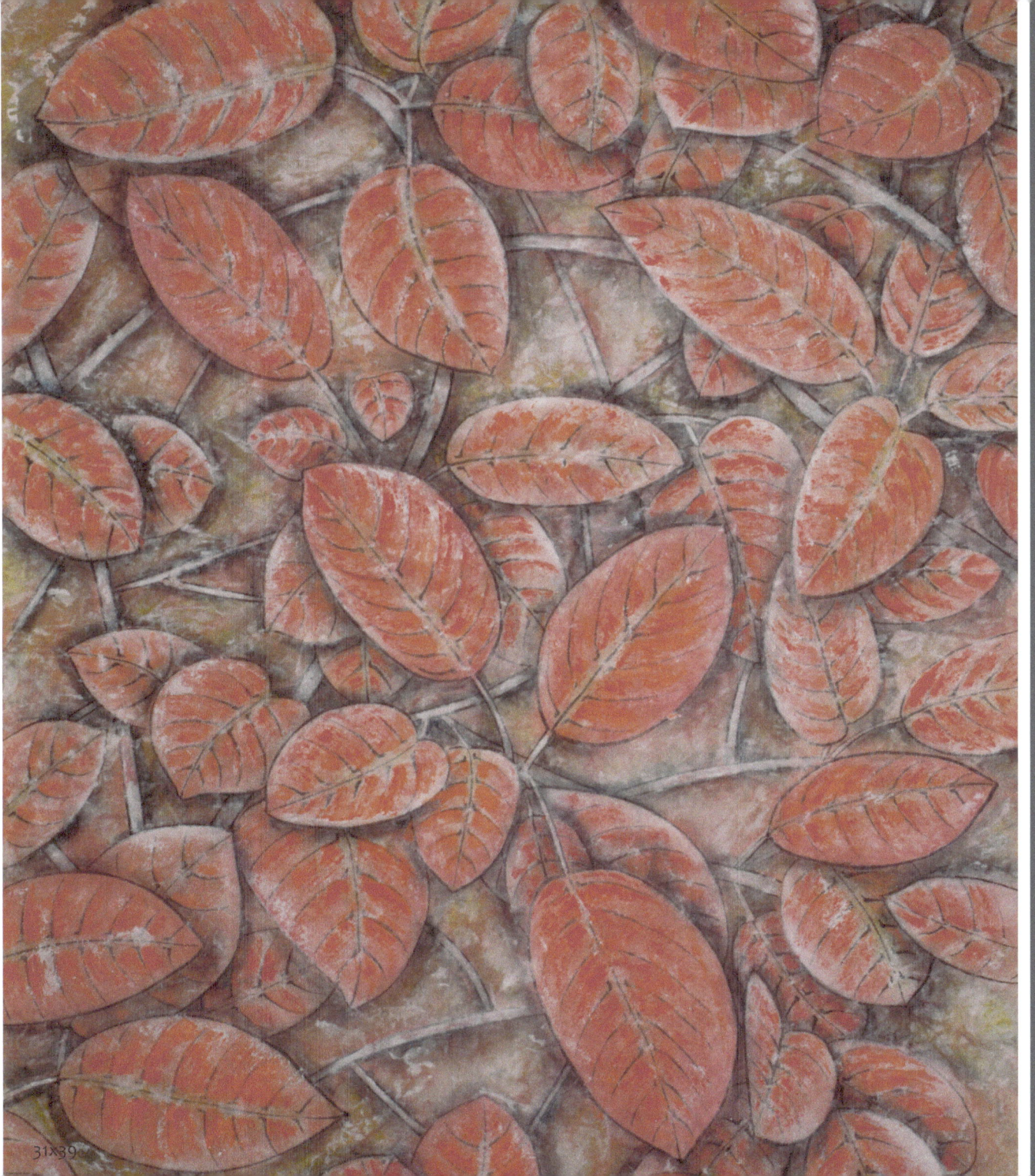

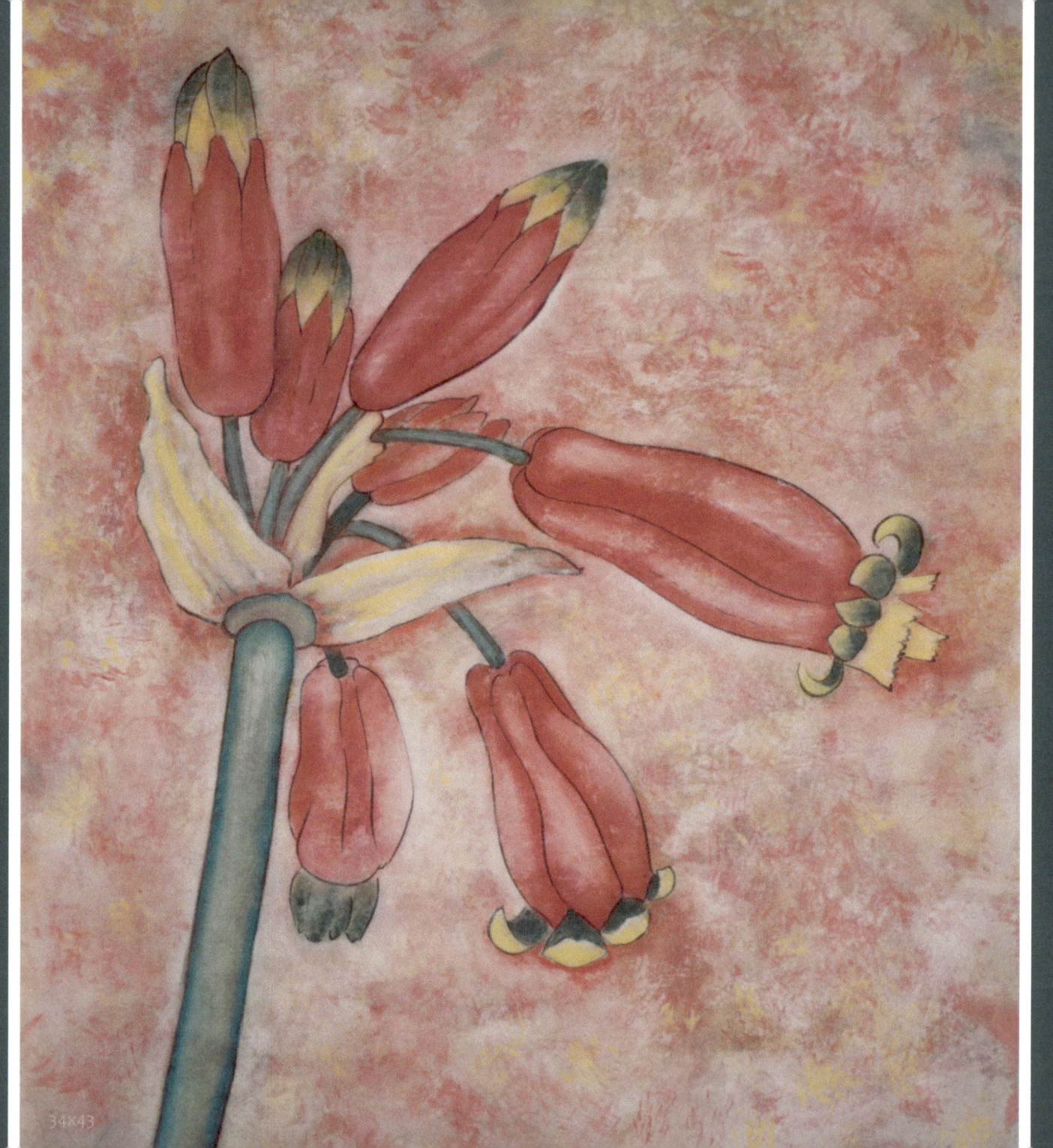

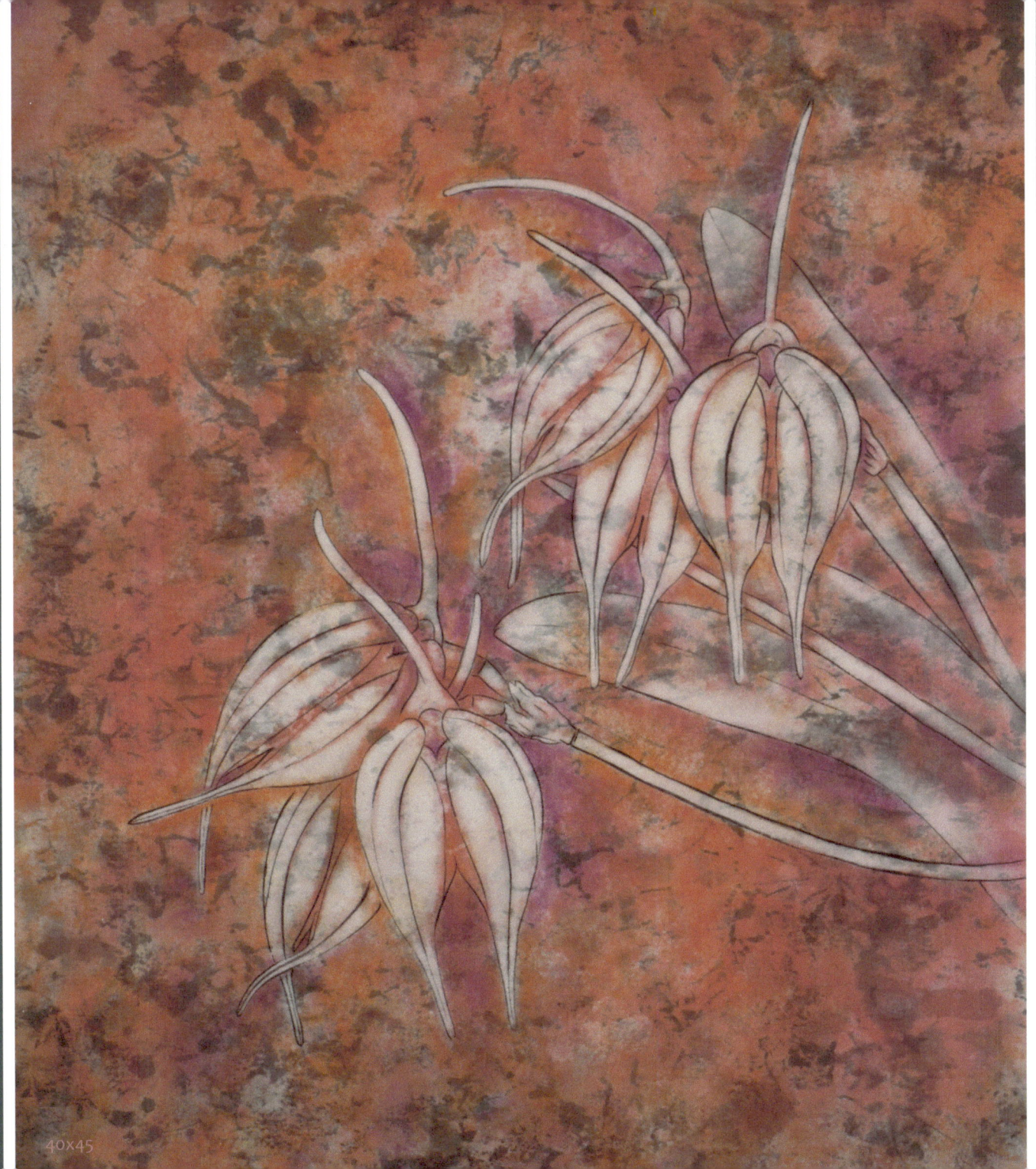

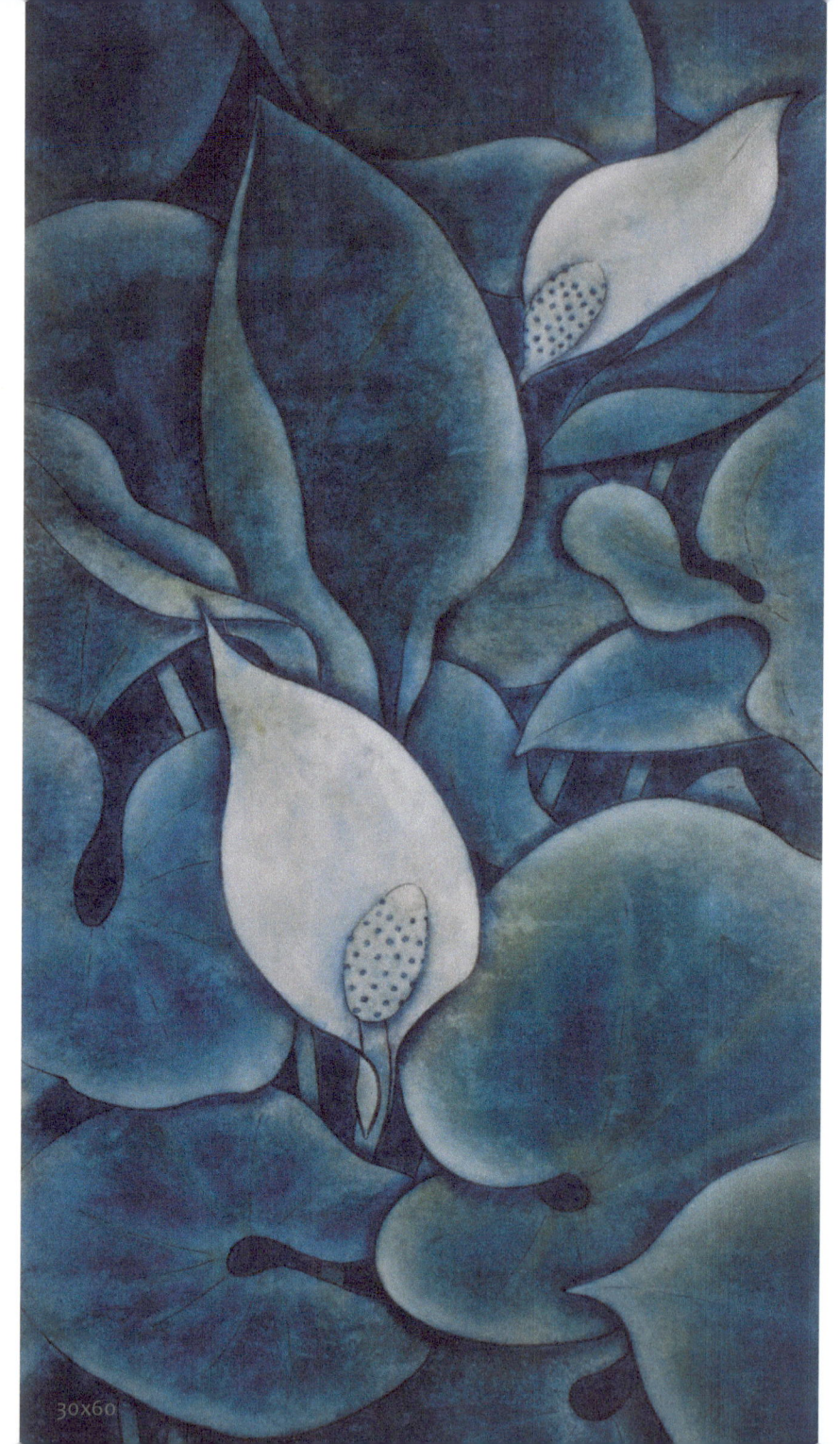

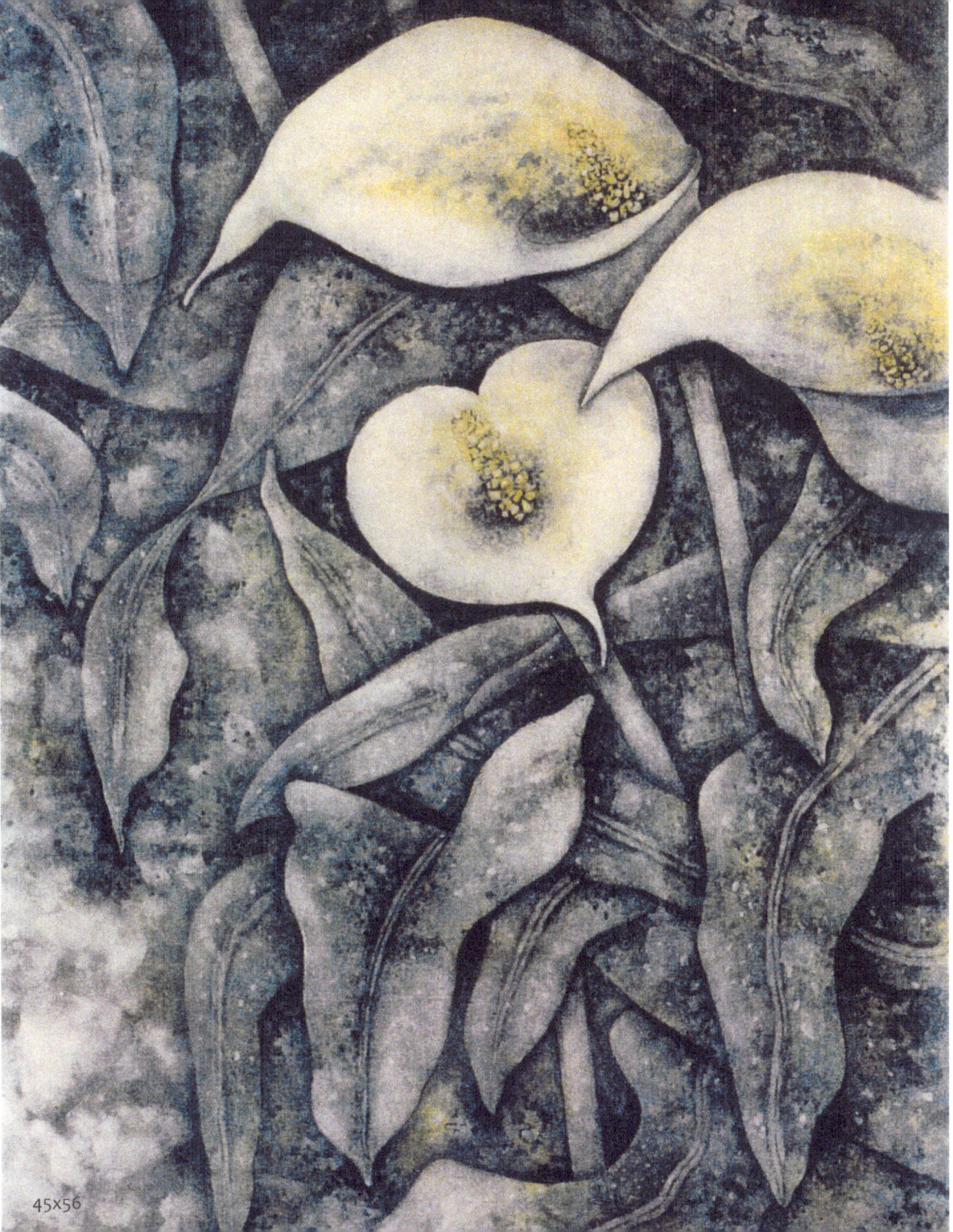

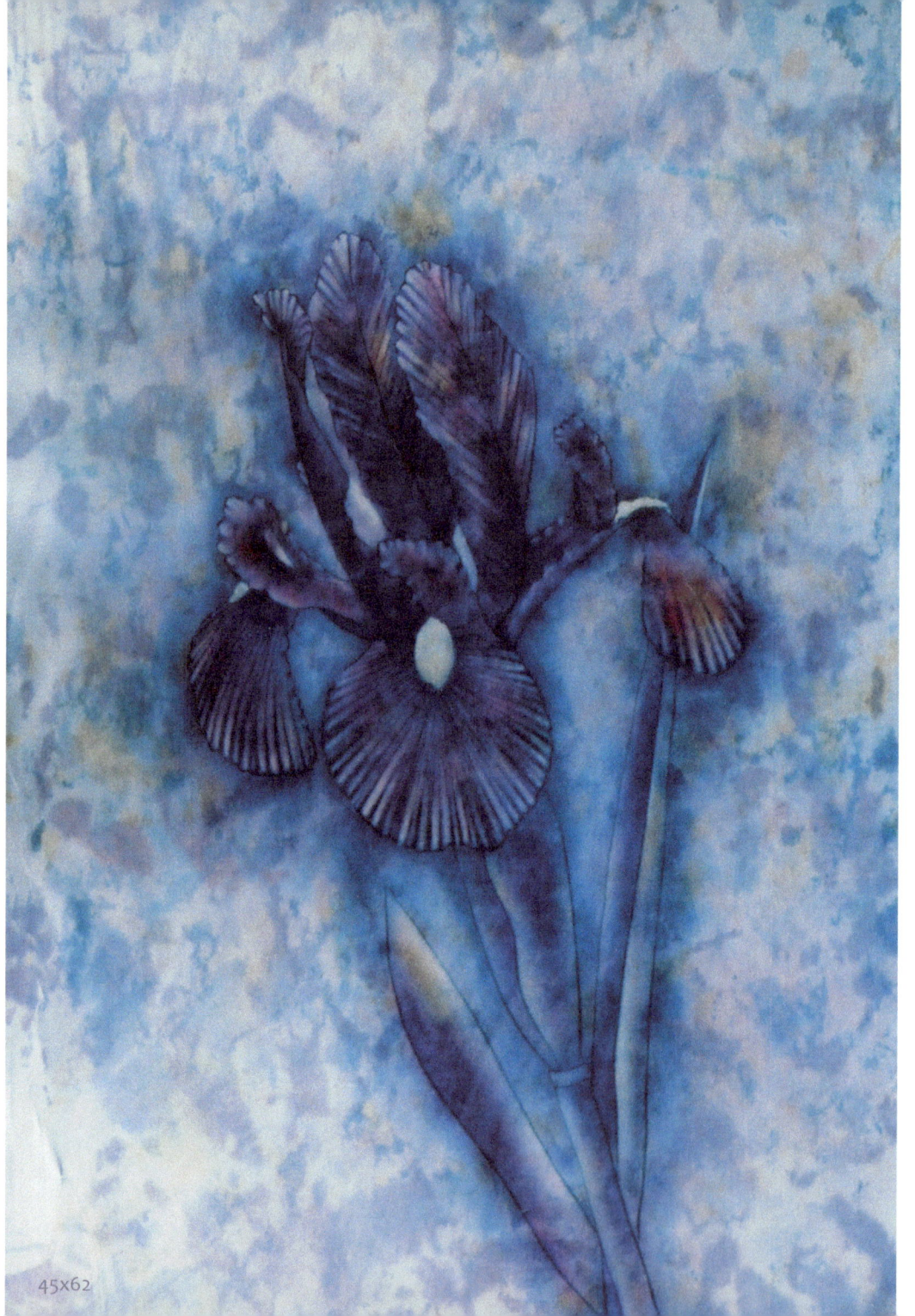

45x62

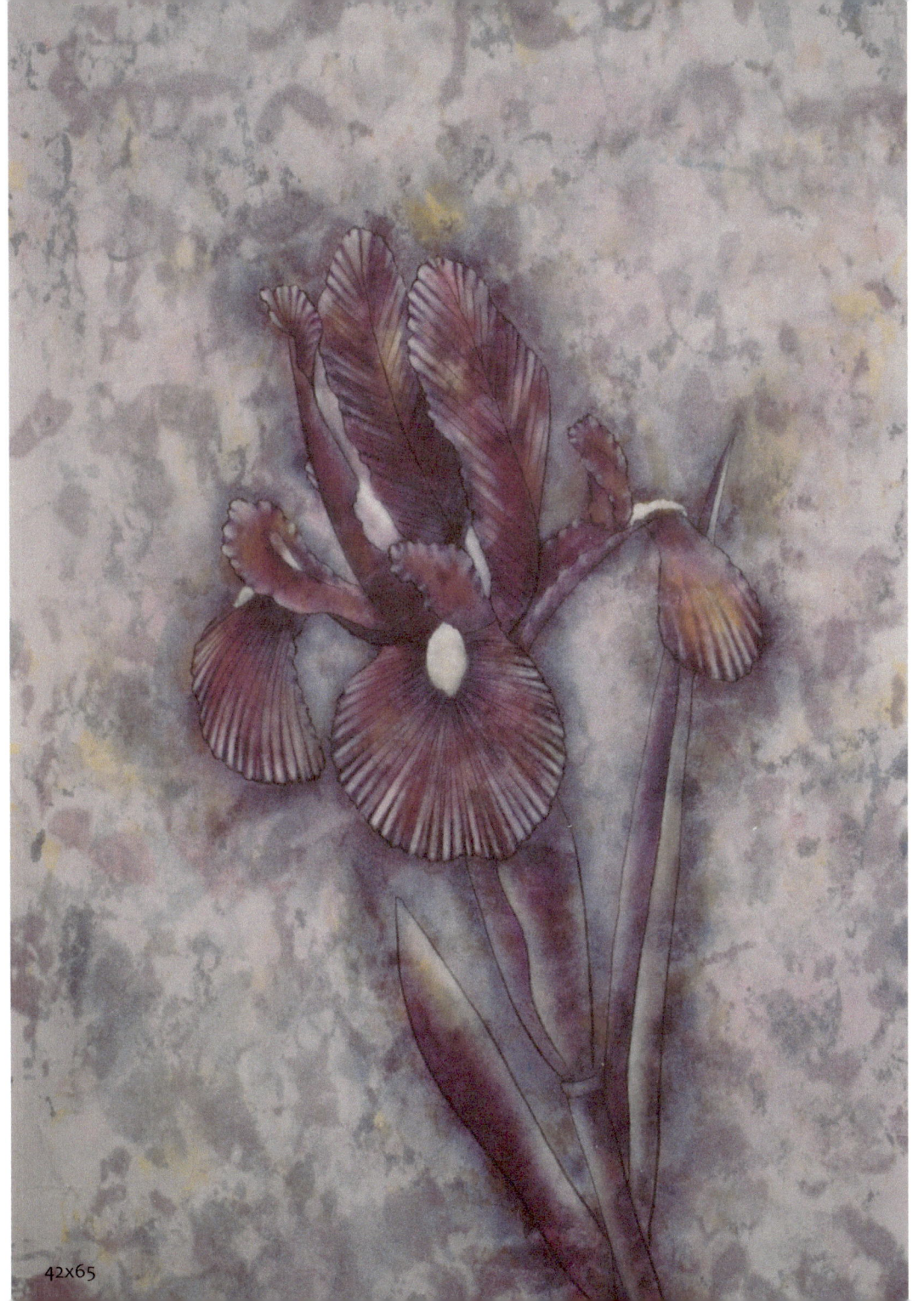

42x65

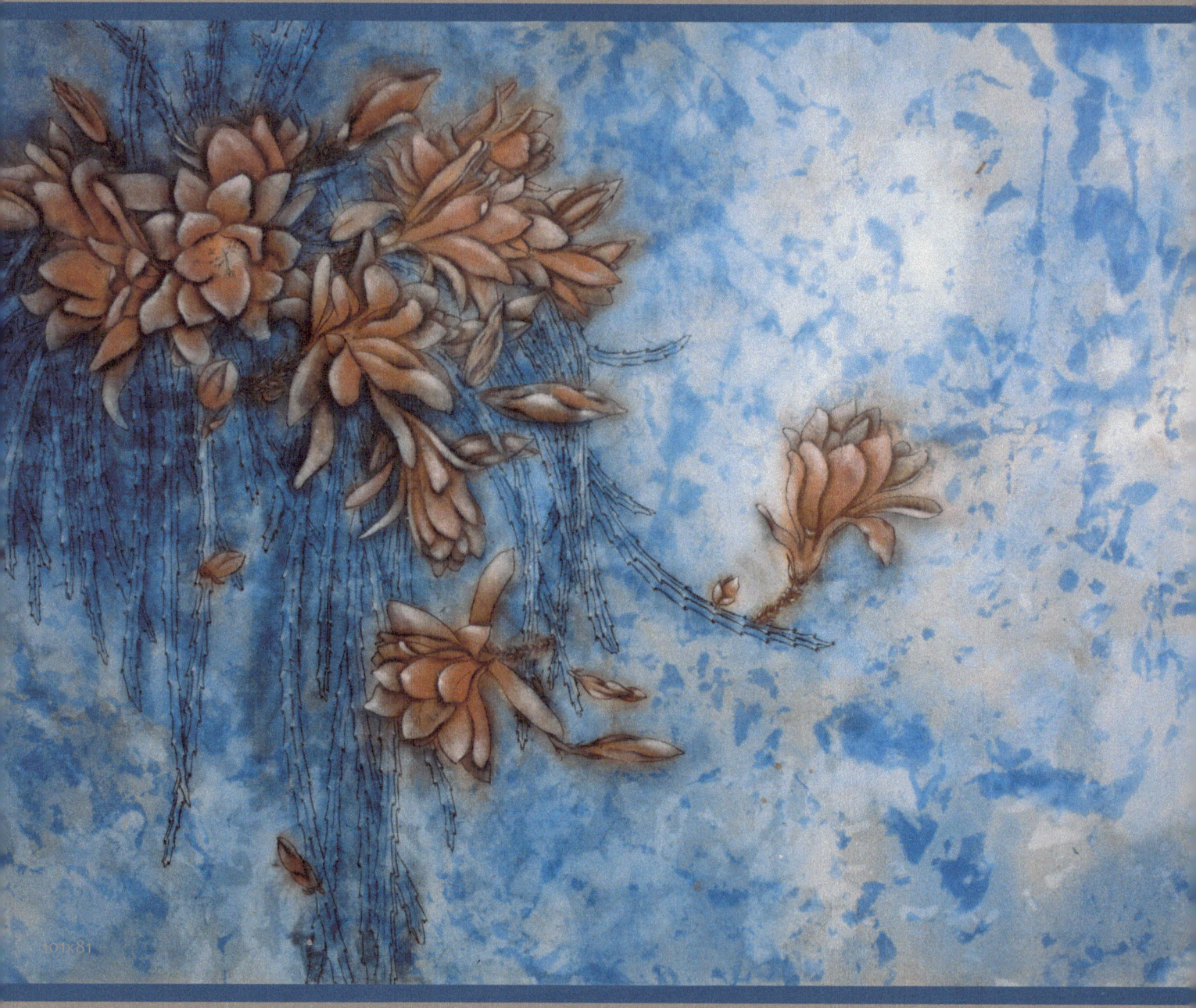

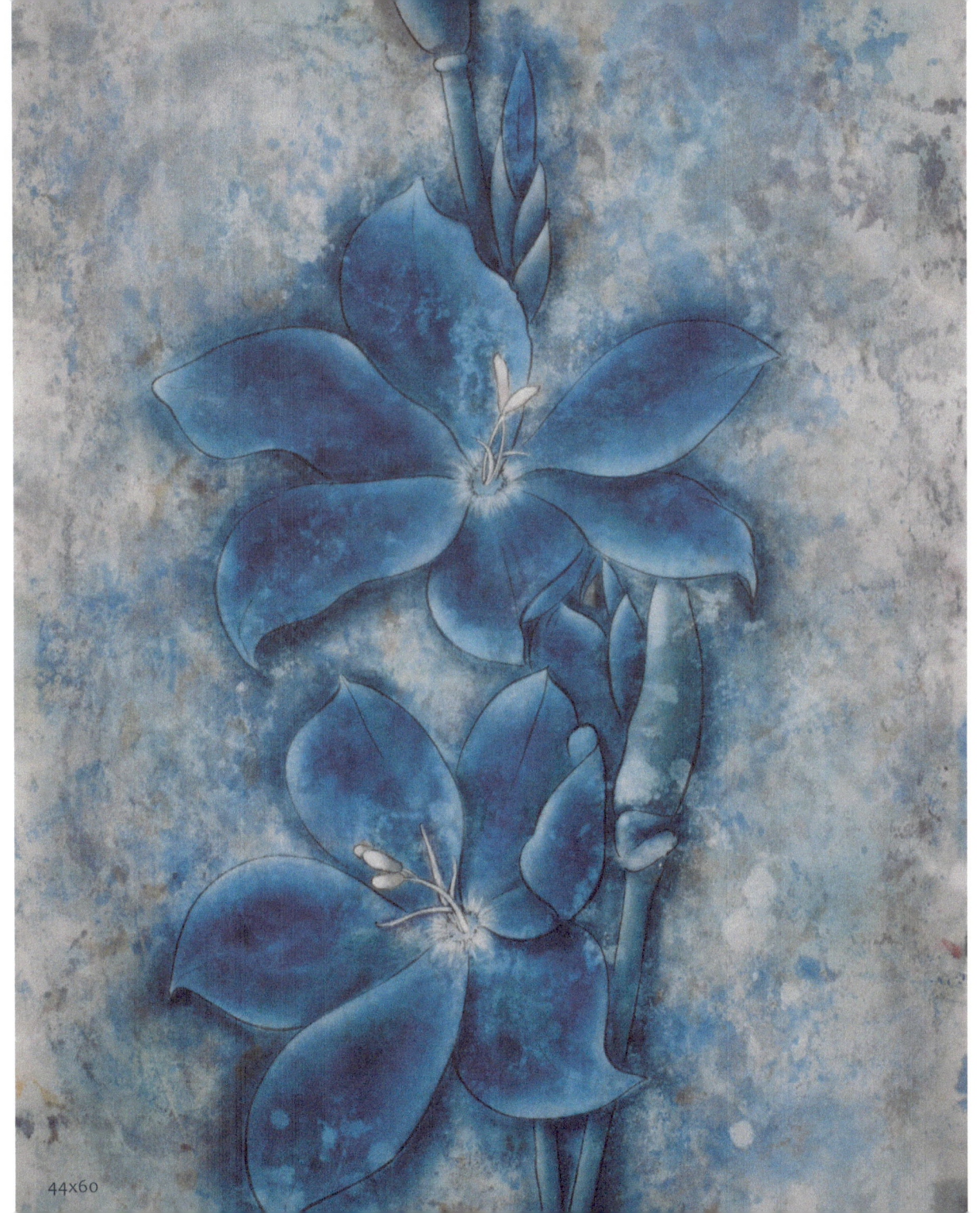

44x60

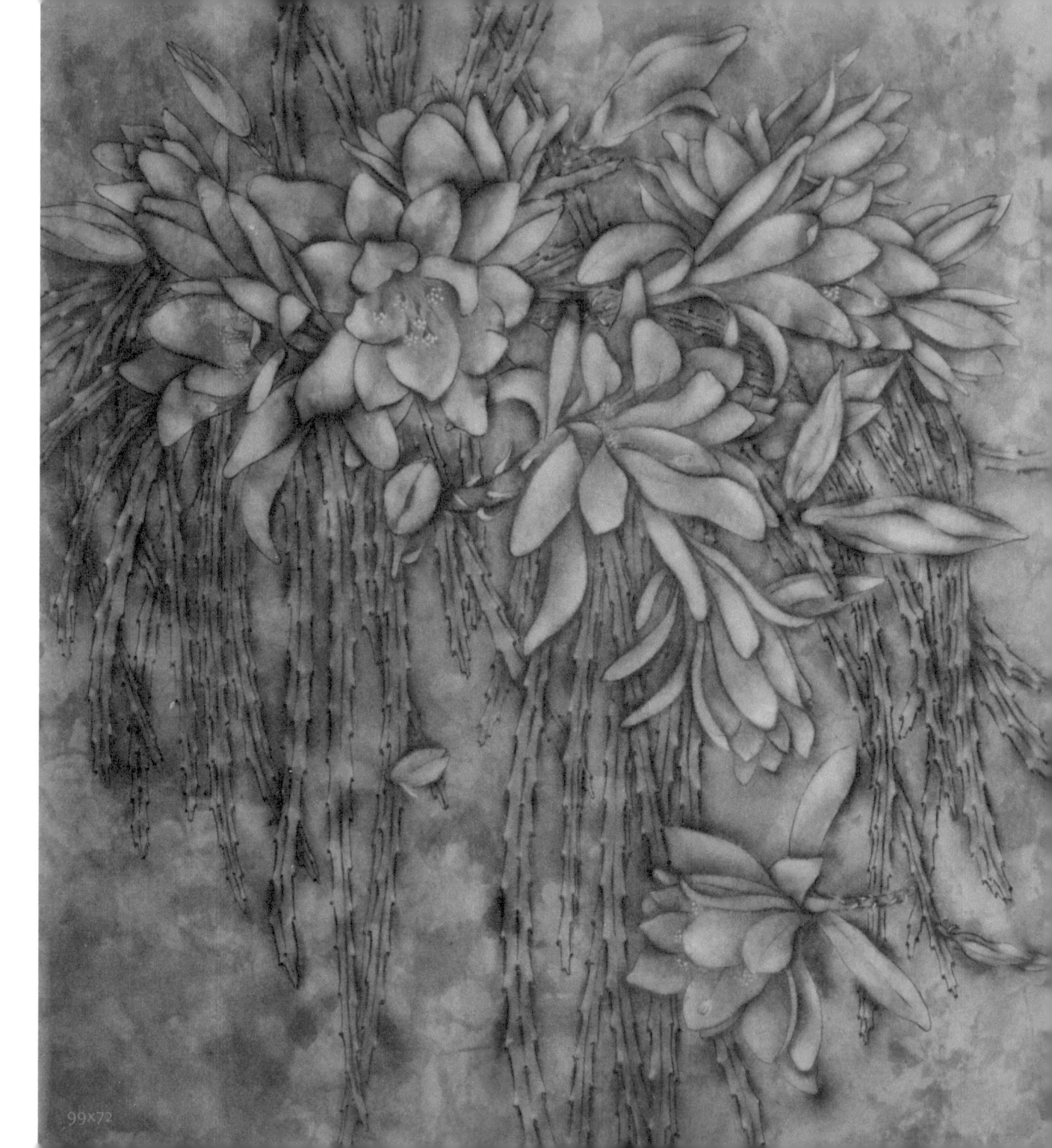

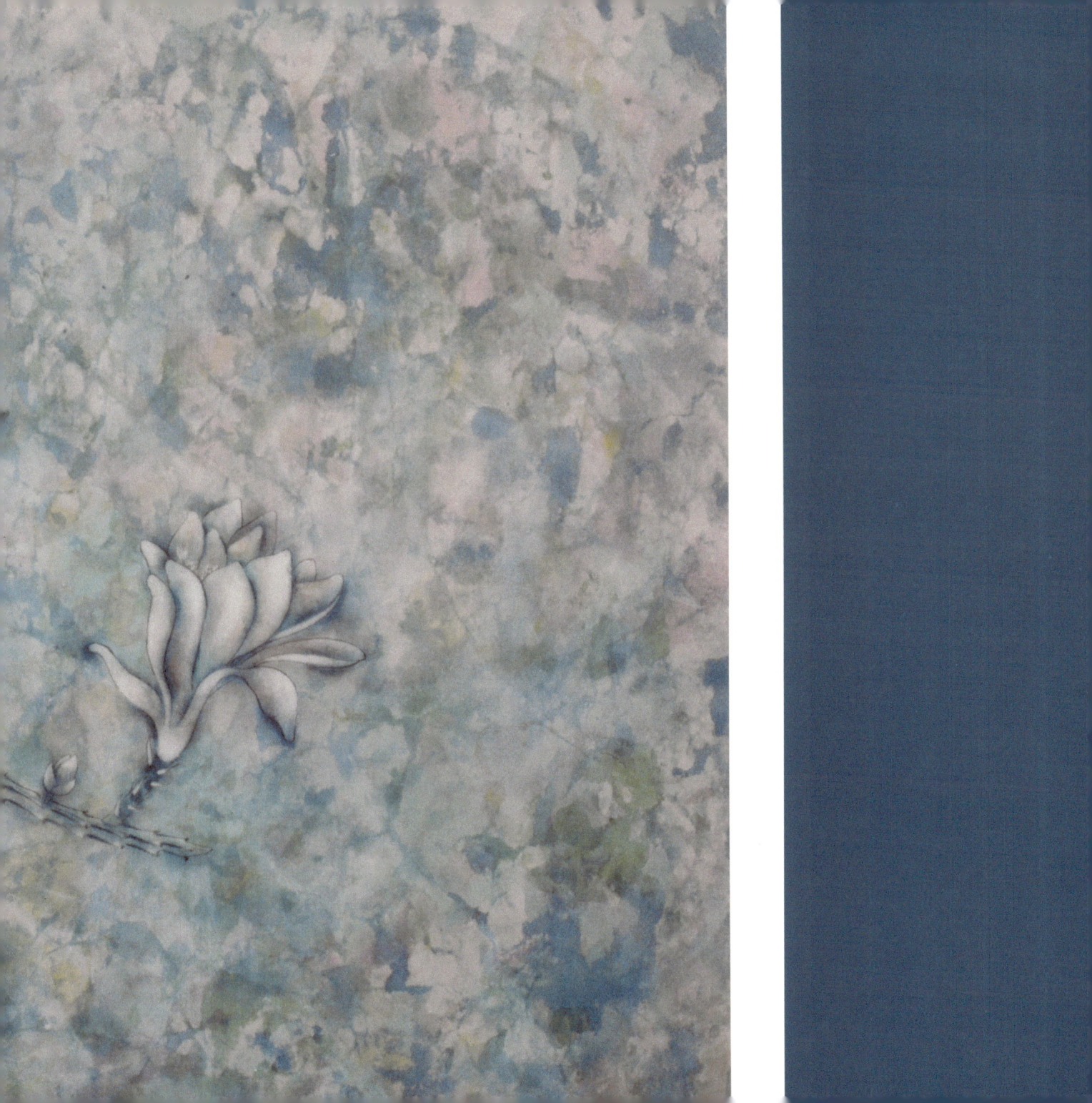

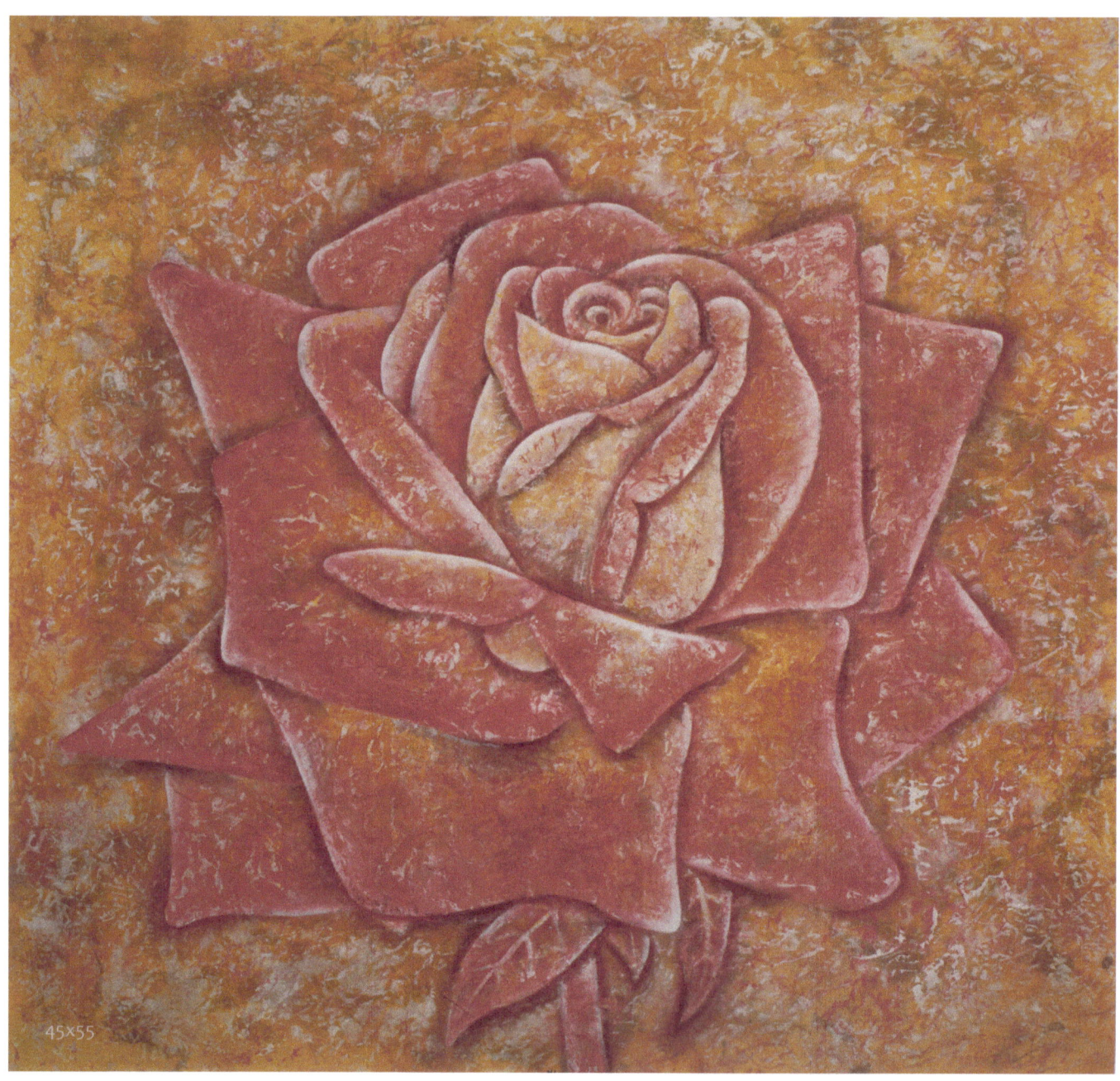
45x55

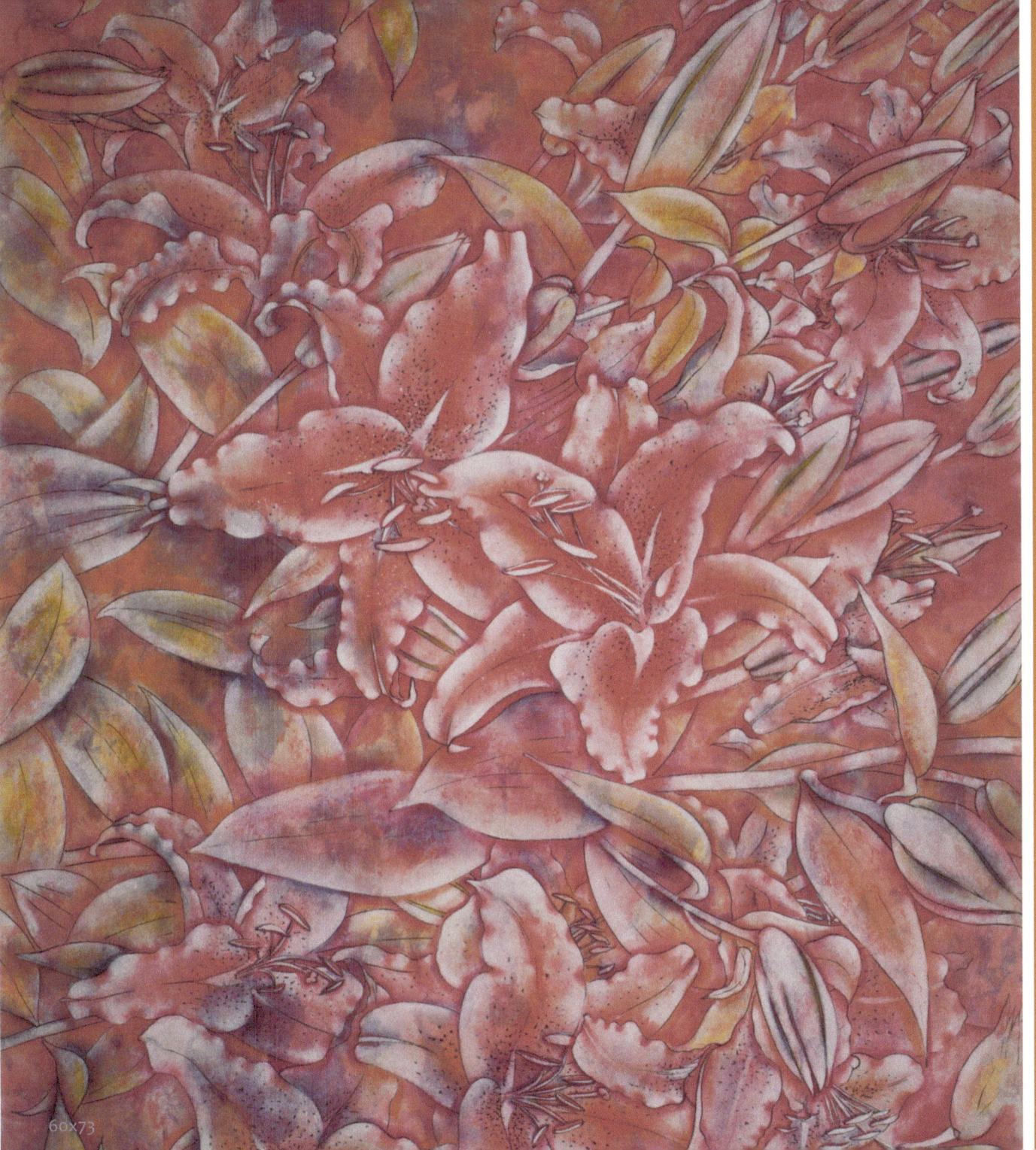

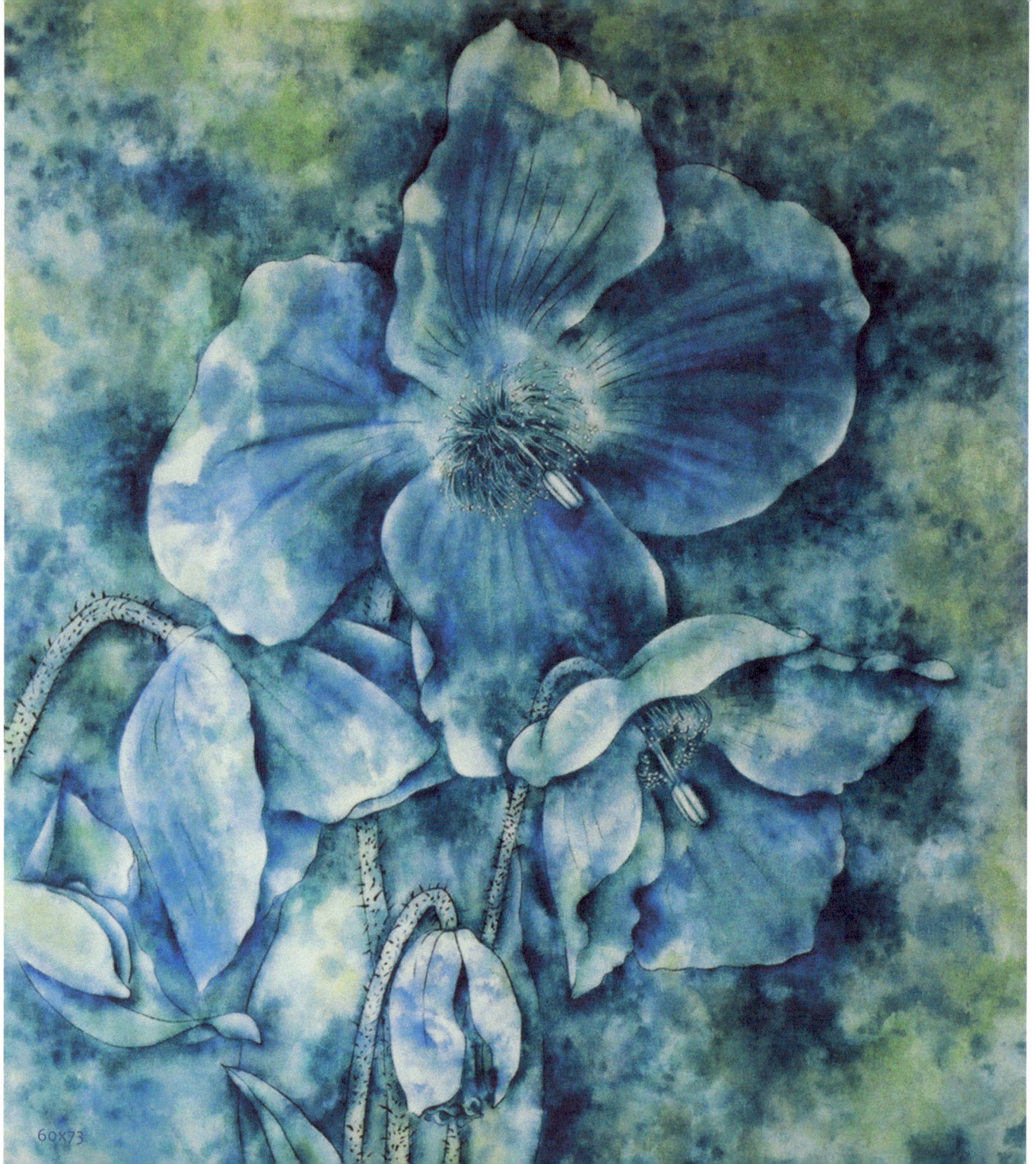

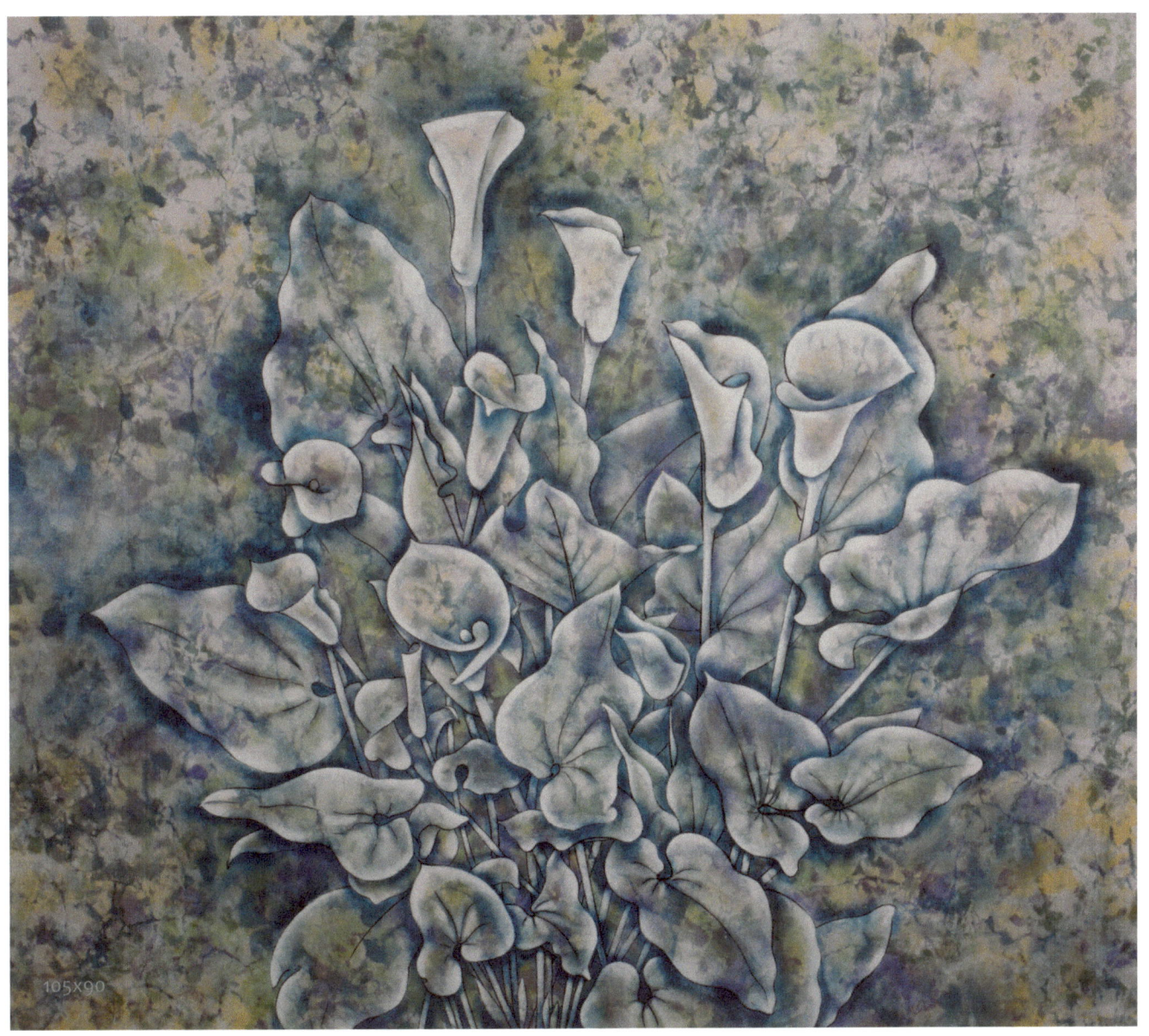

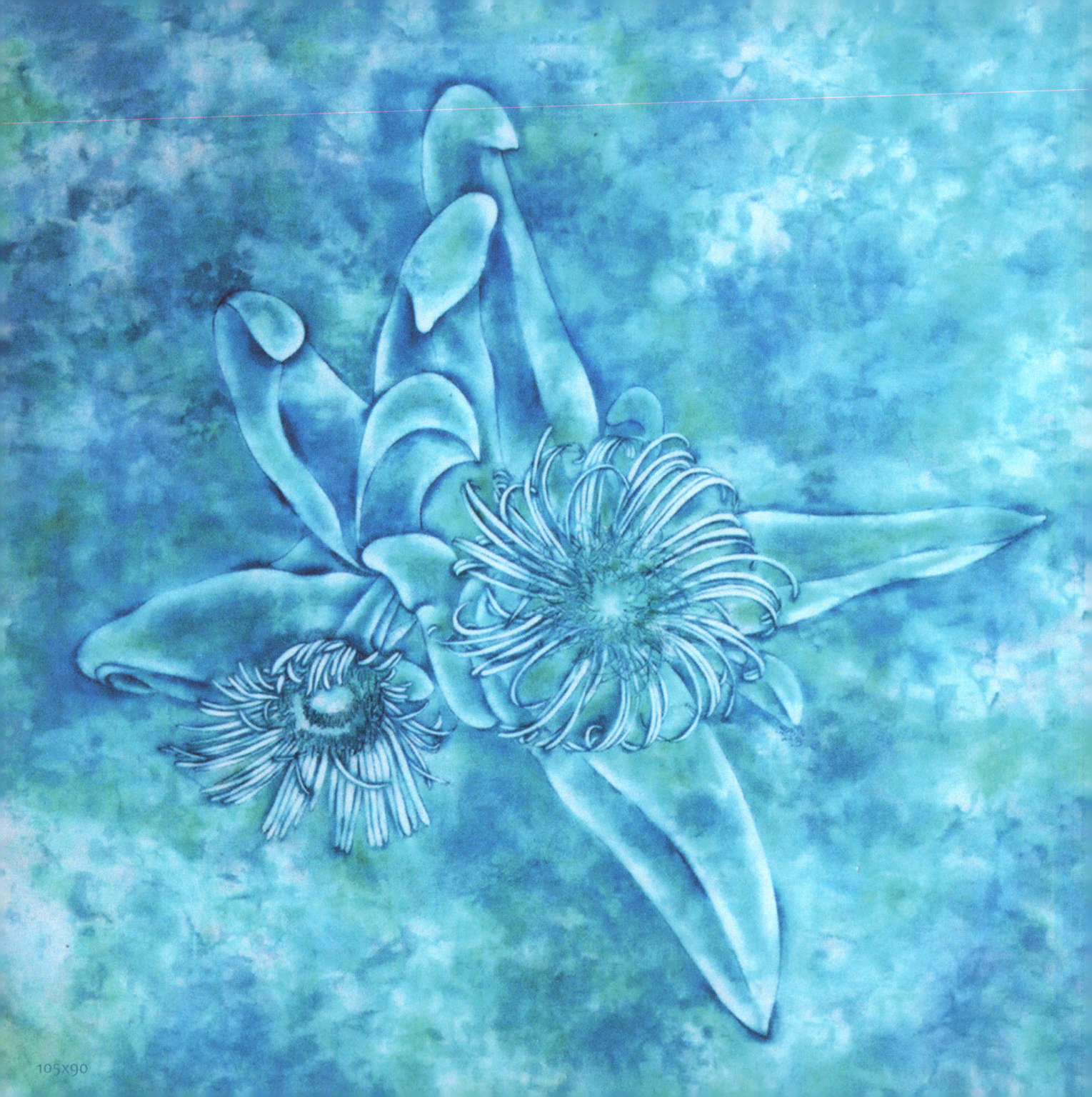

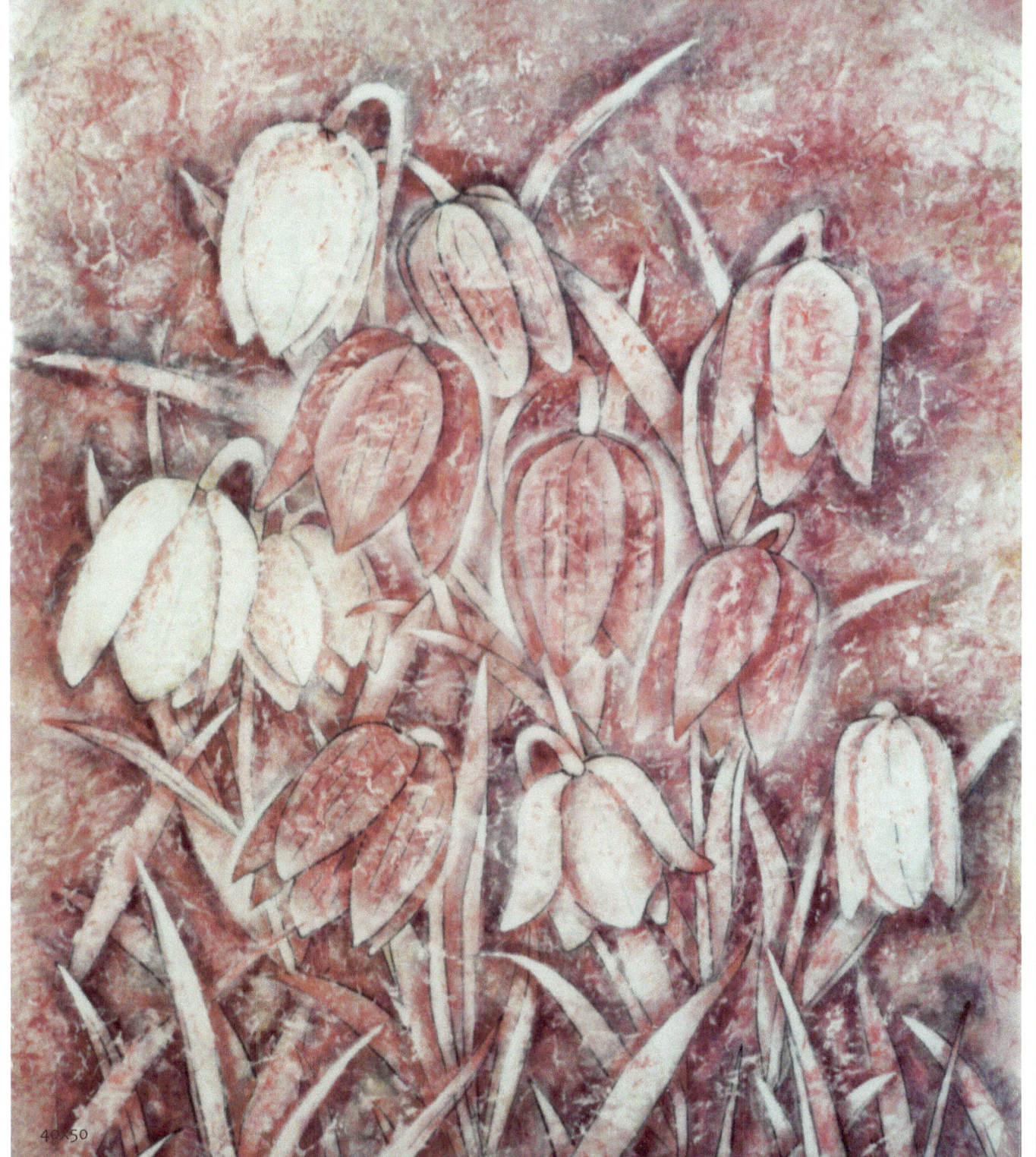

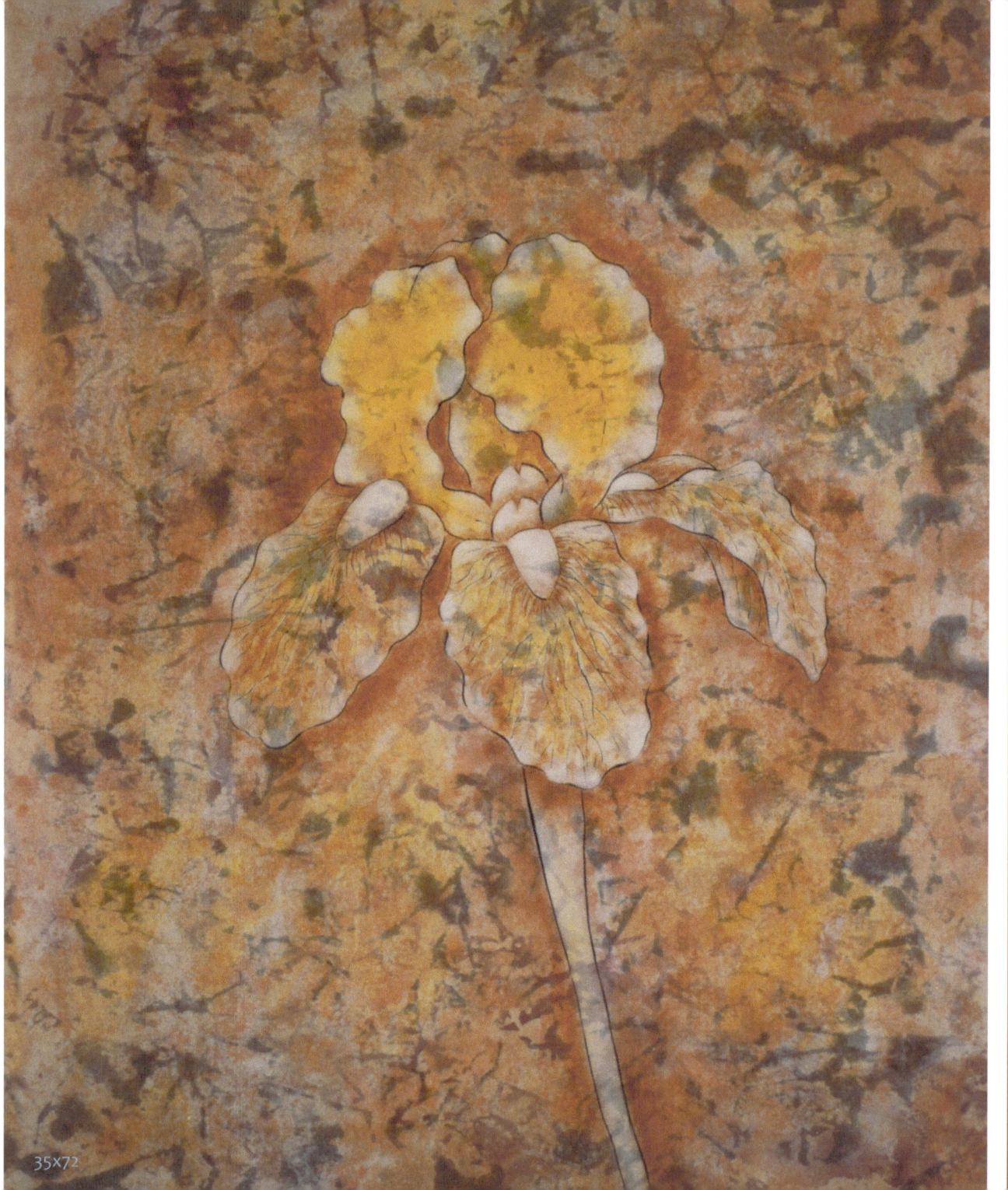

35x72

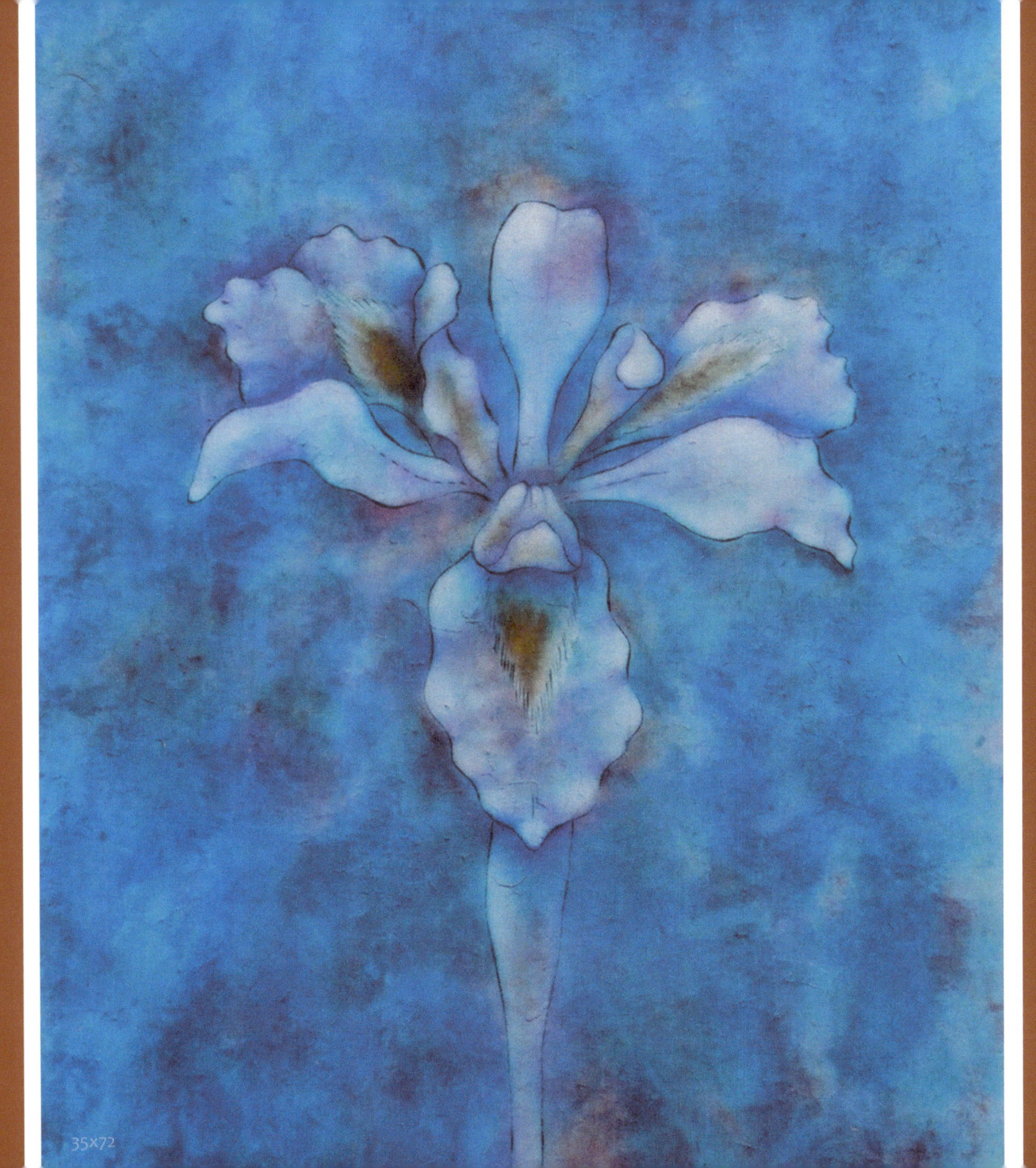

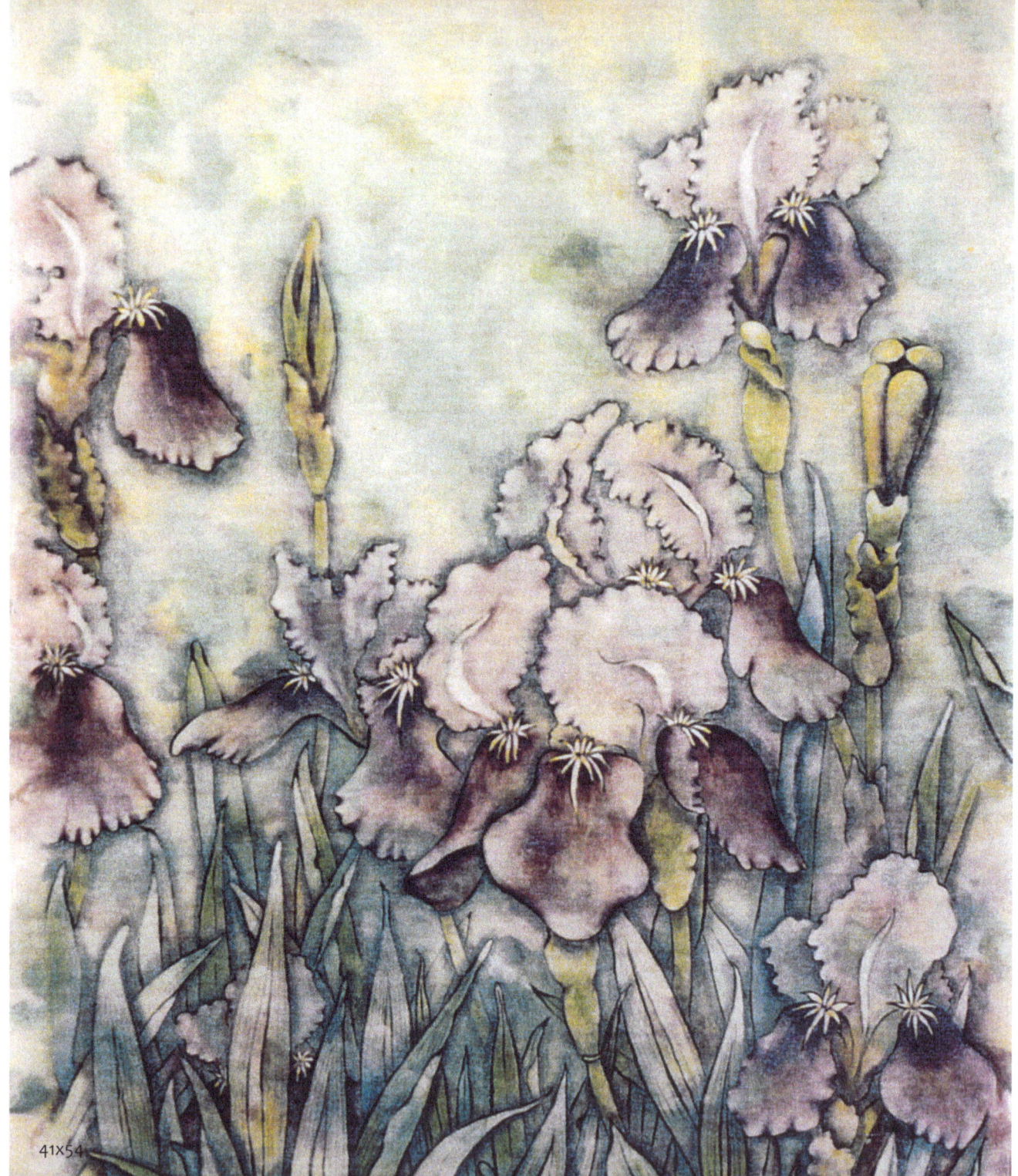

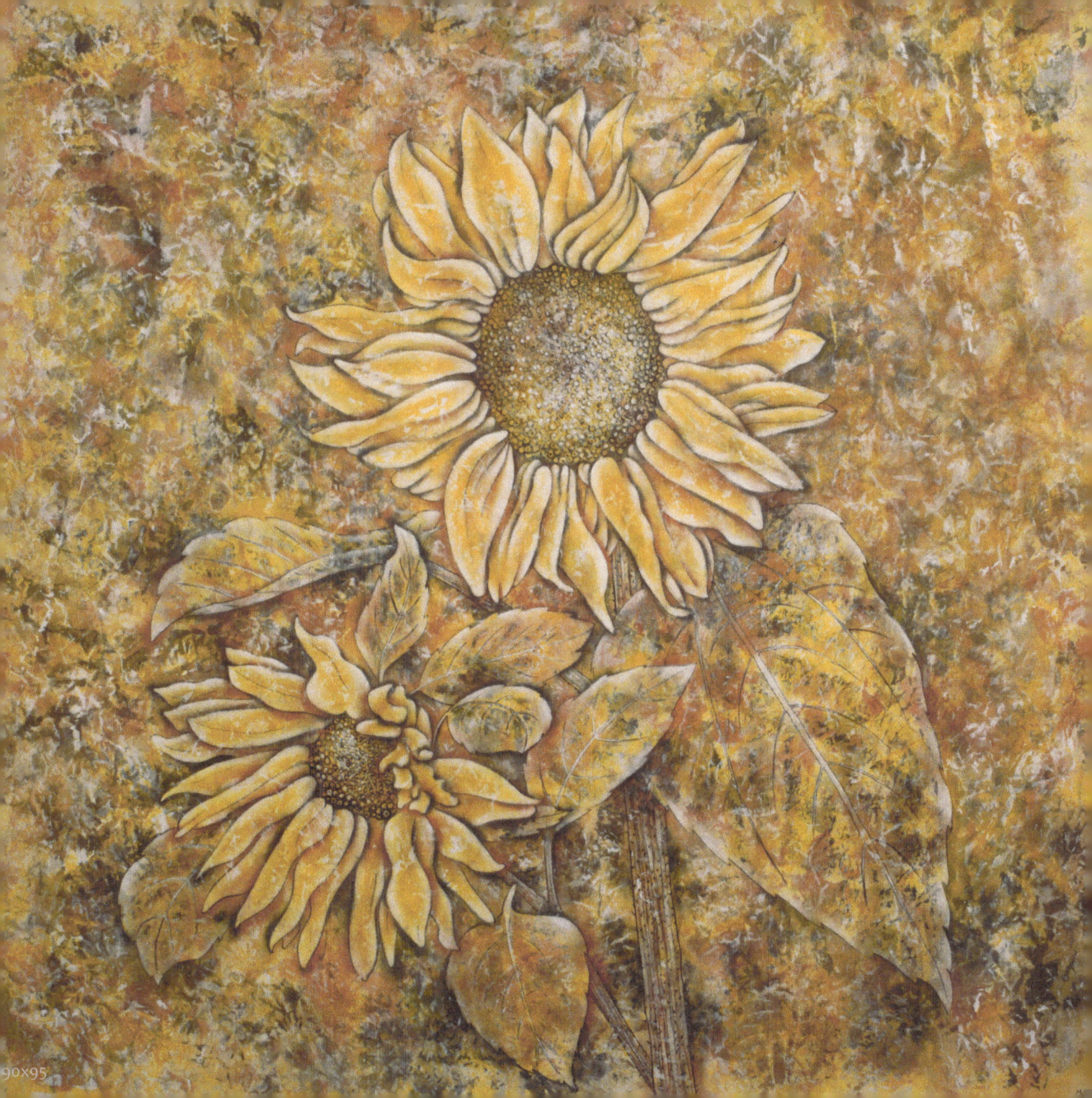

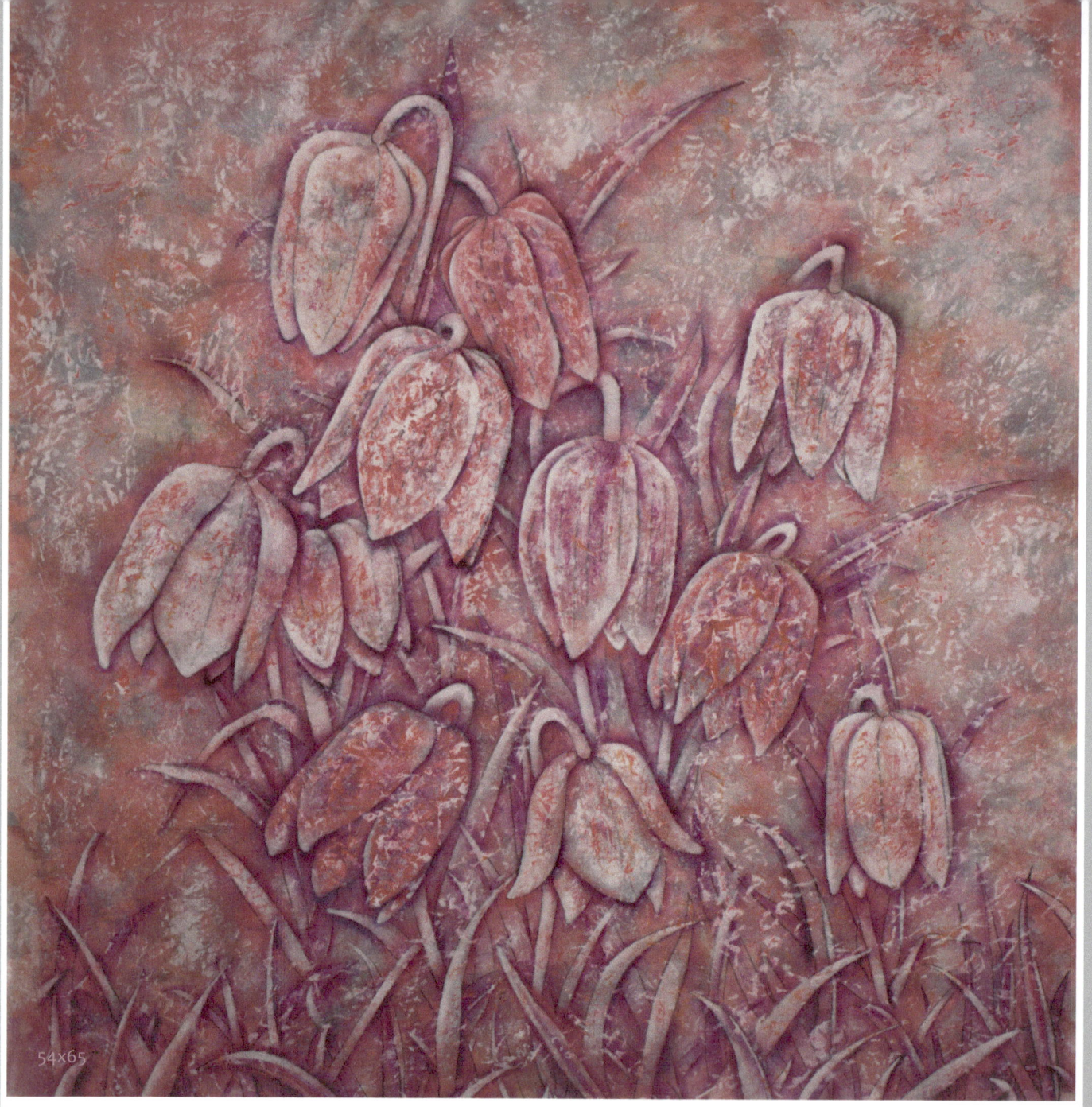
54x65

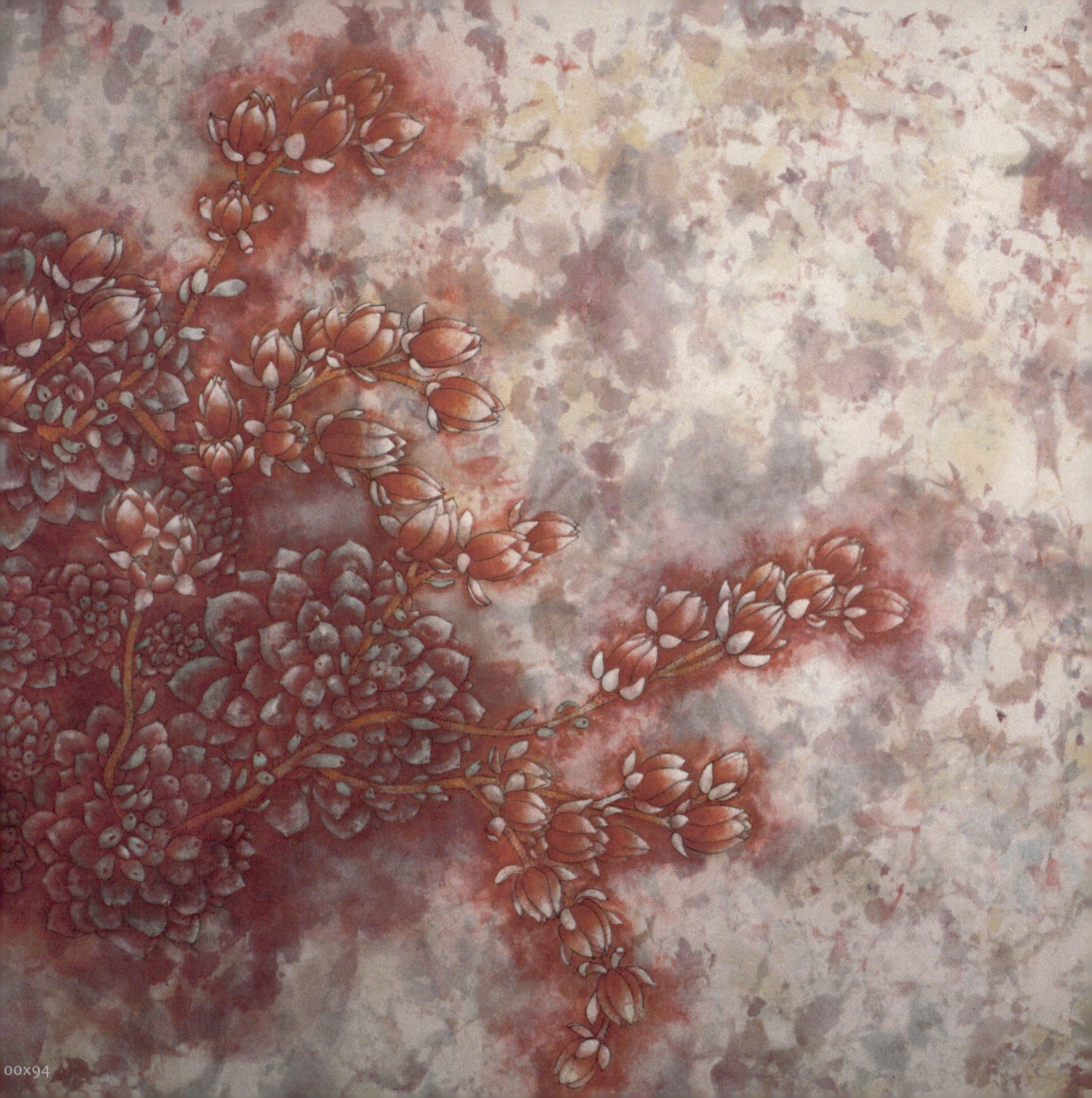

MEDIEVAL SAINTS

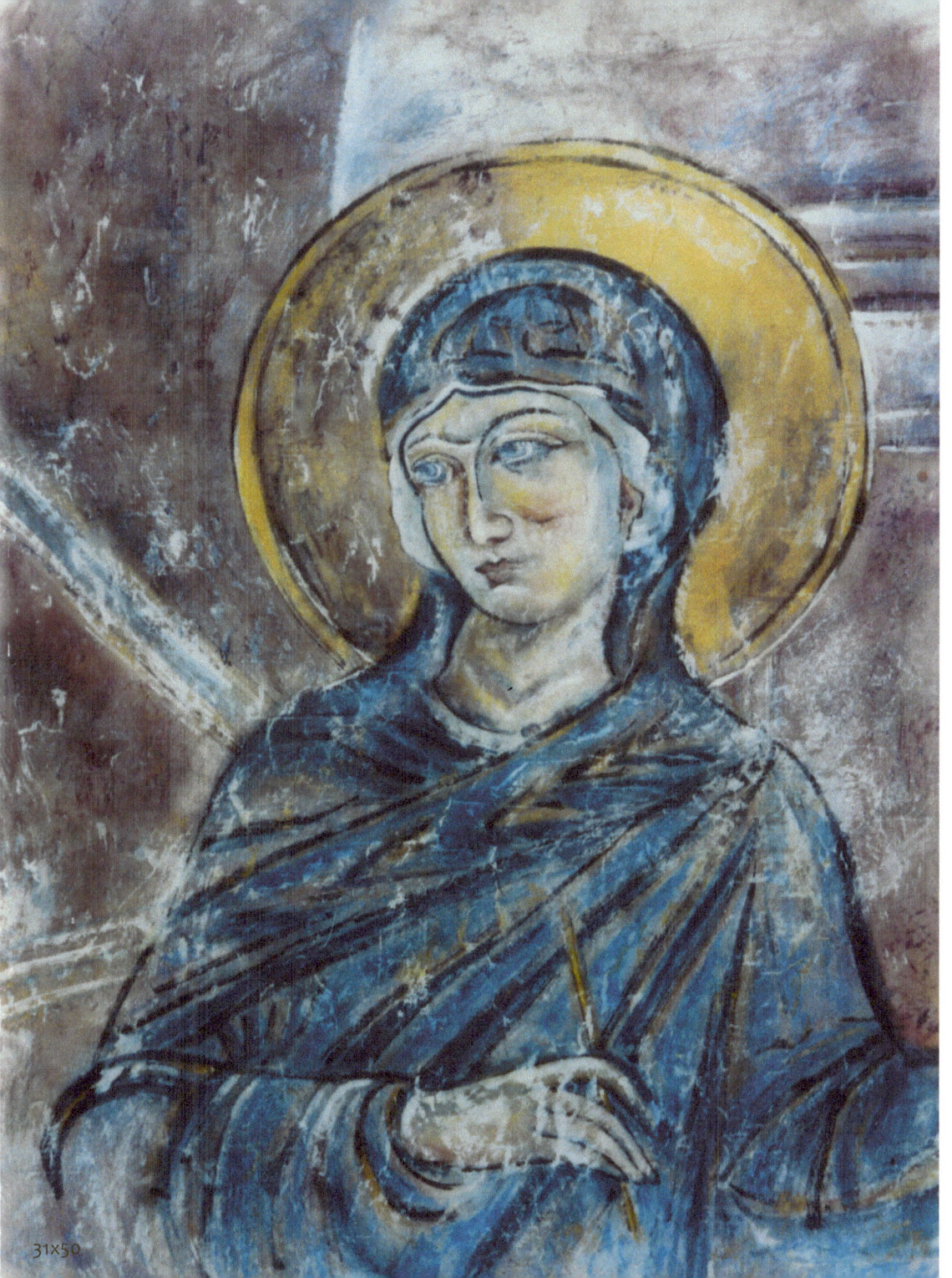

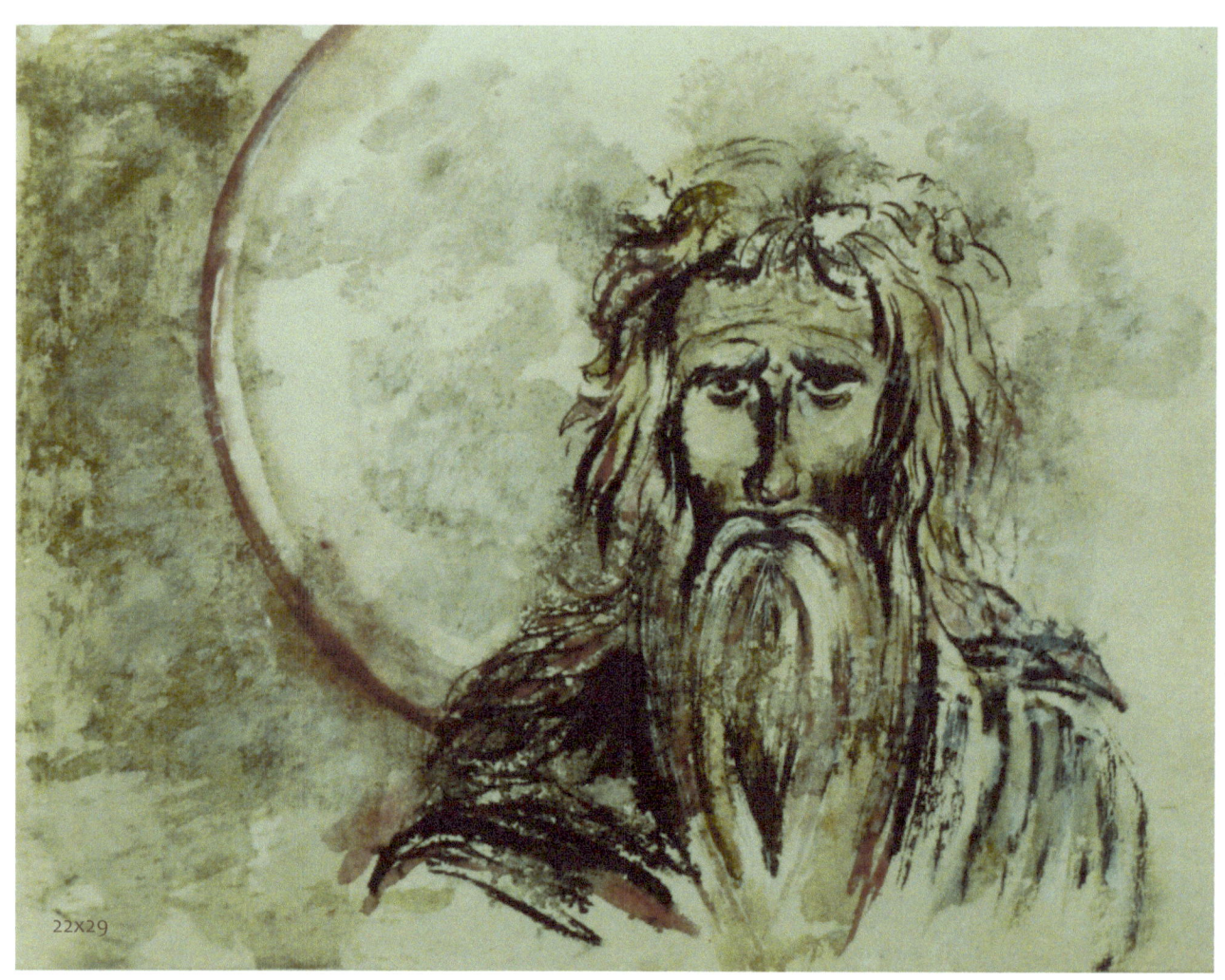

22x29

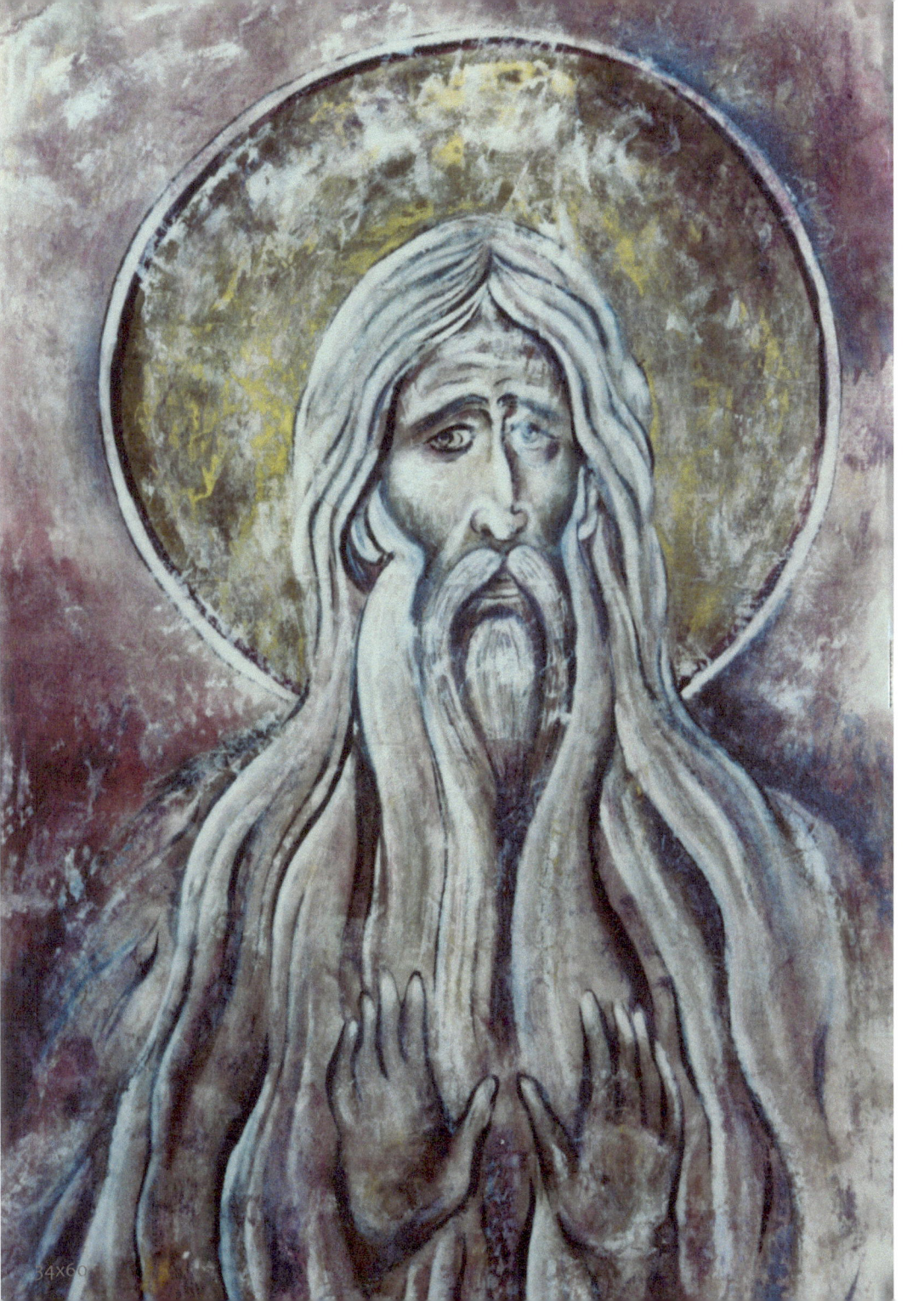

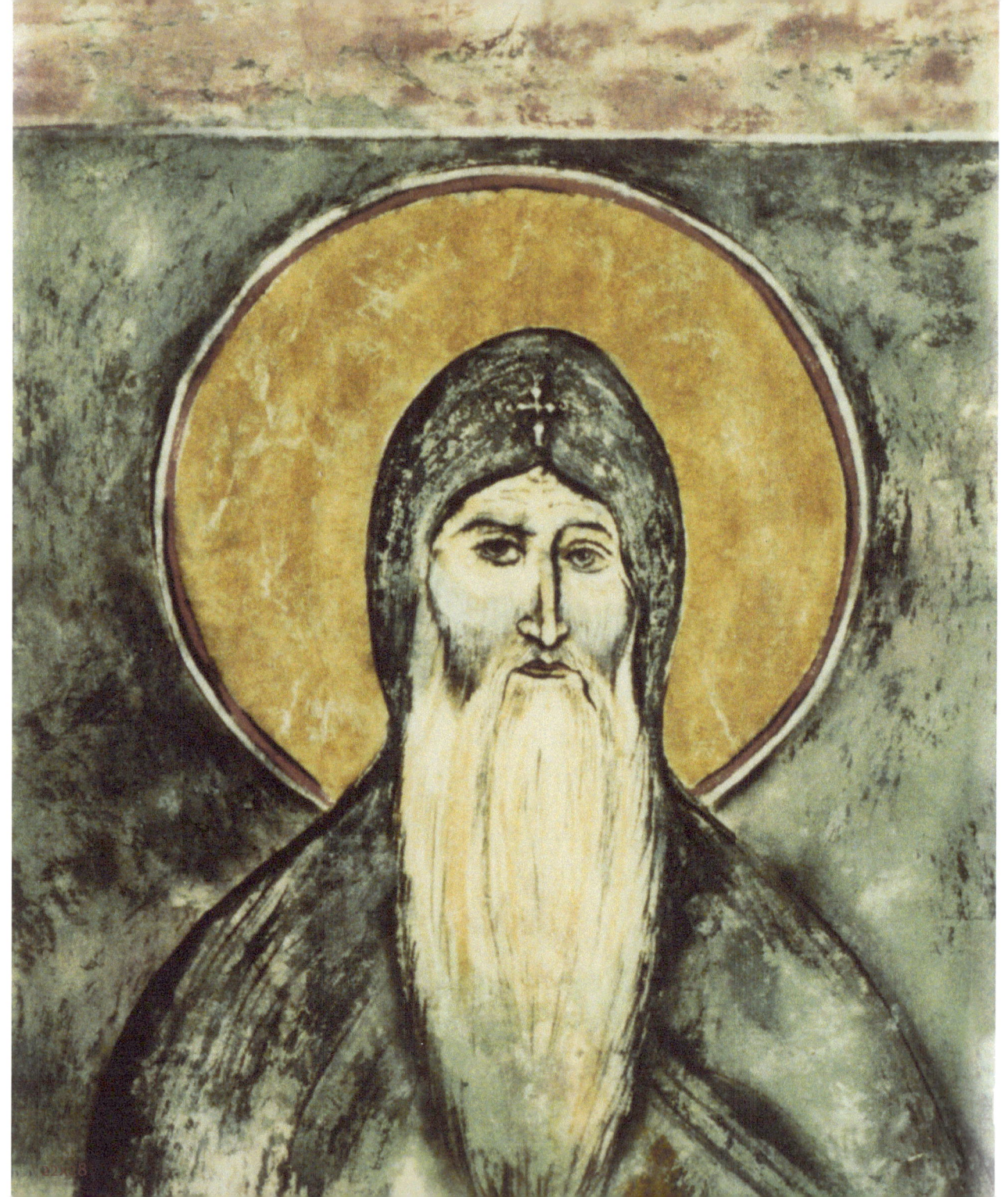

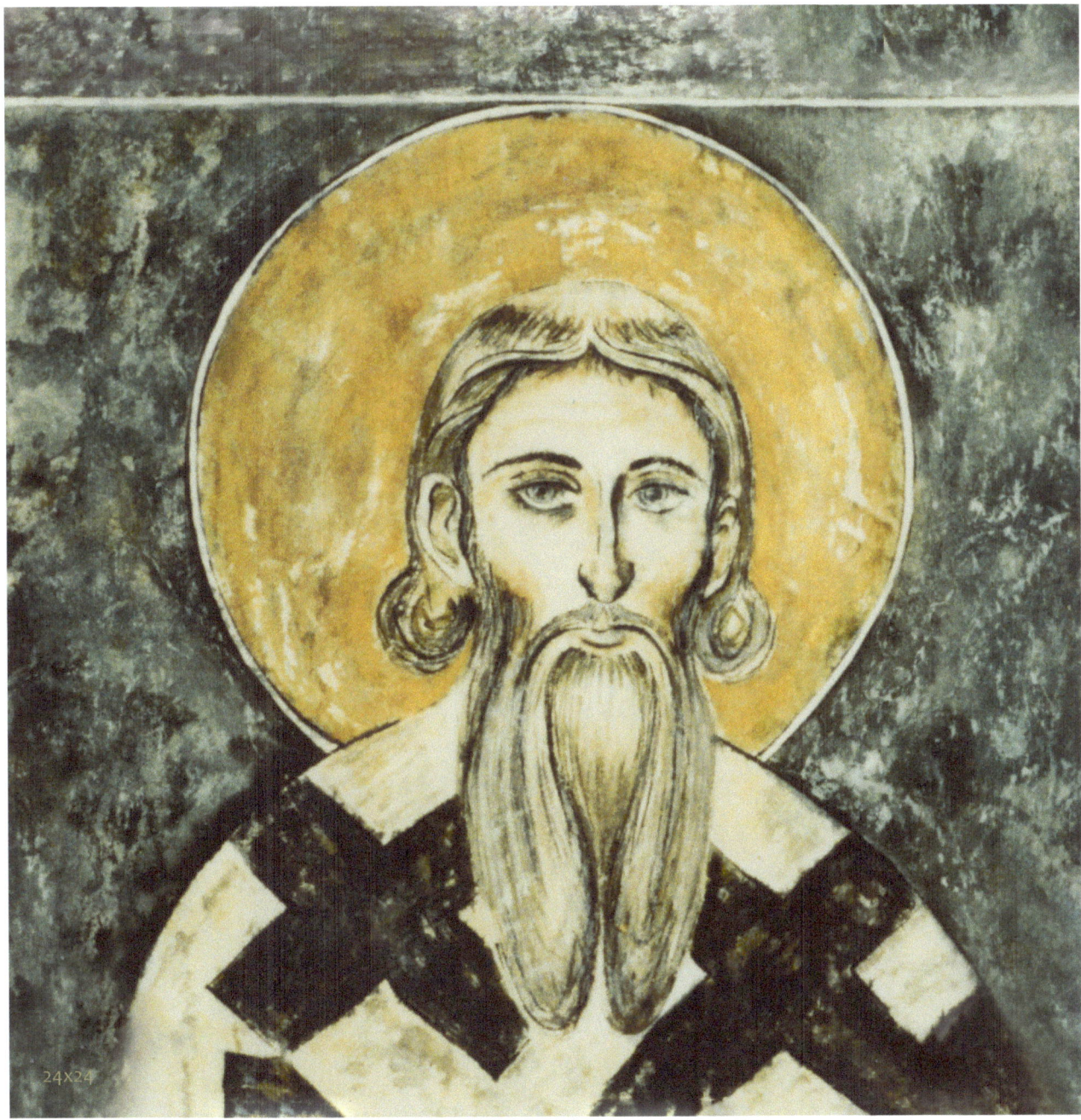

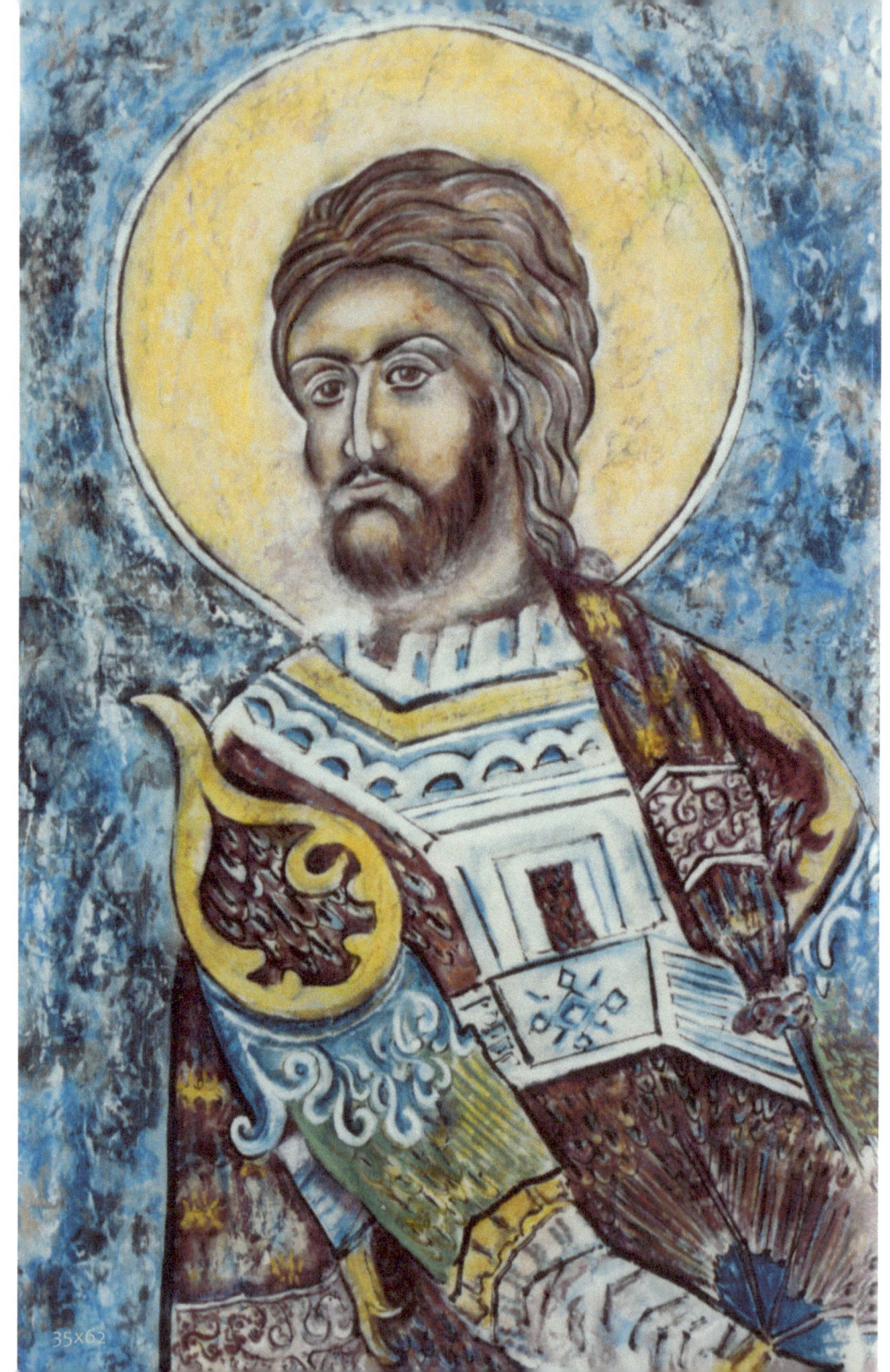

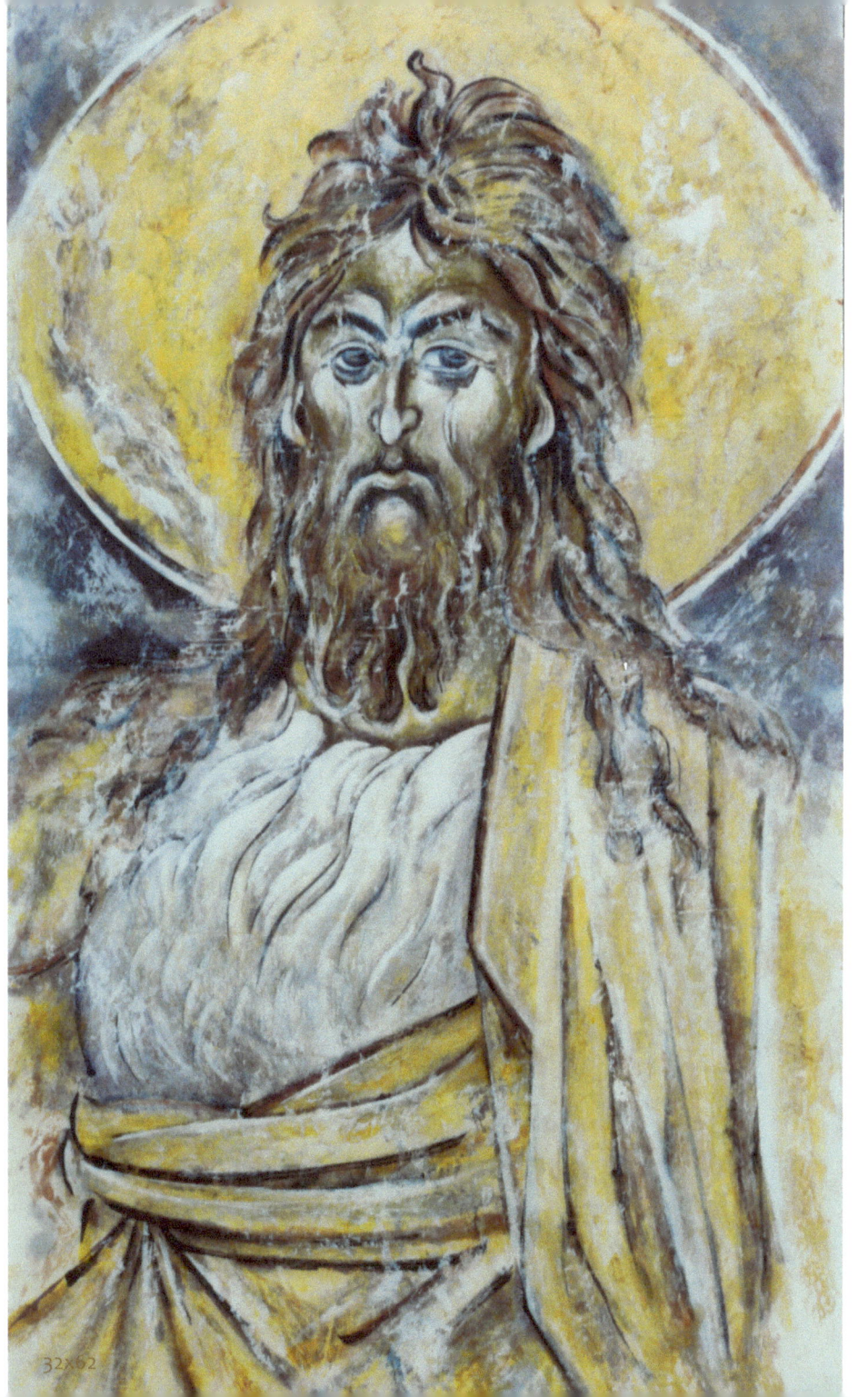

BEYOND
THOUGHTS

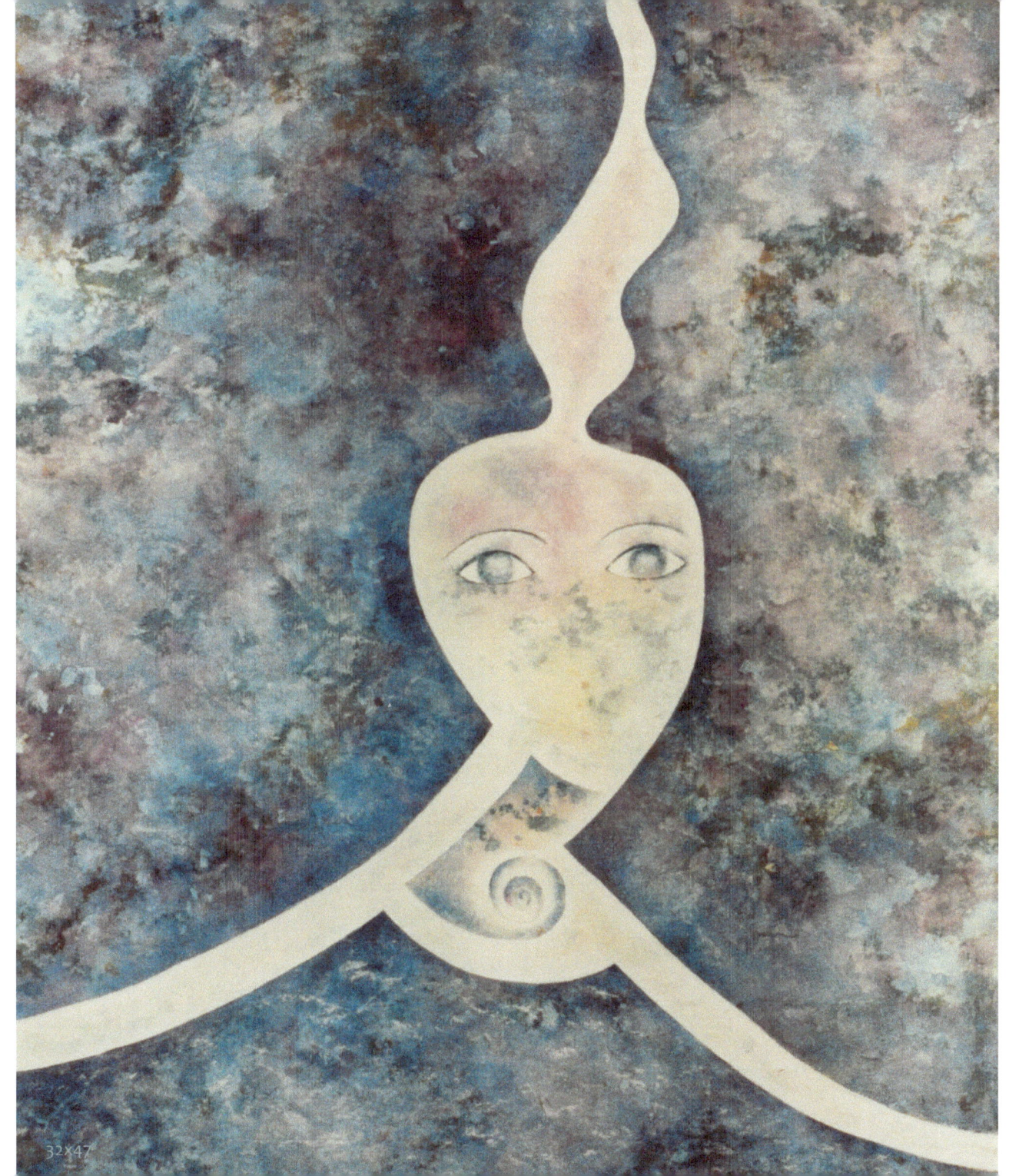

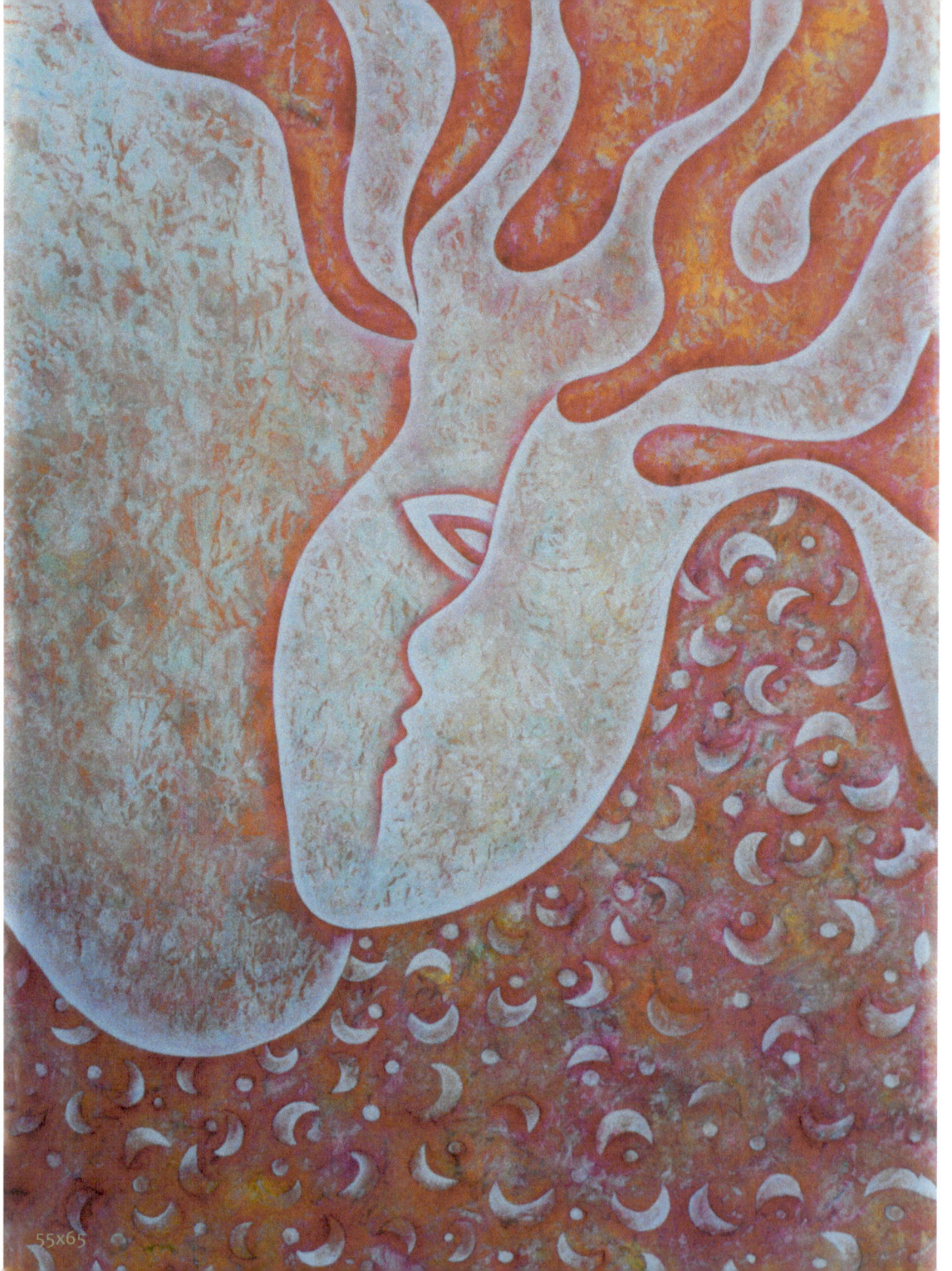

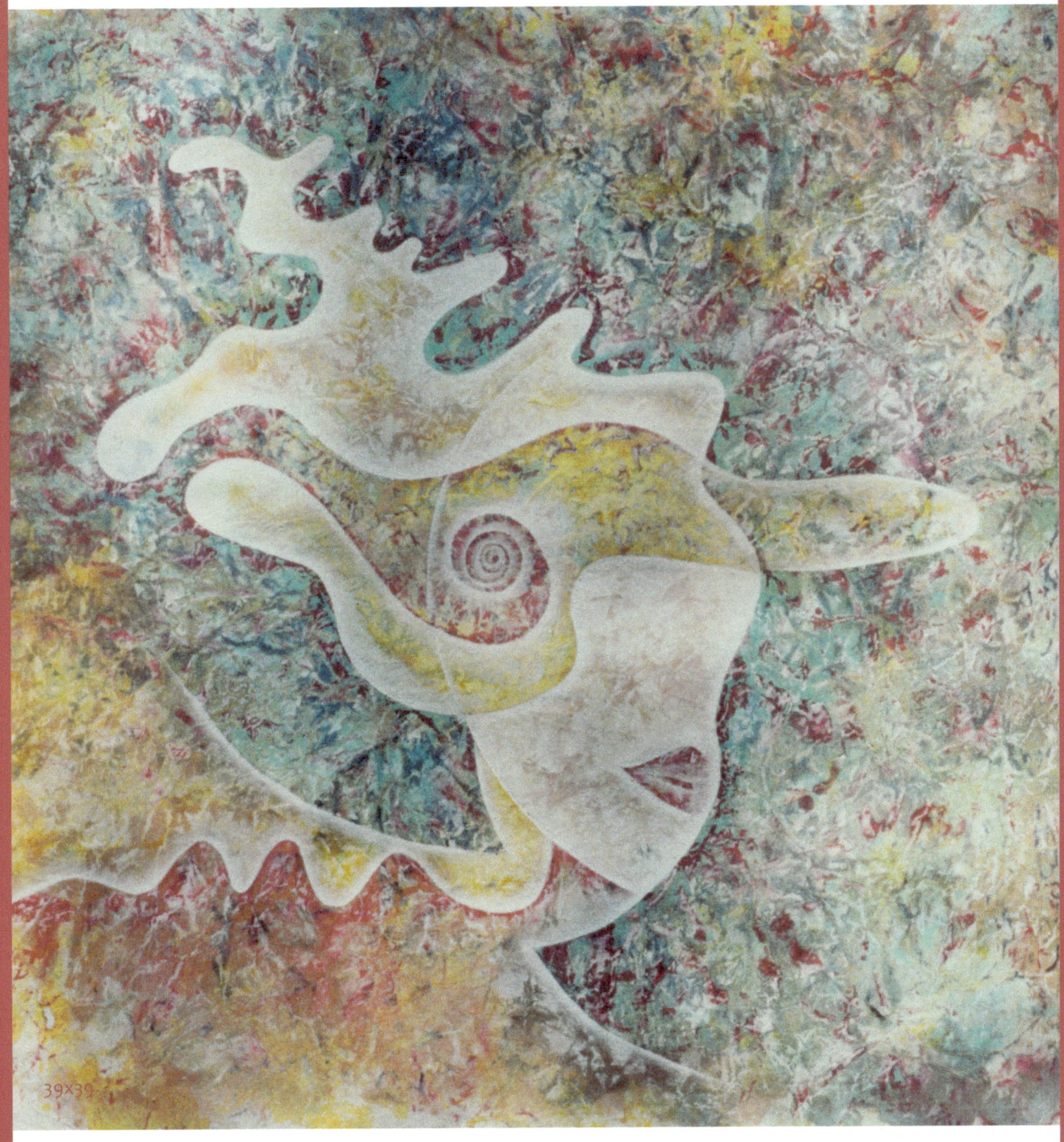

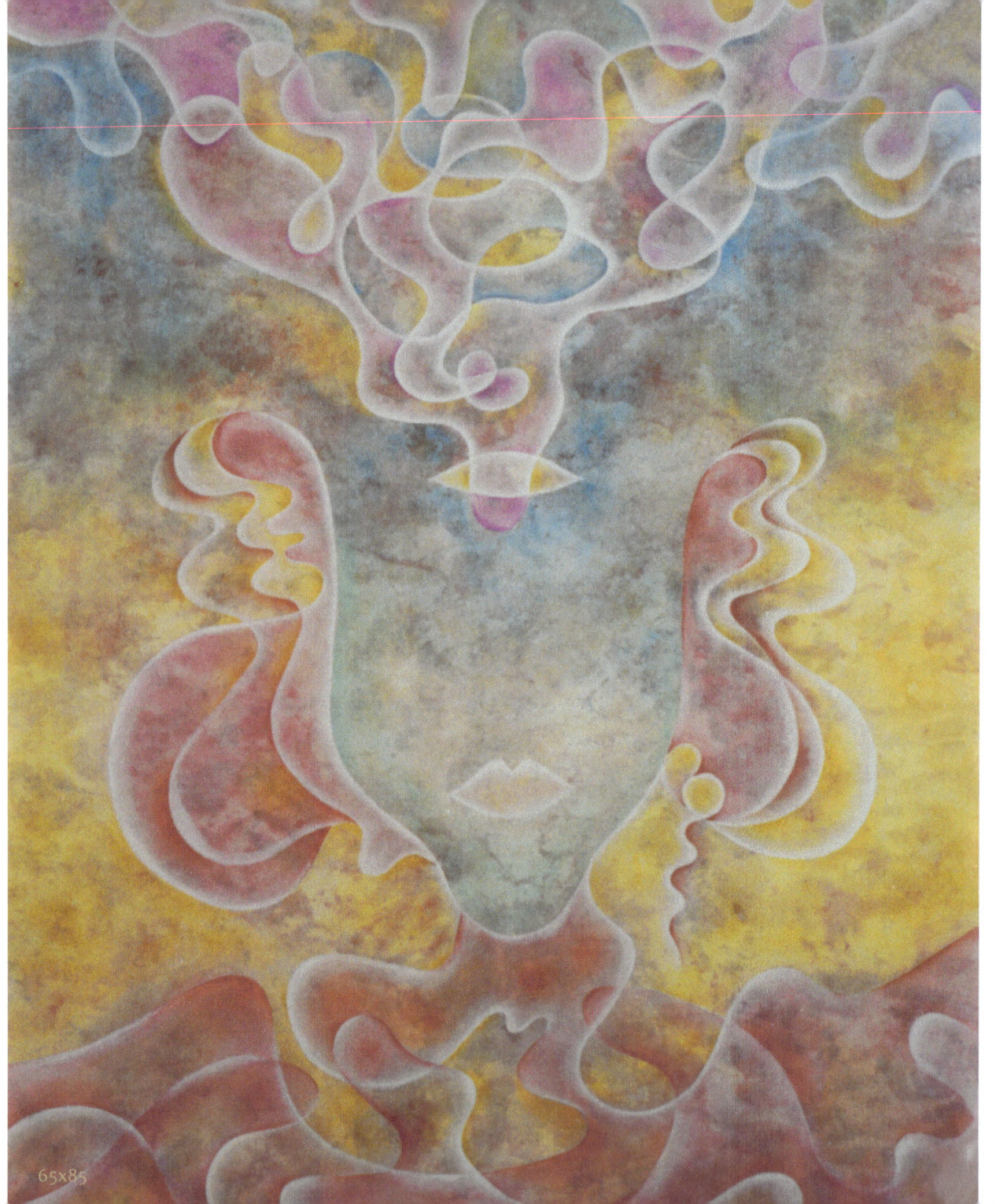

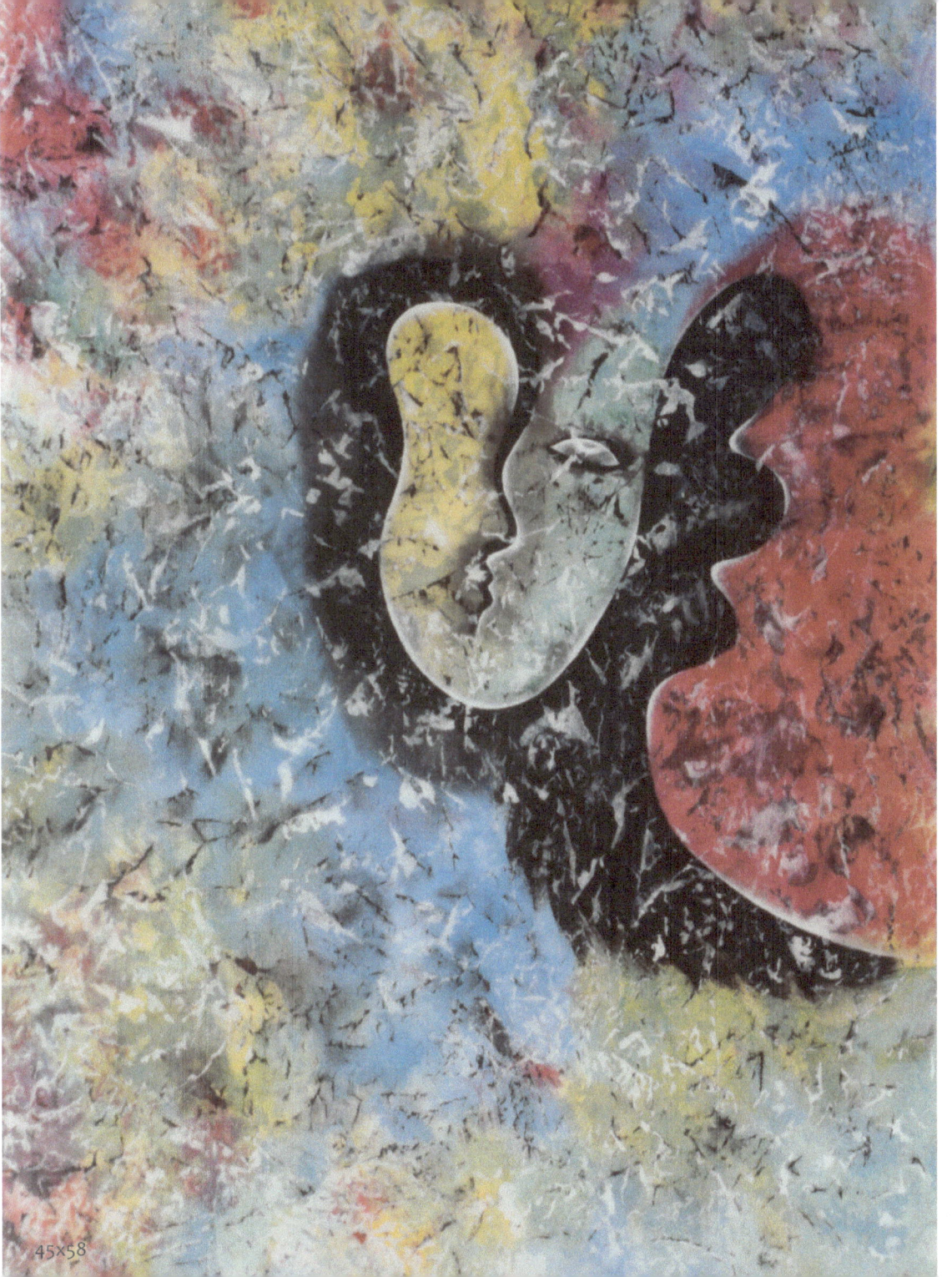

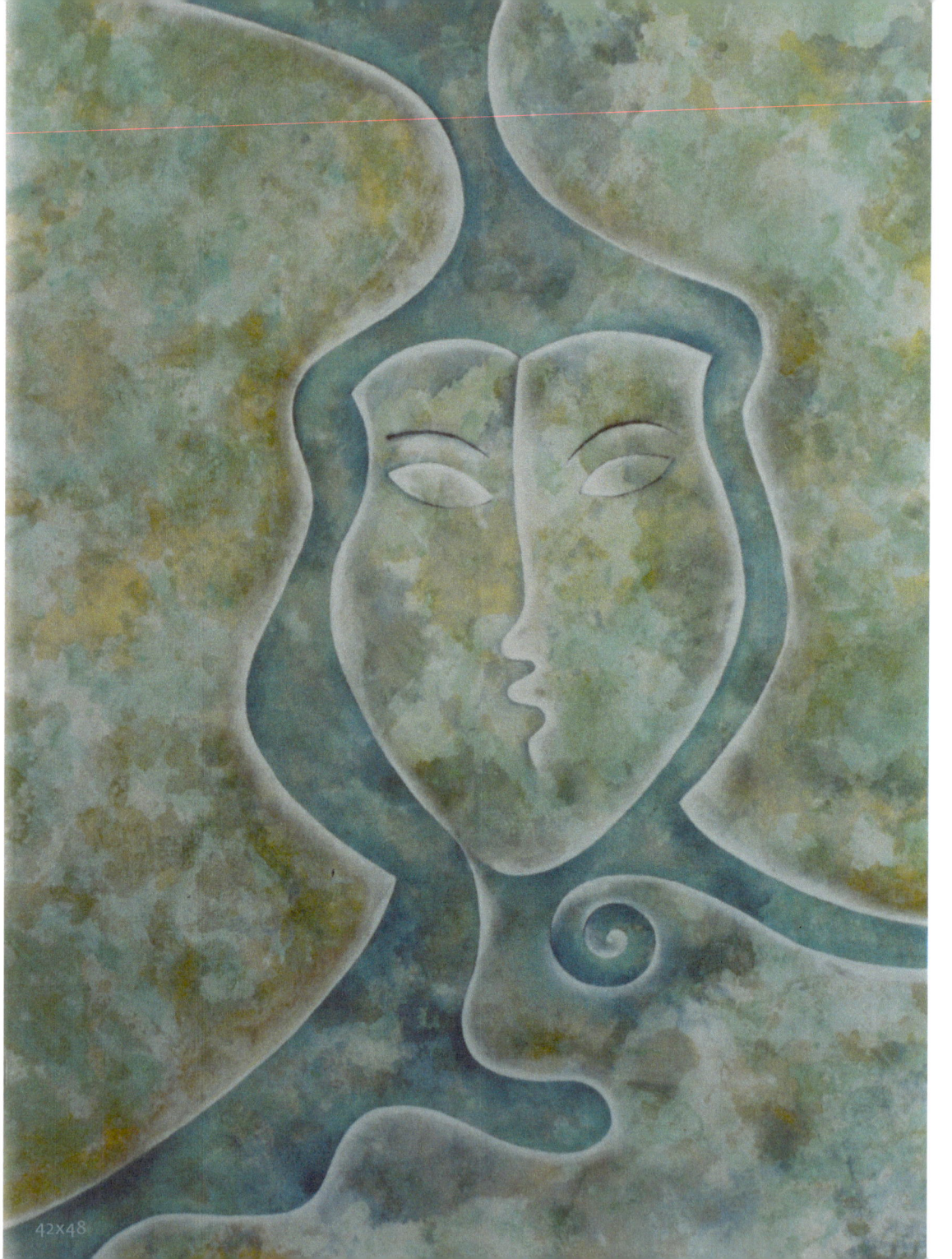

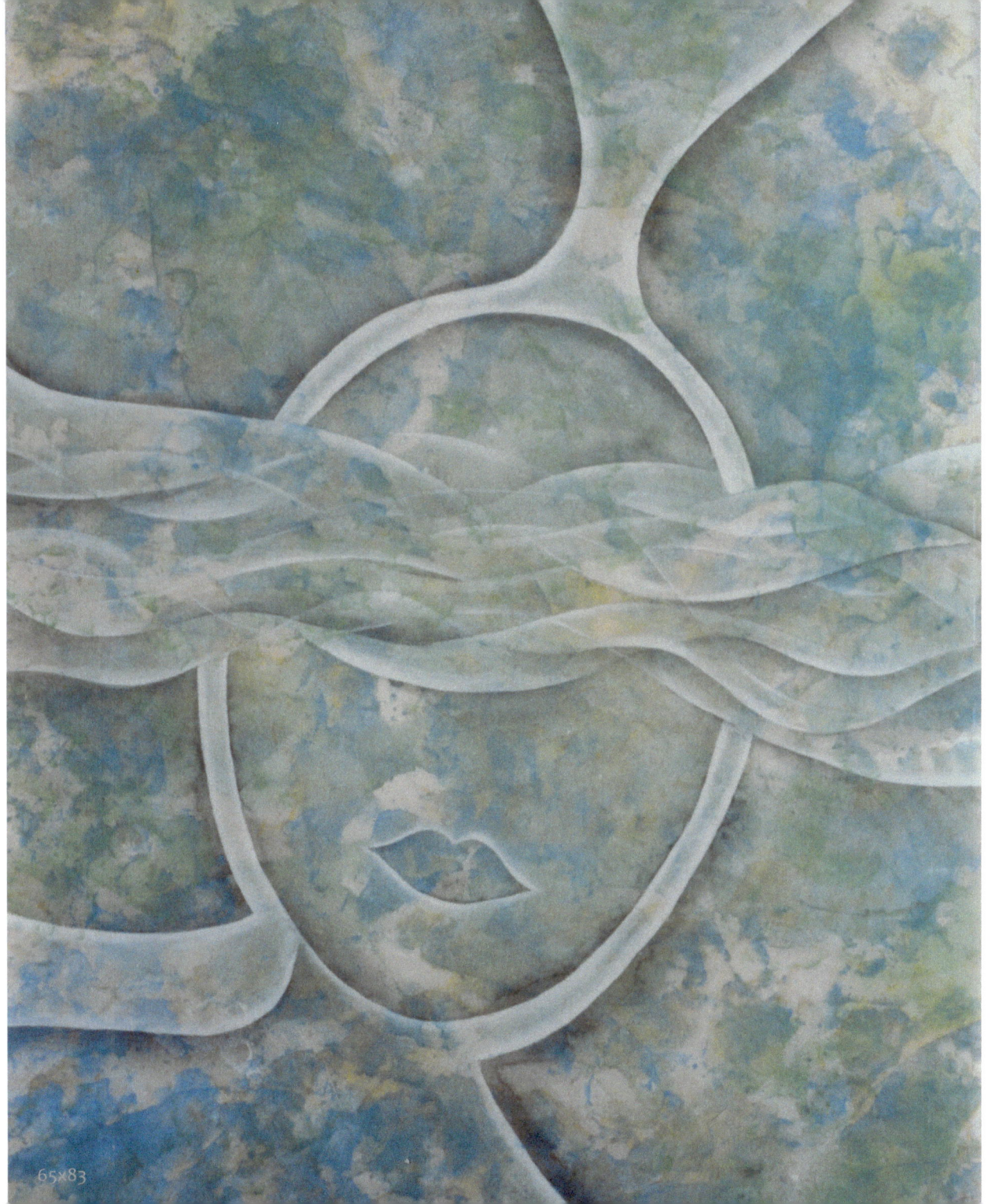

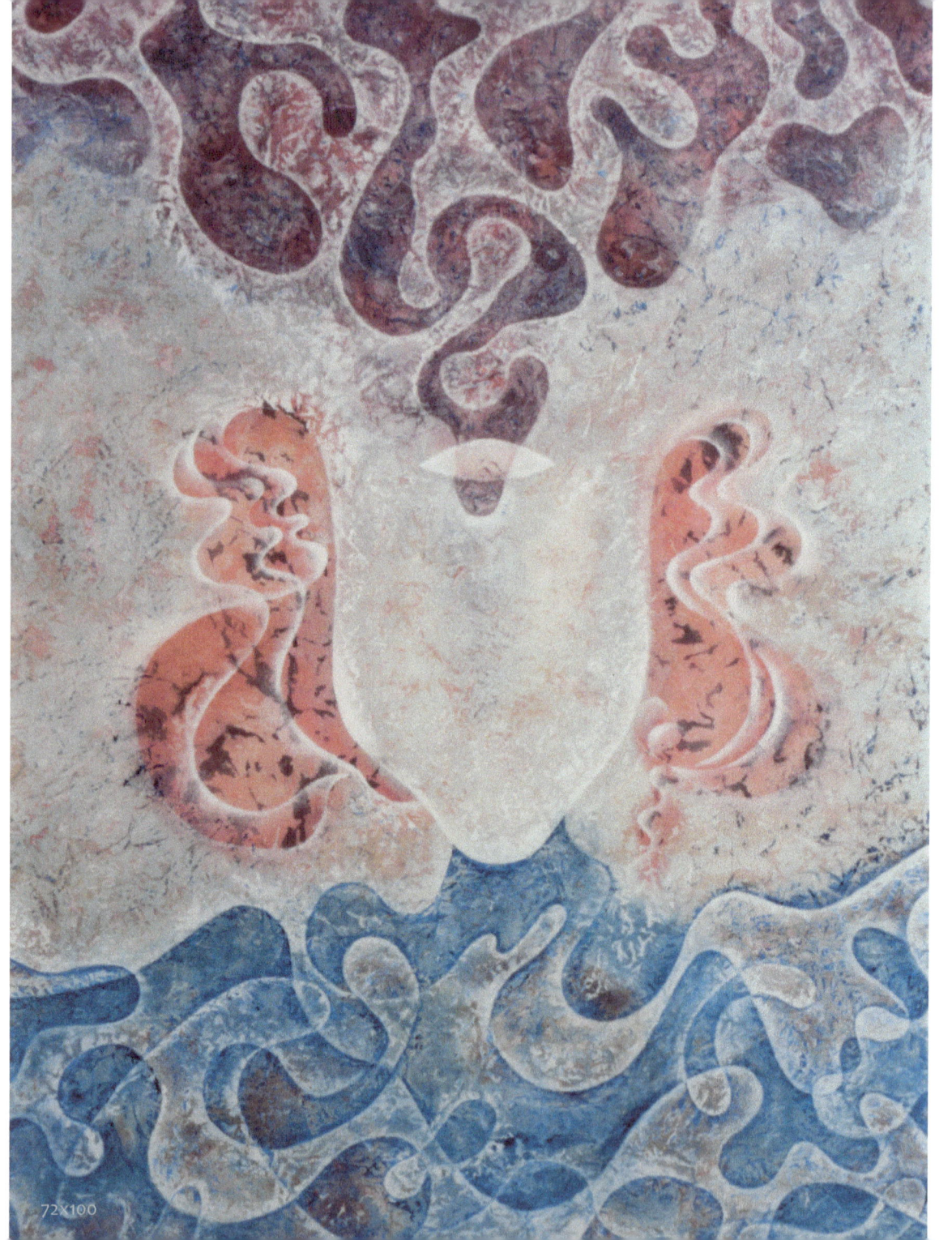

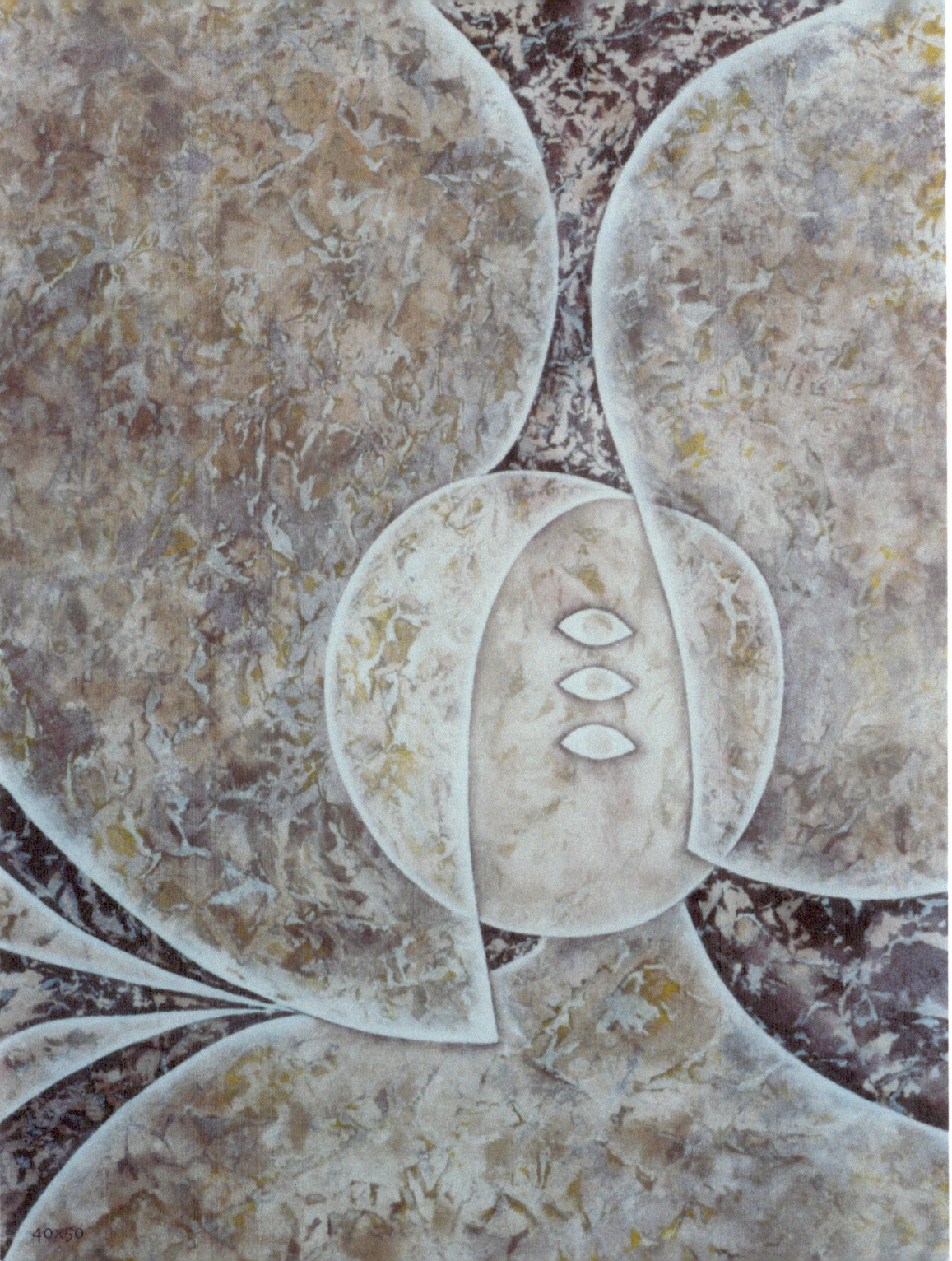

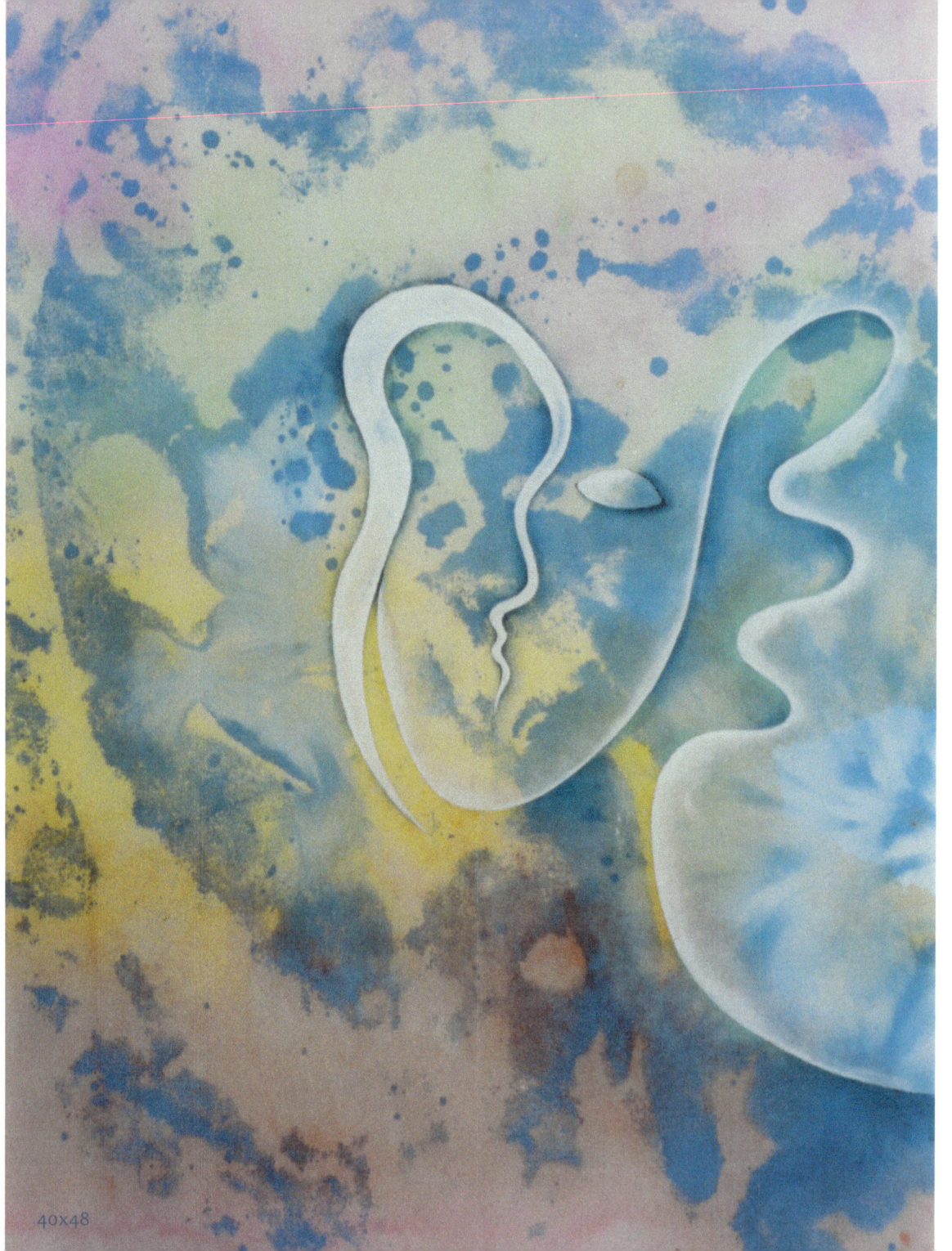

40x48

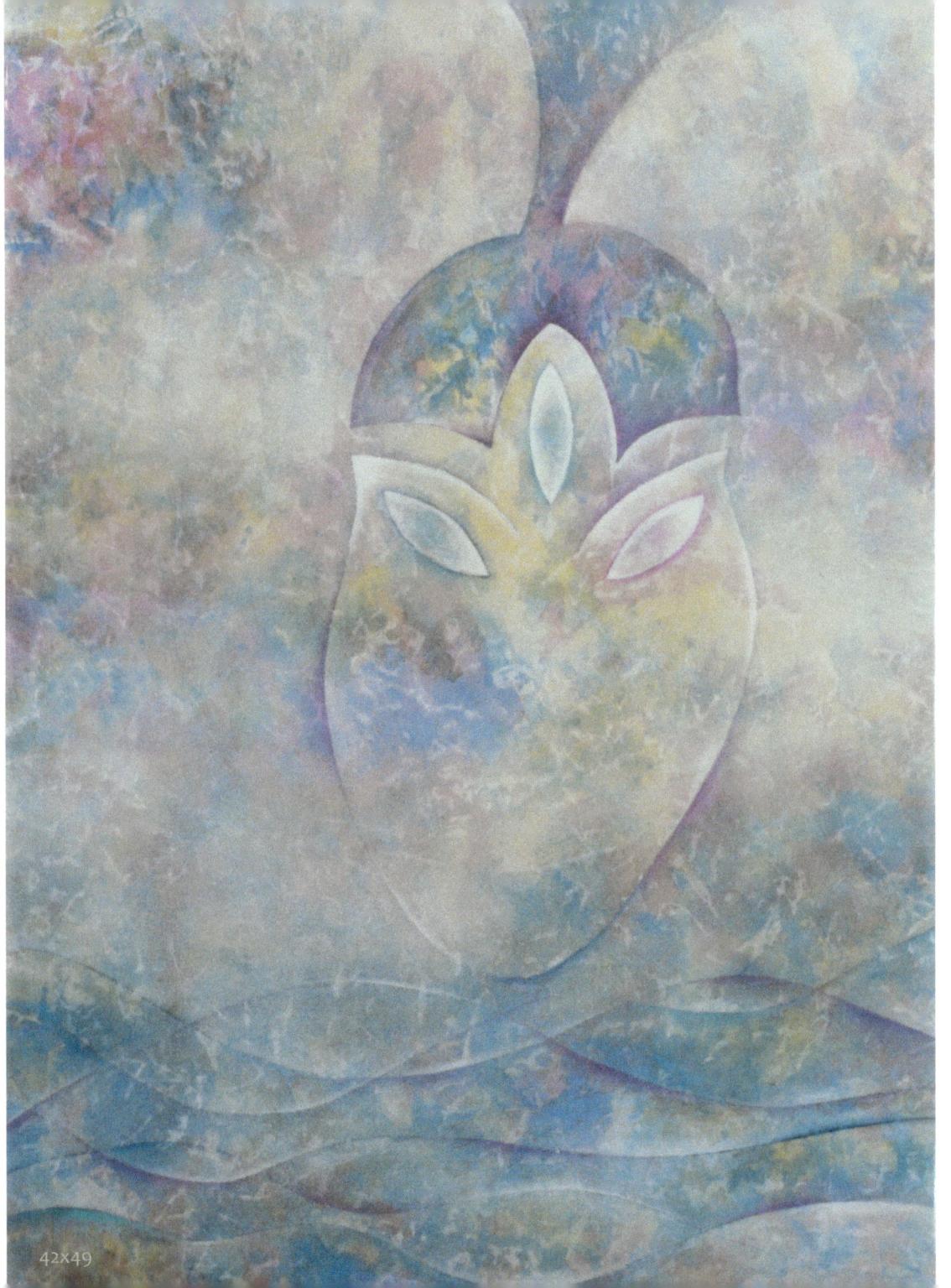

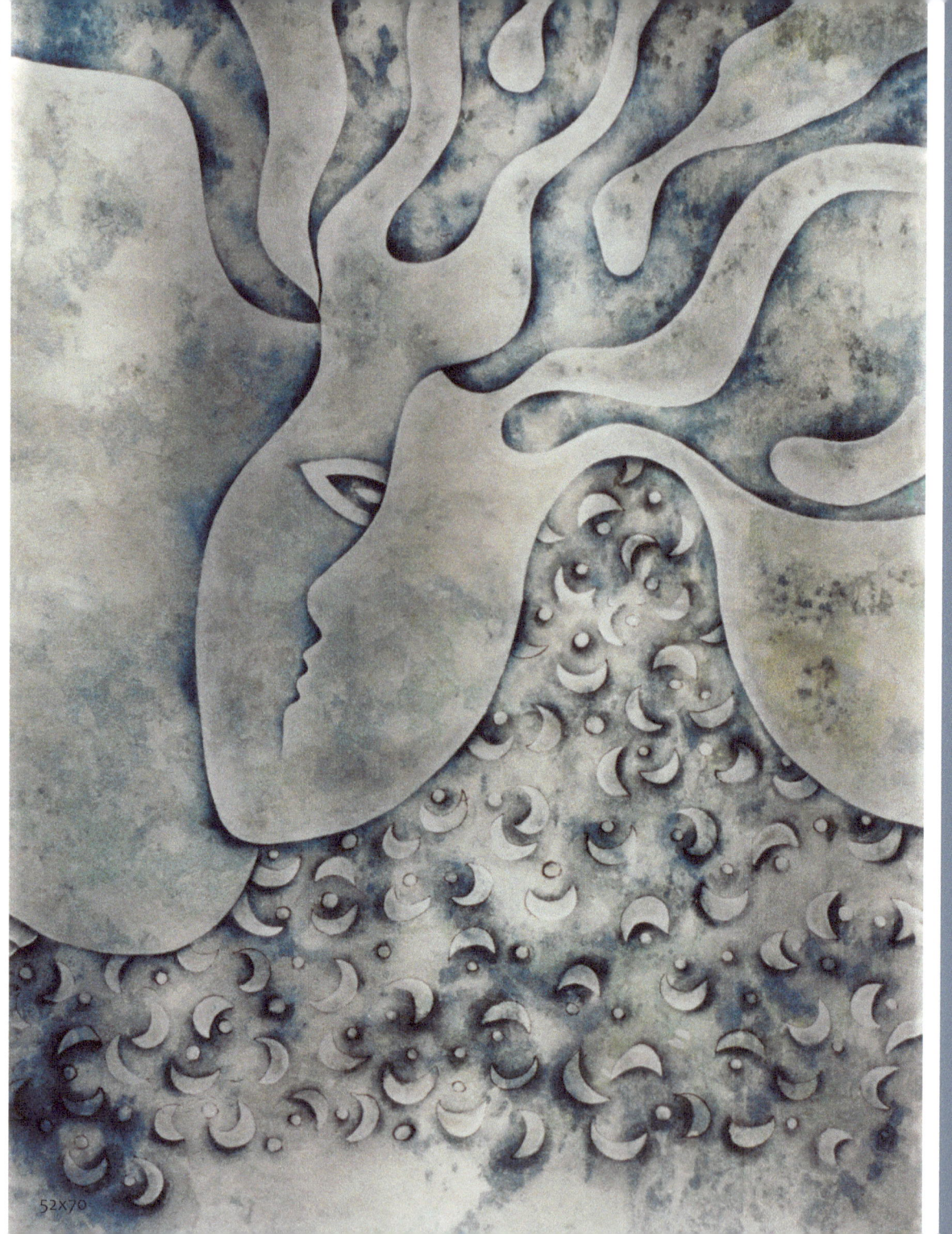

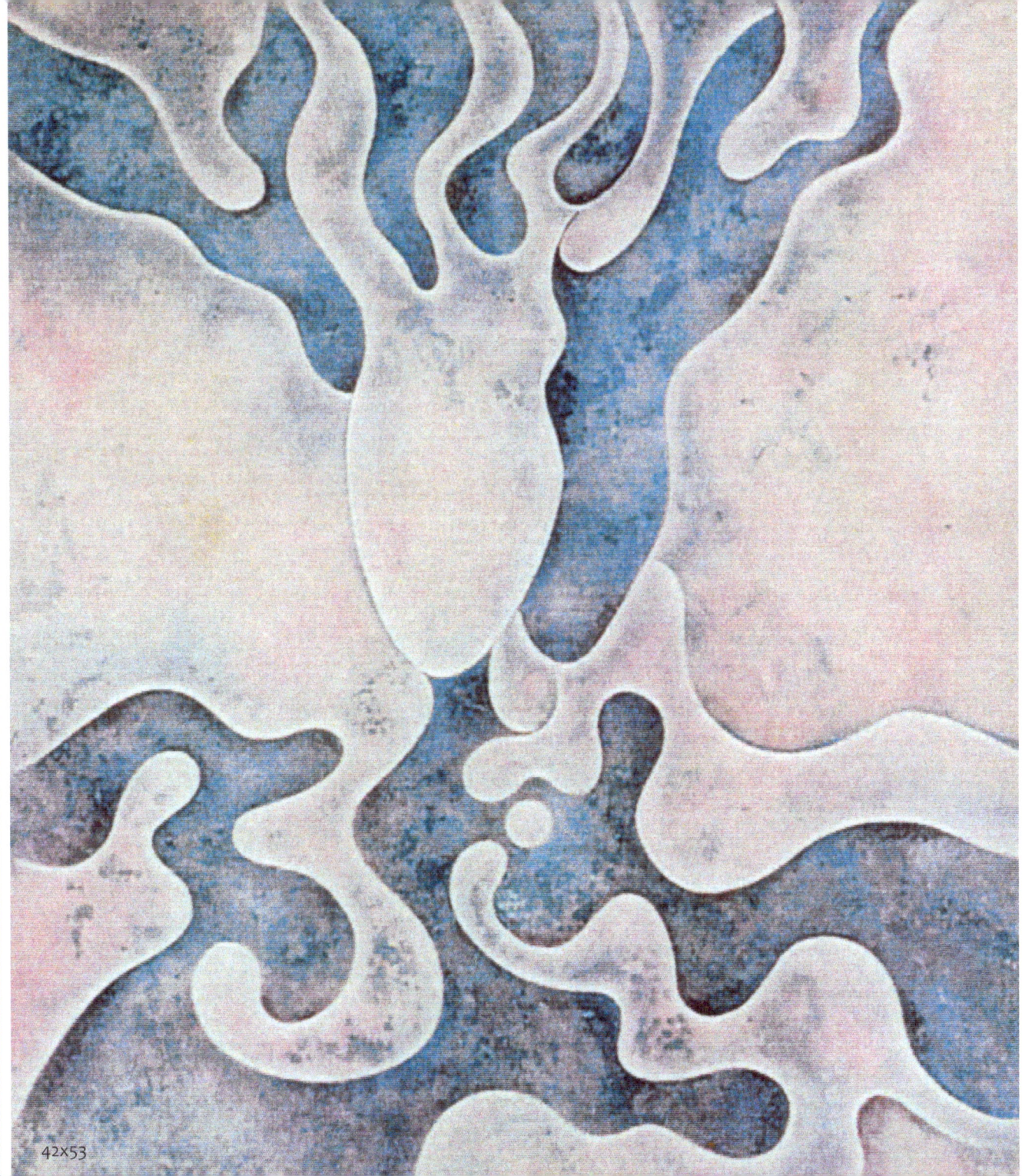
42x53

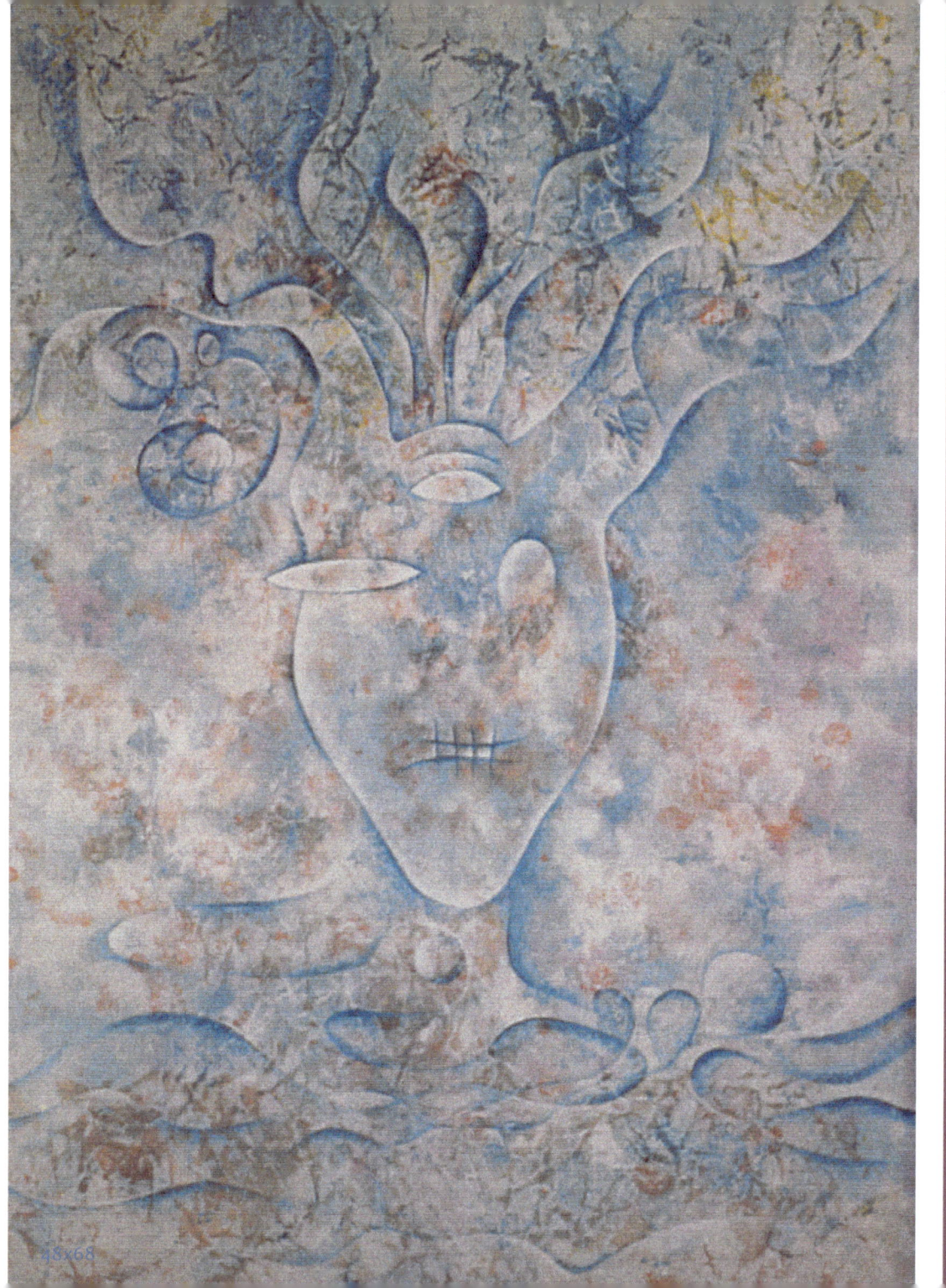

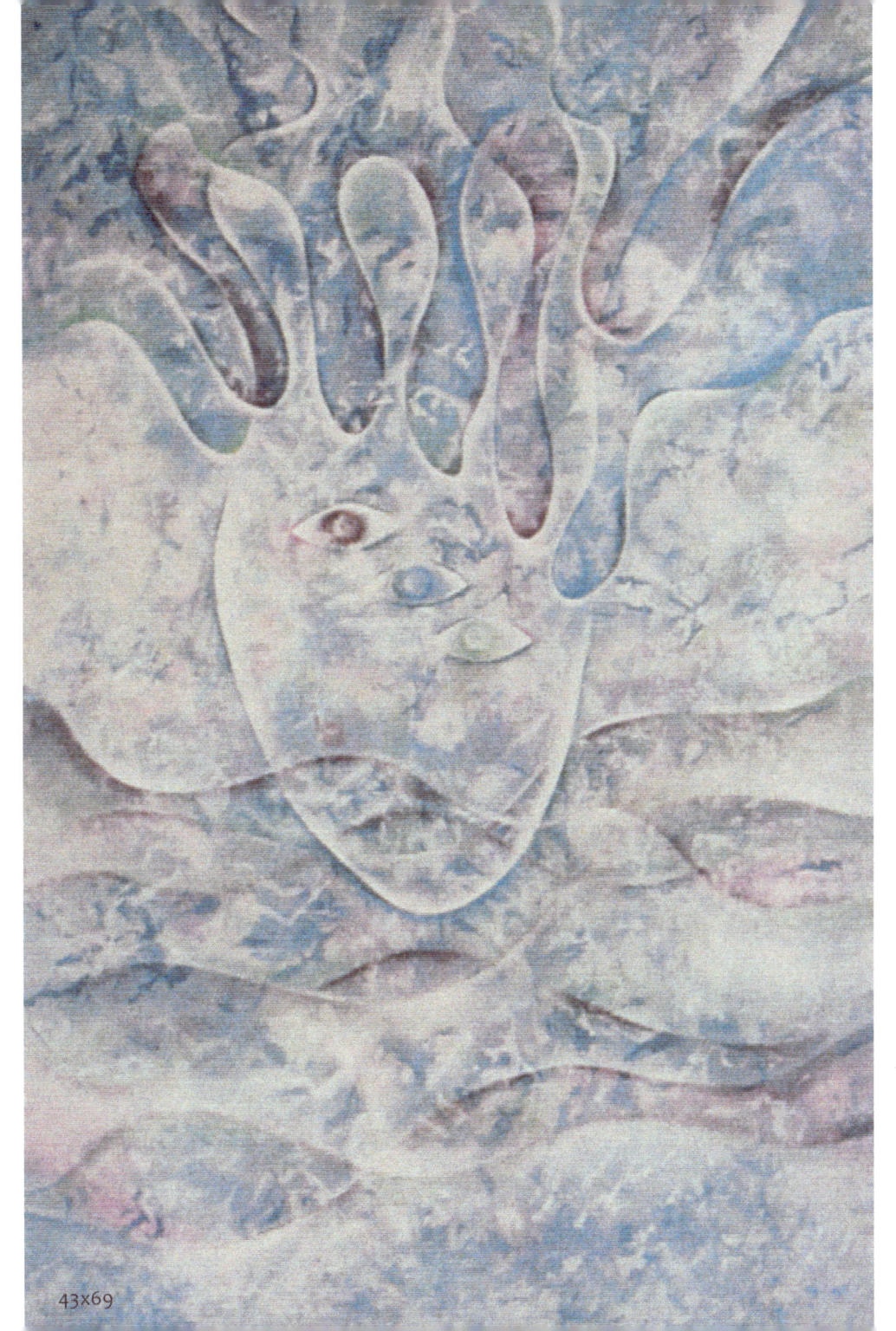

43x69

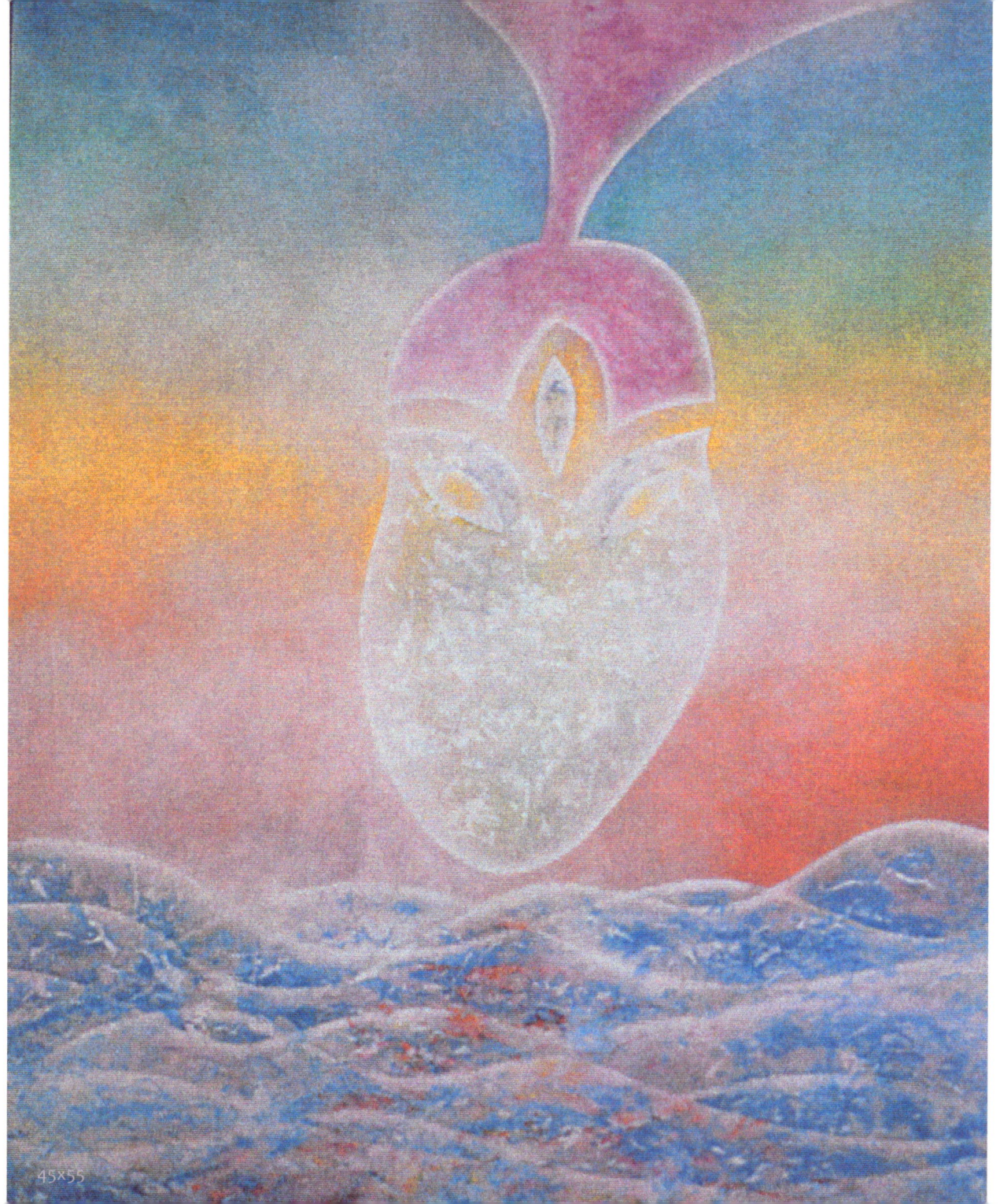

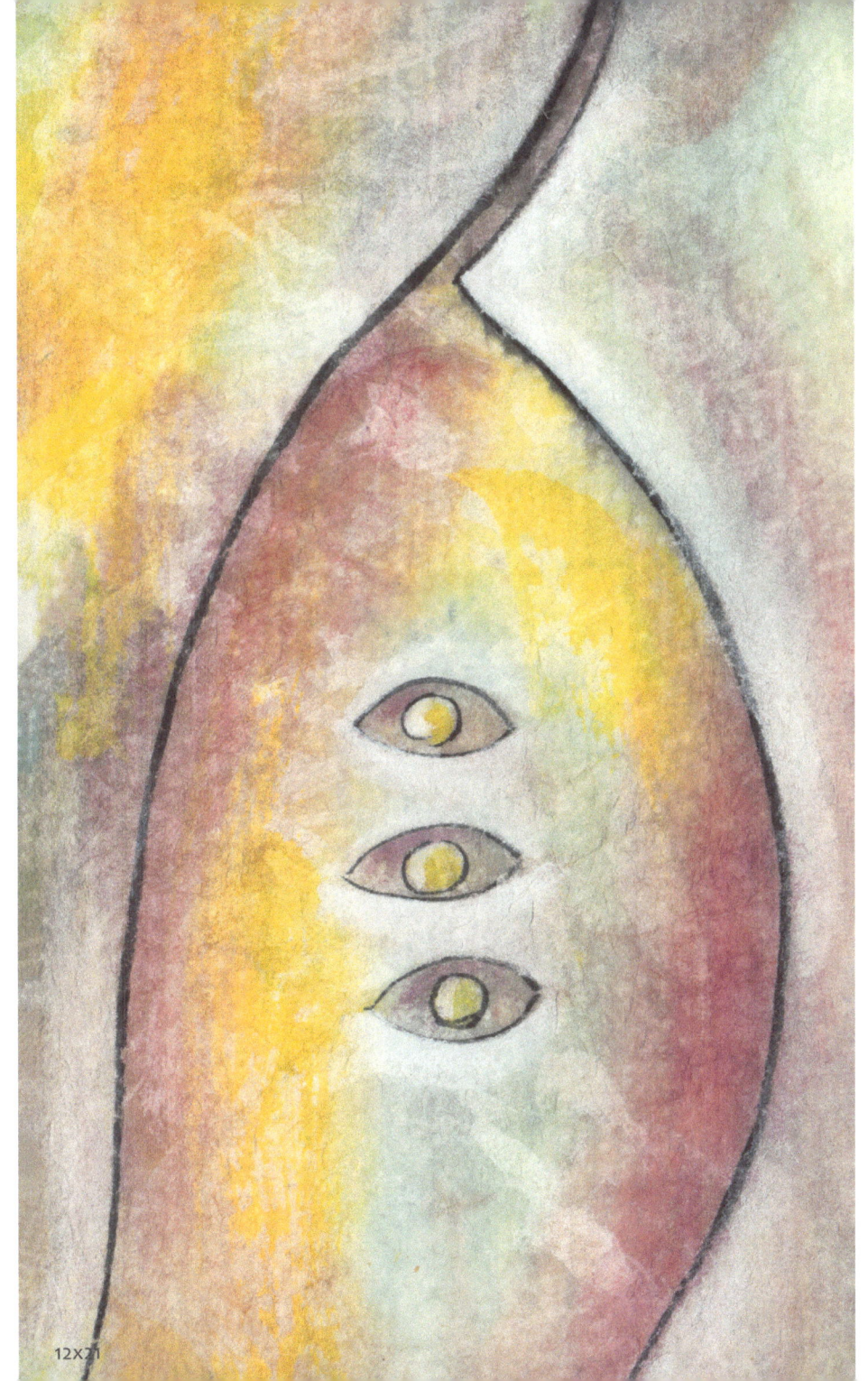

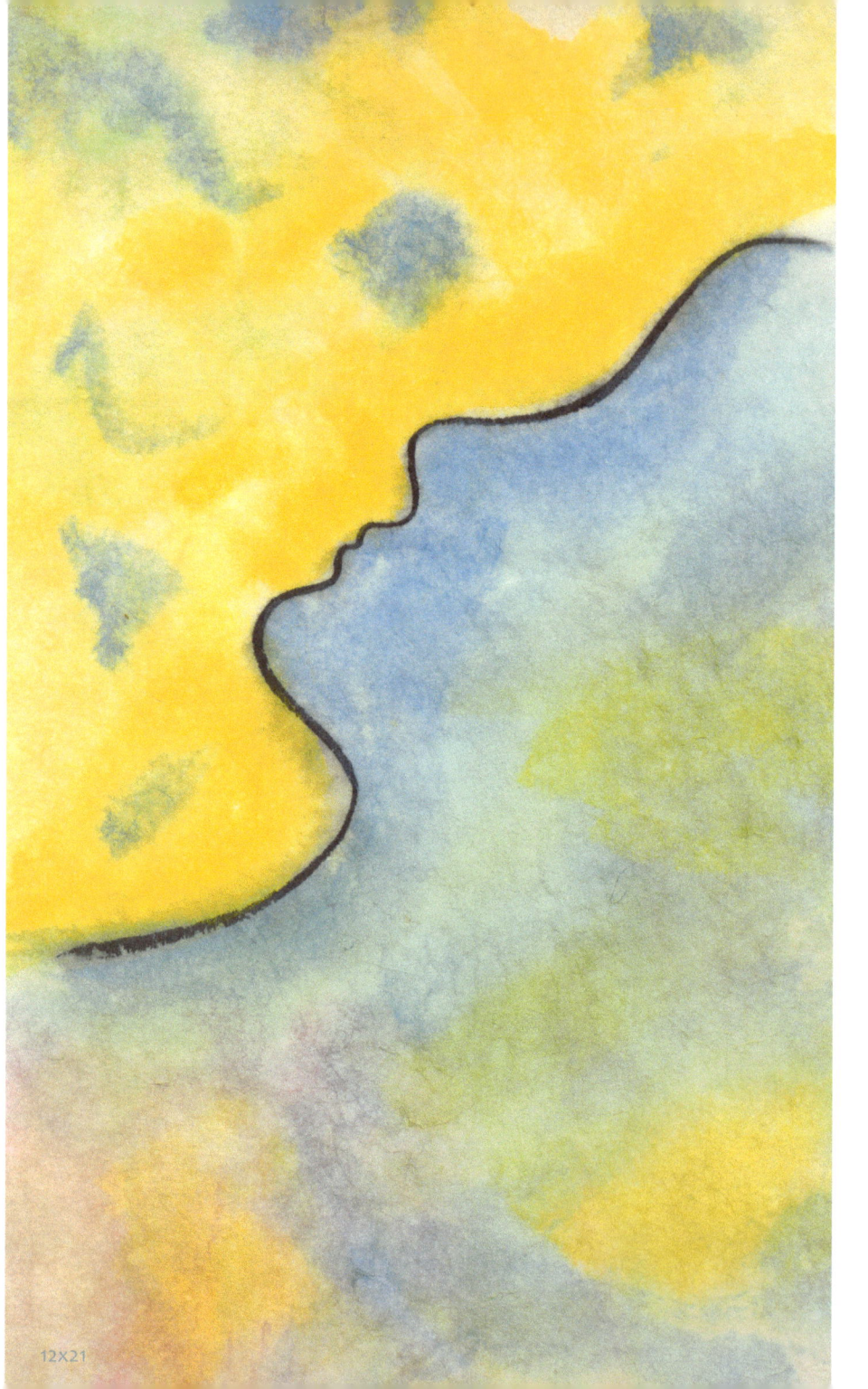

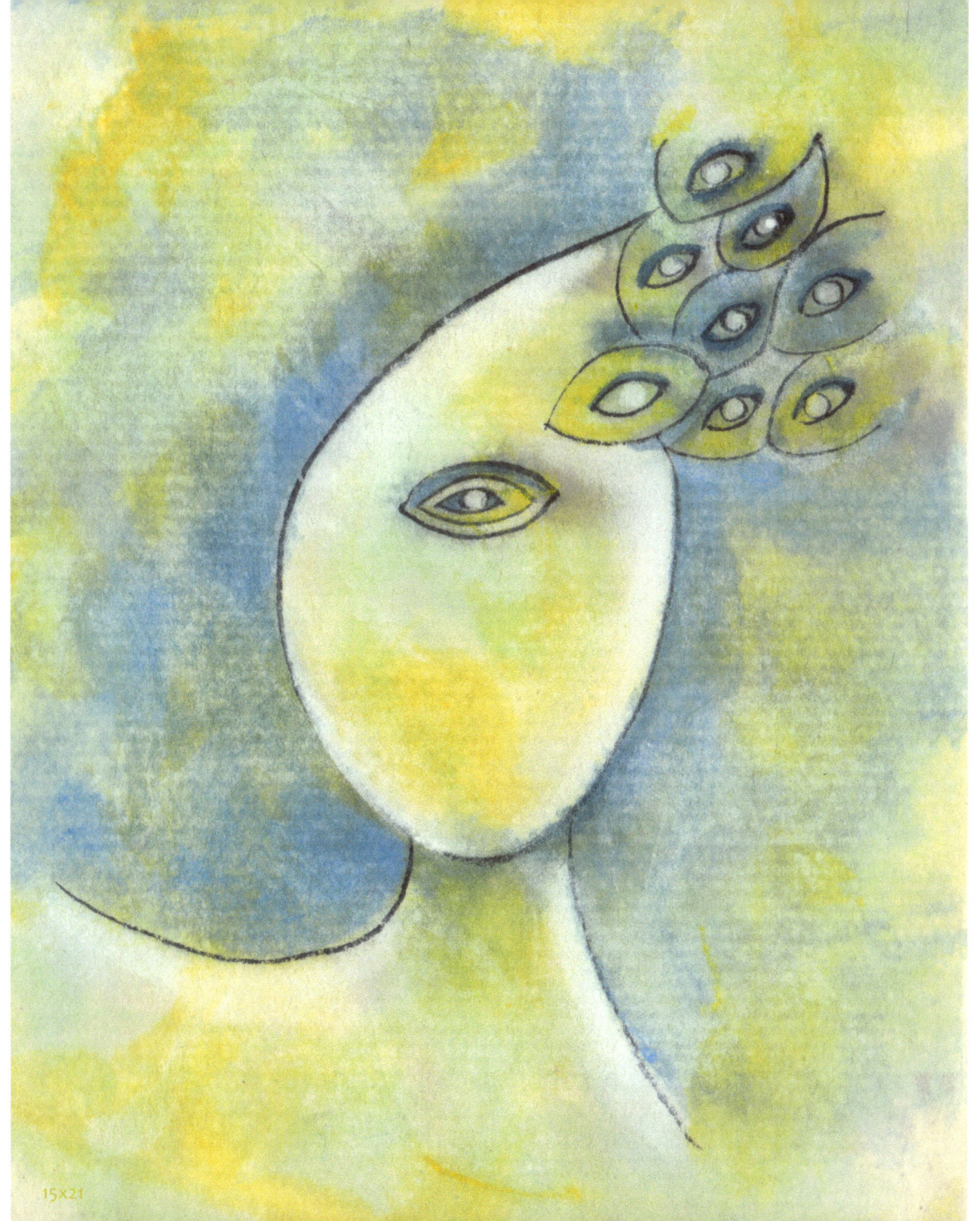

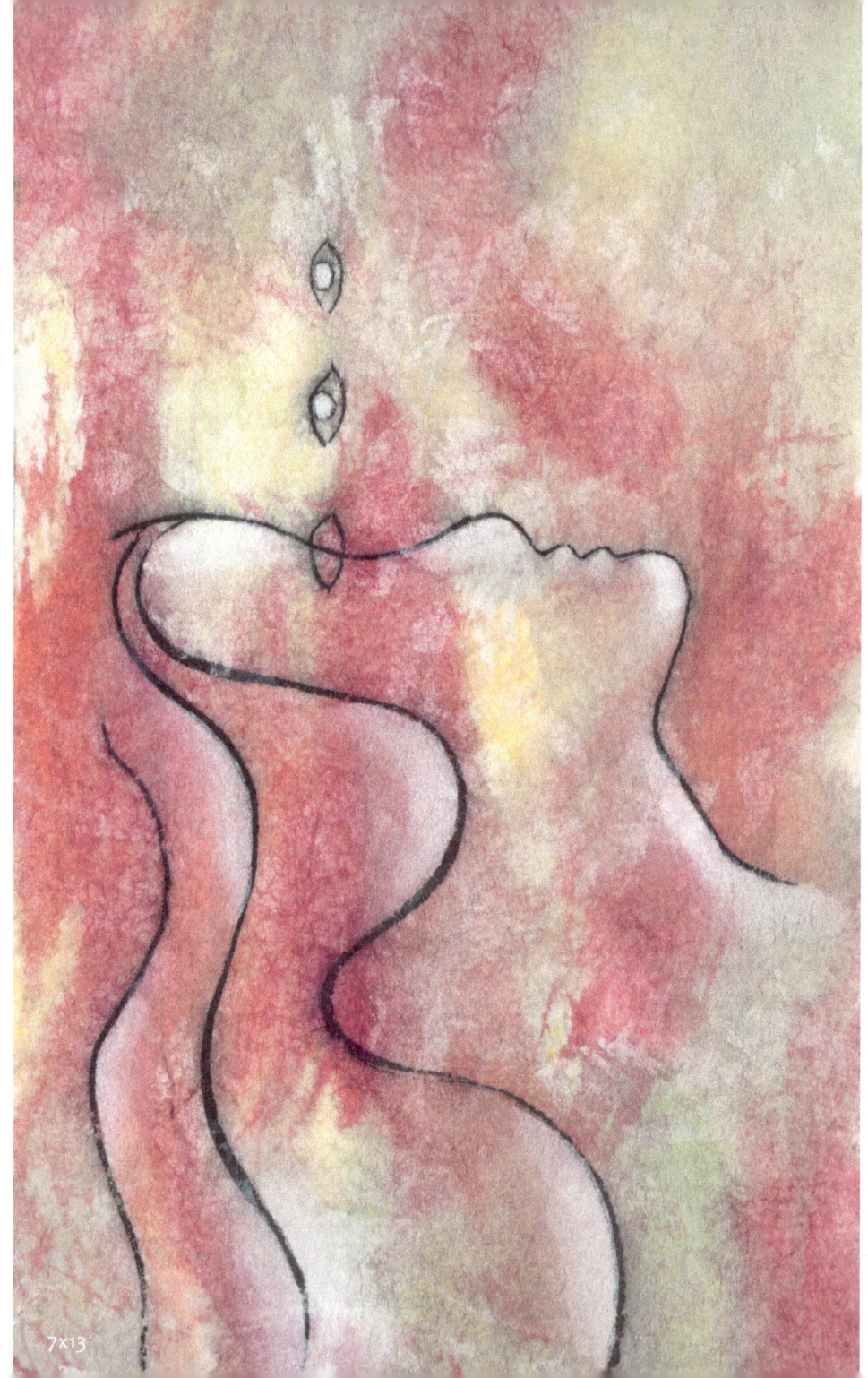

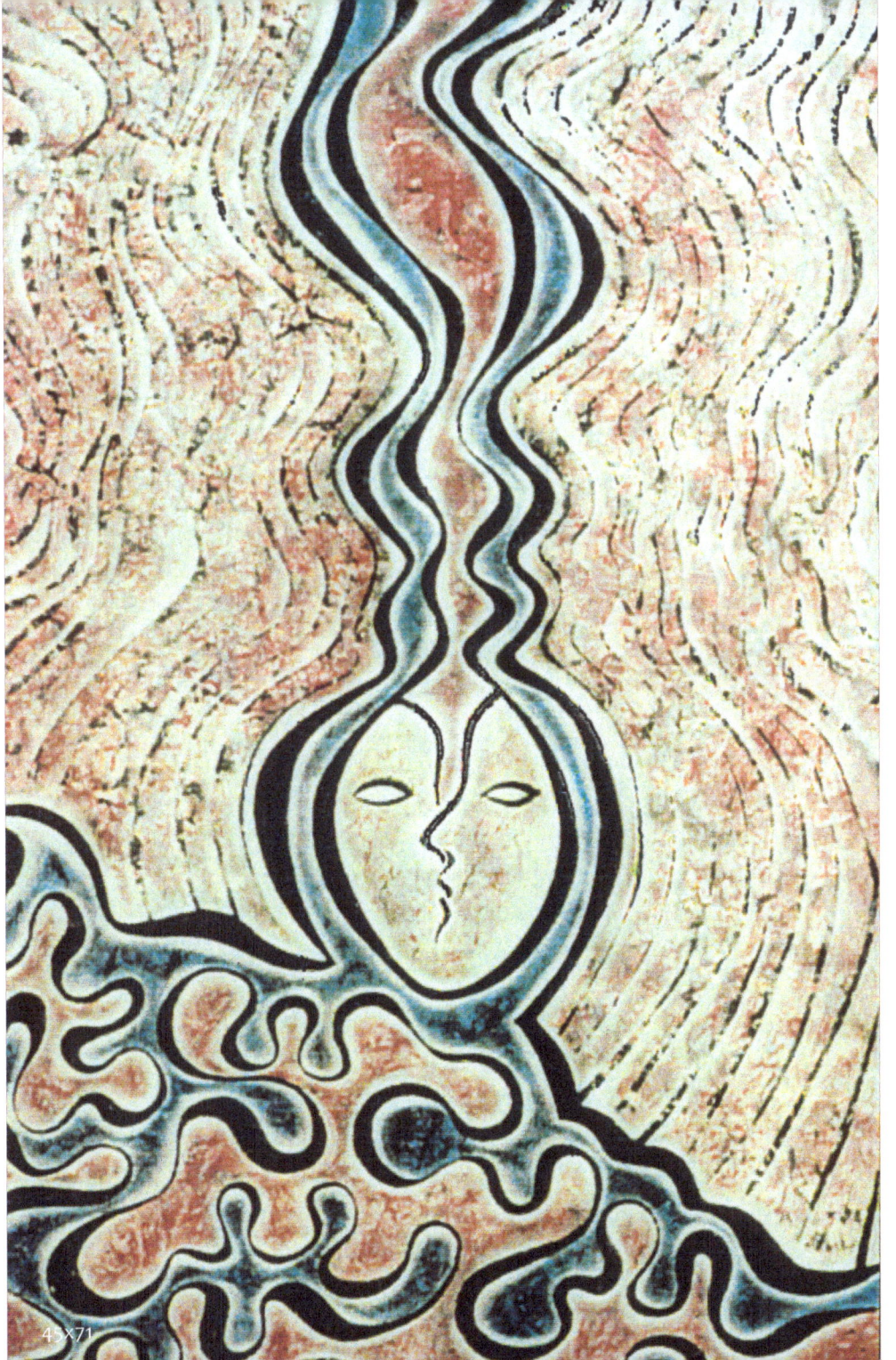

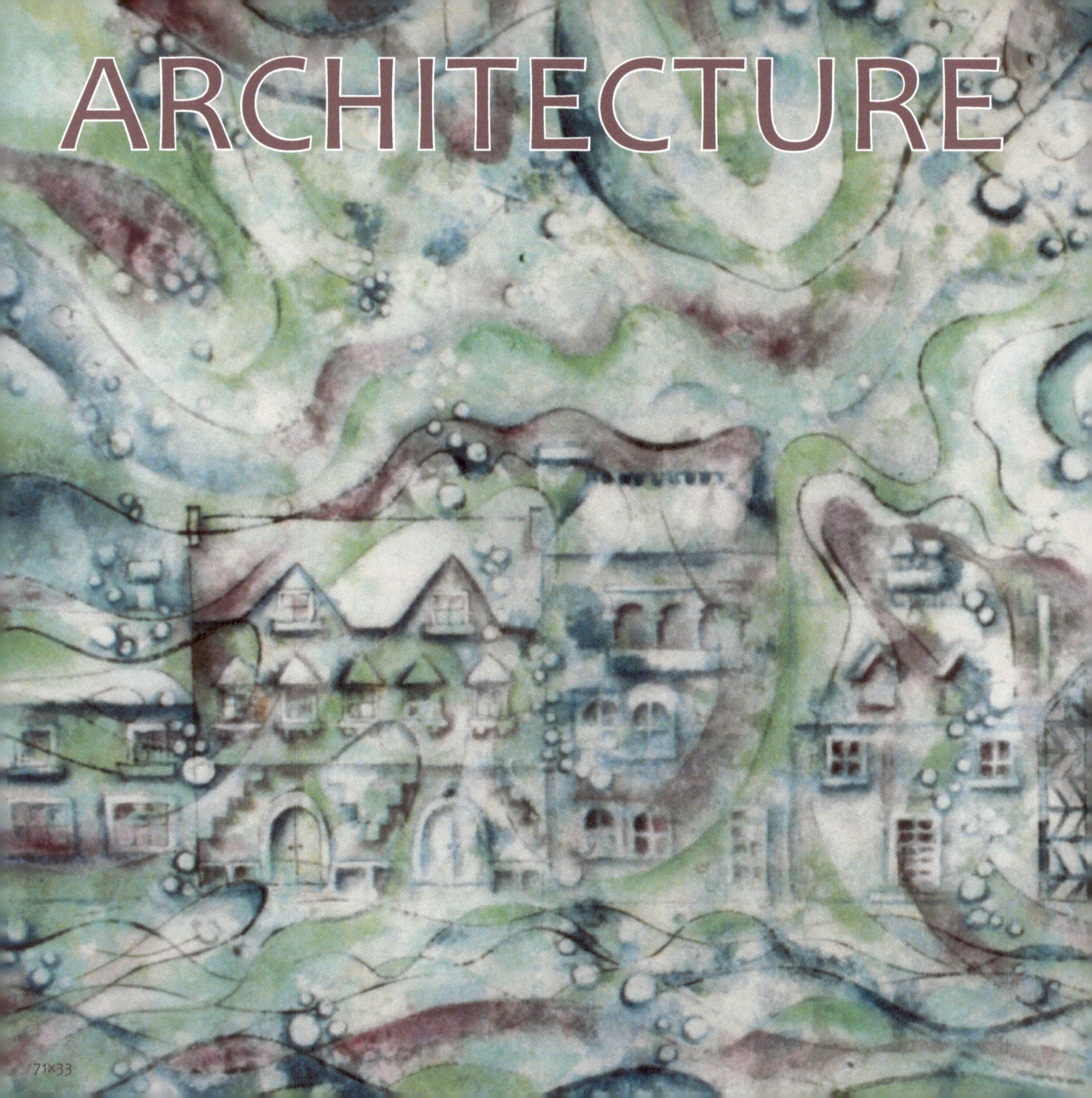

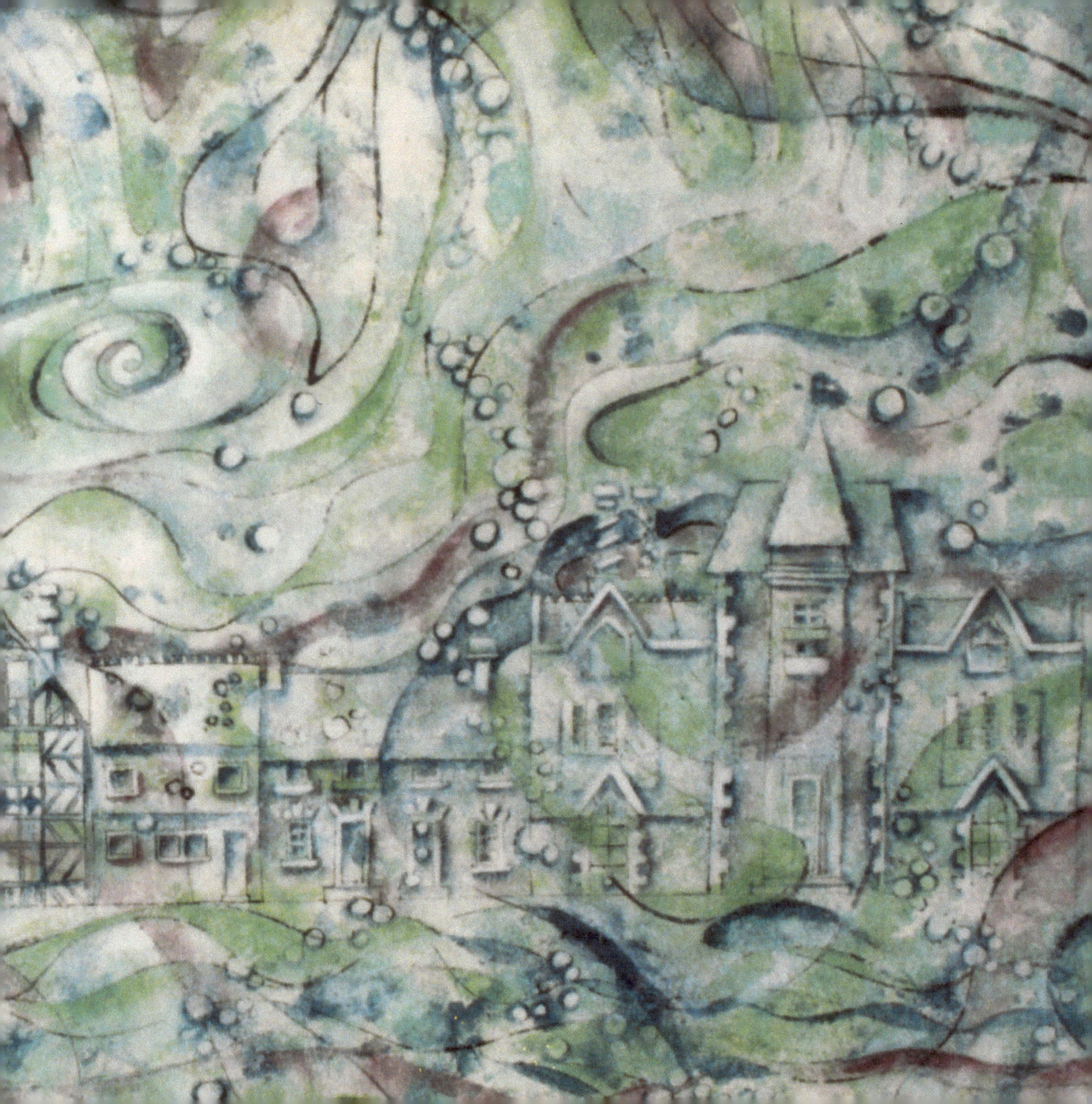

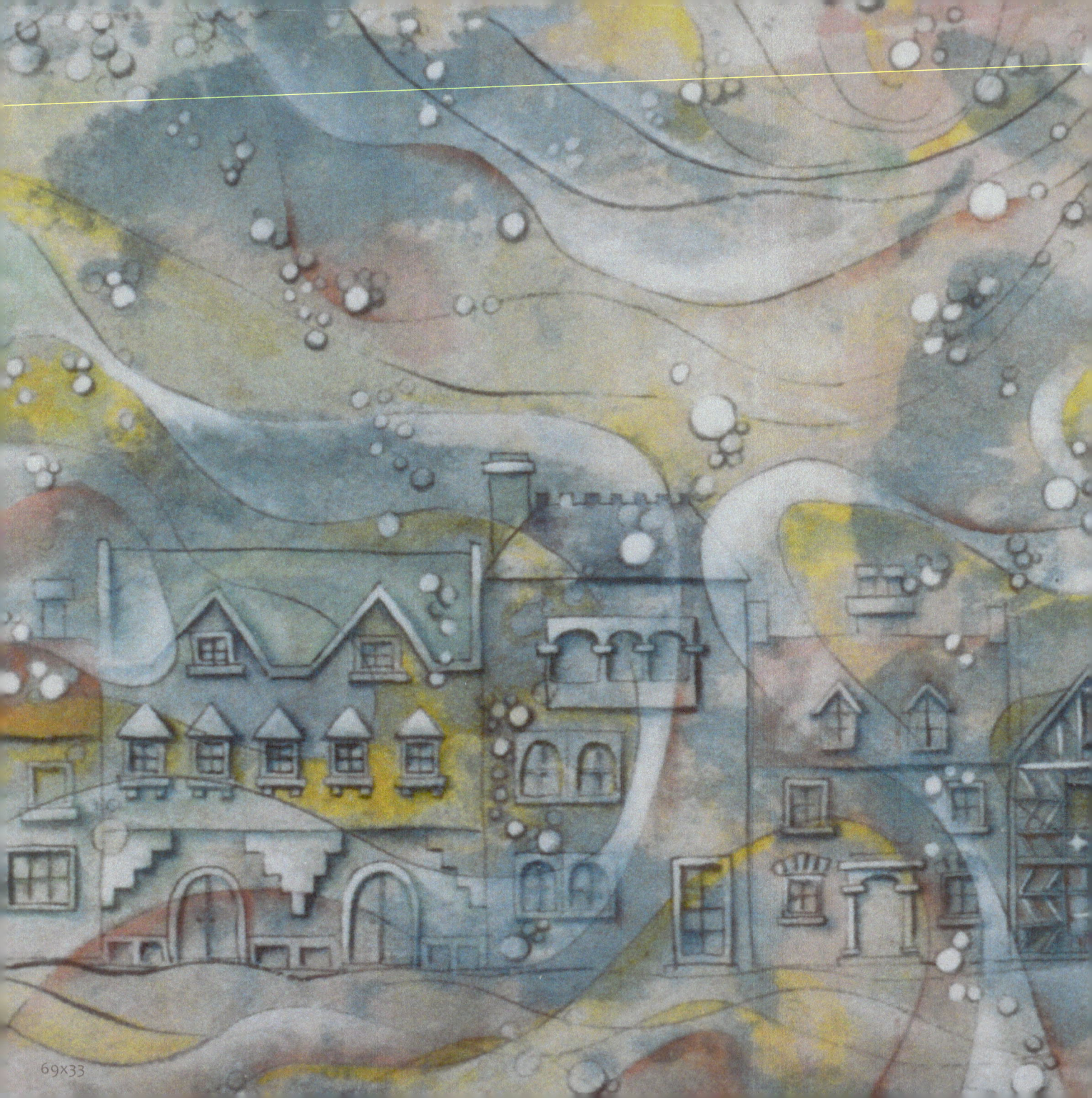

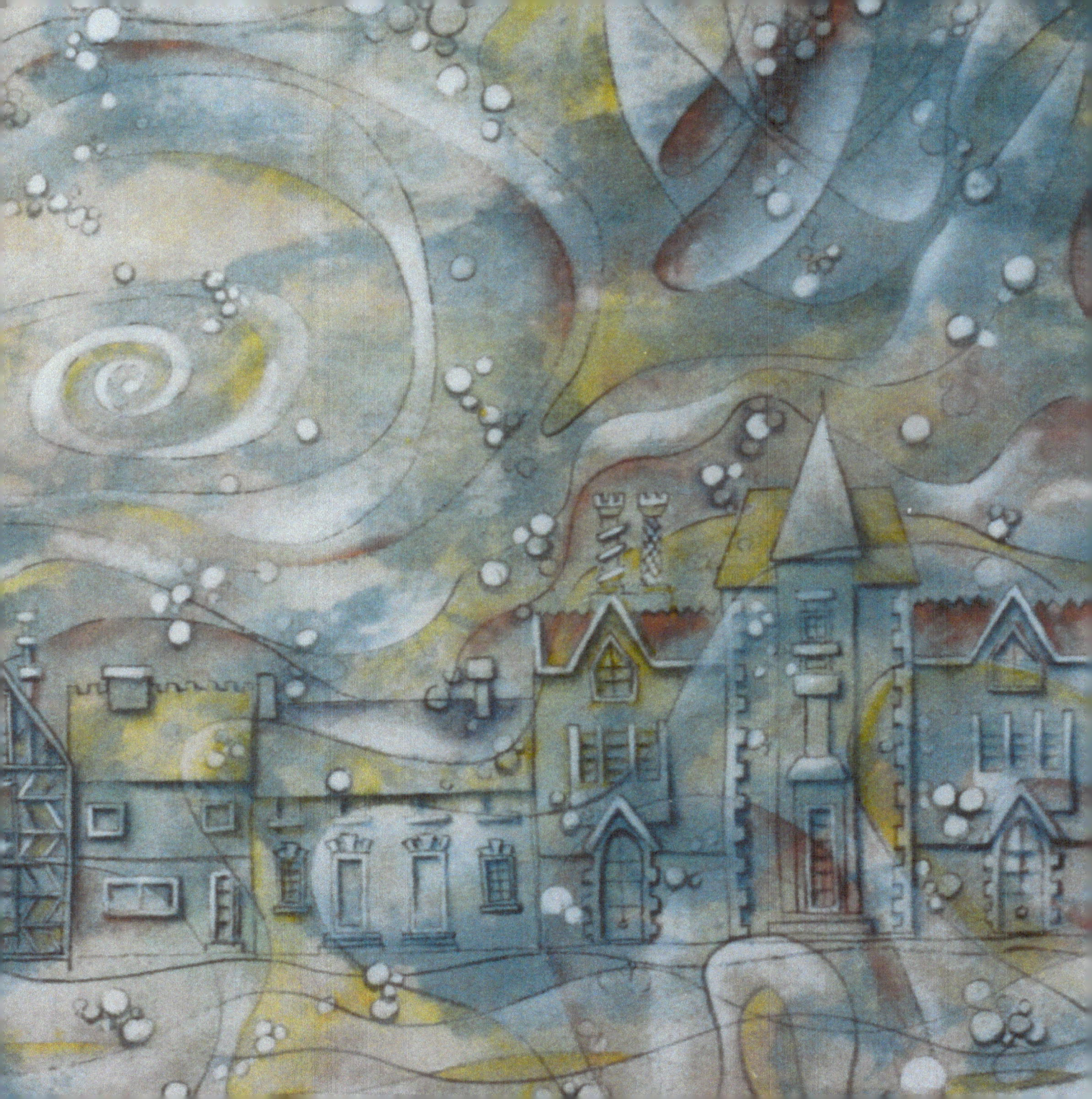

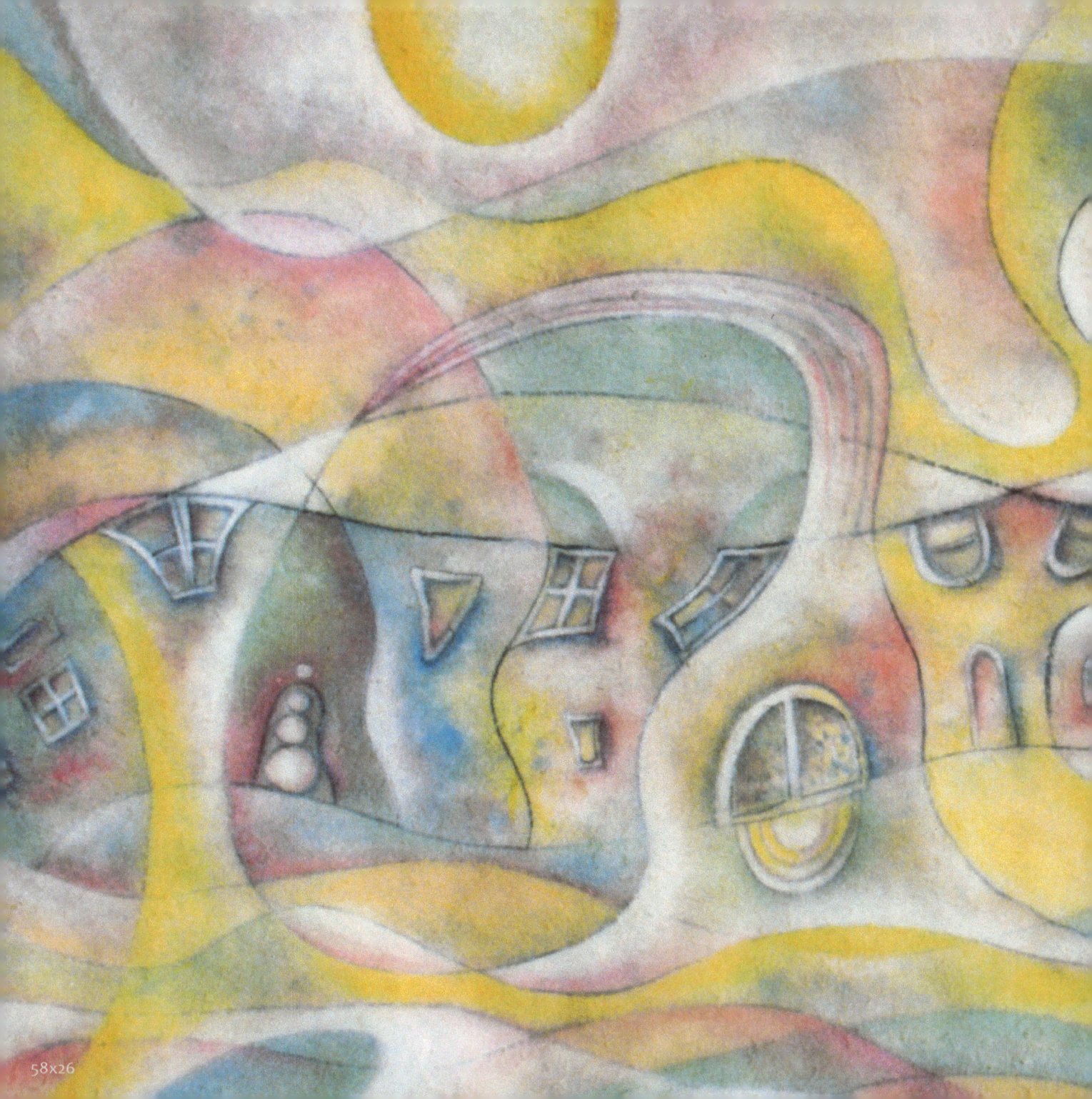

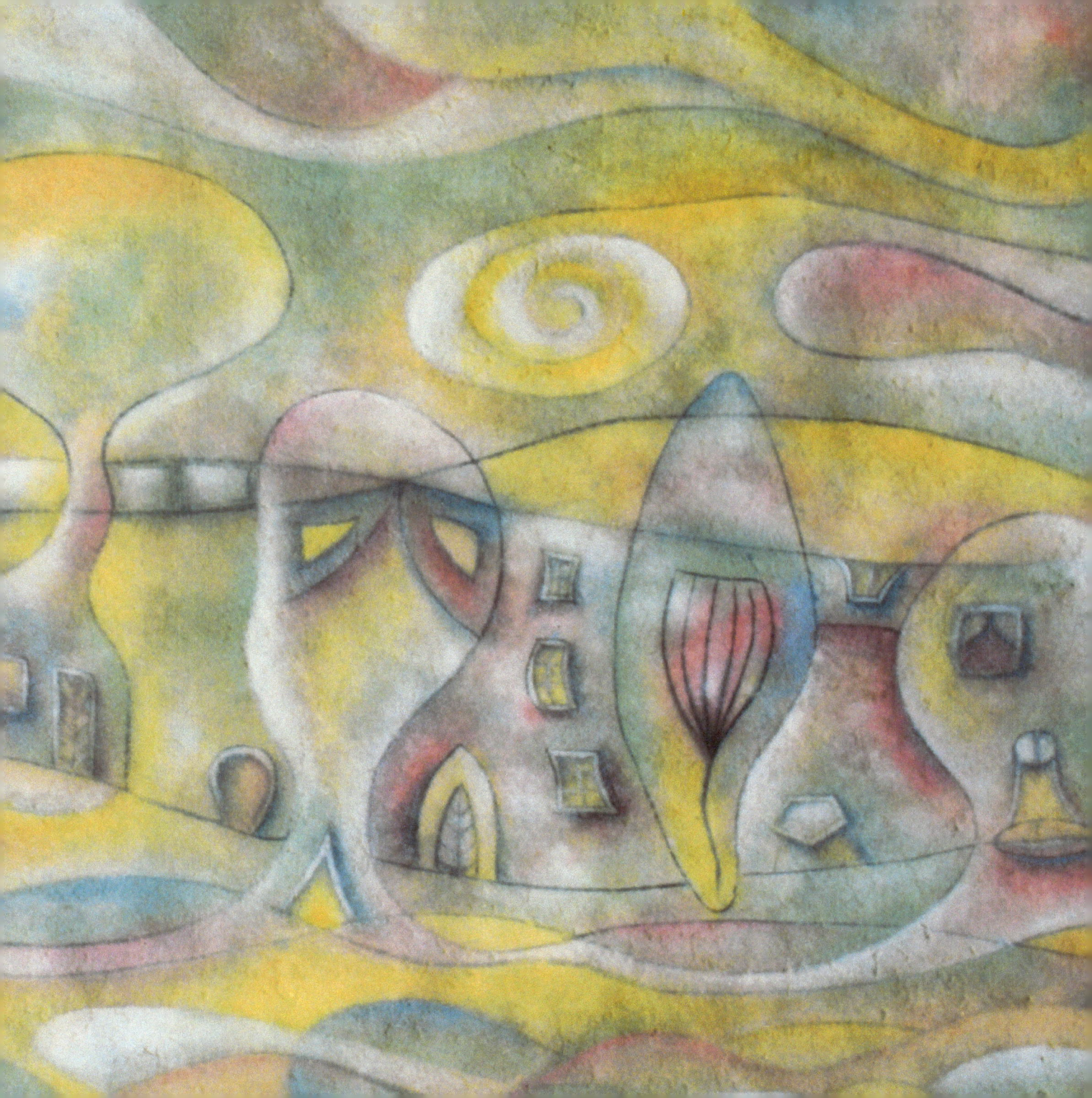

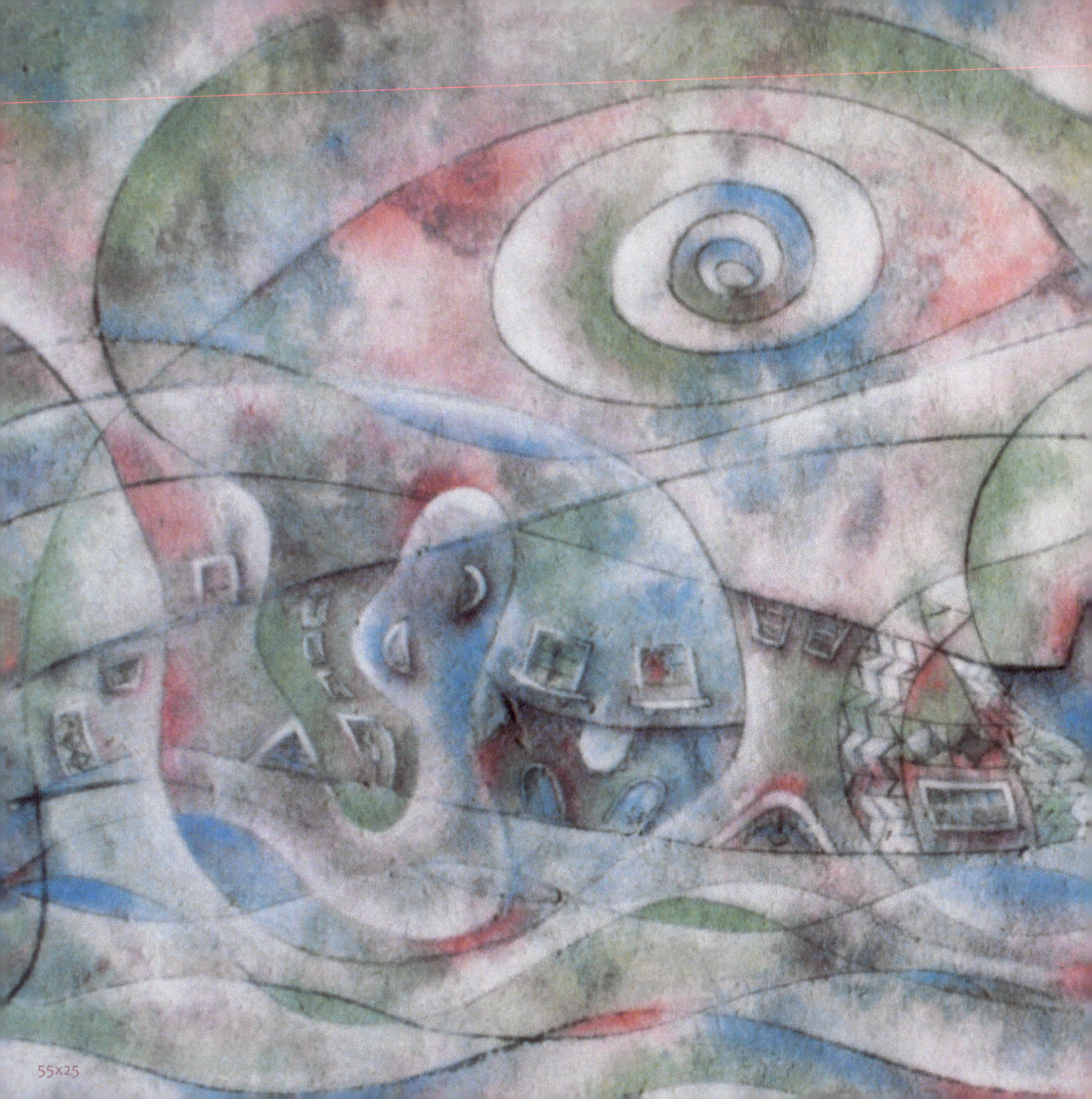

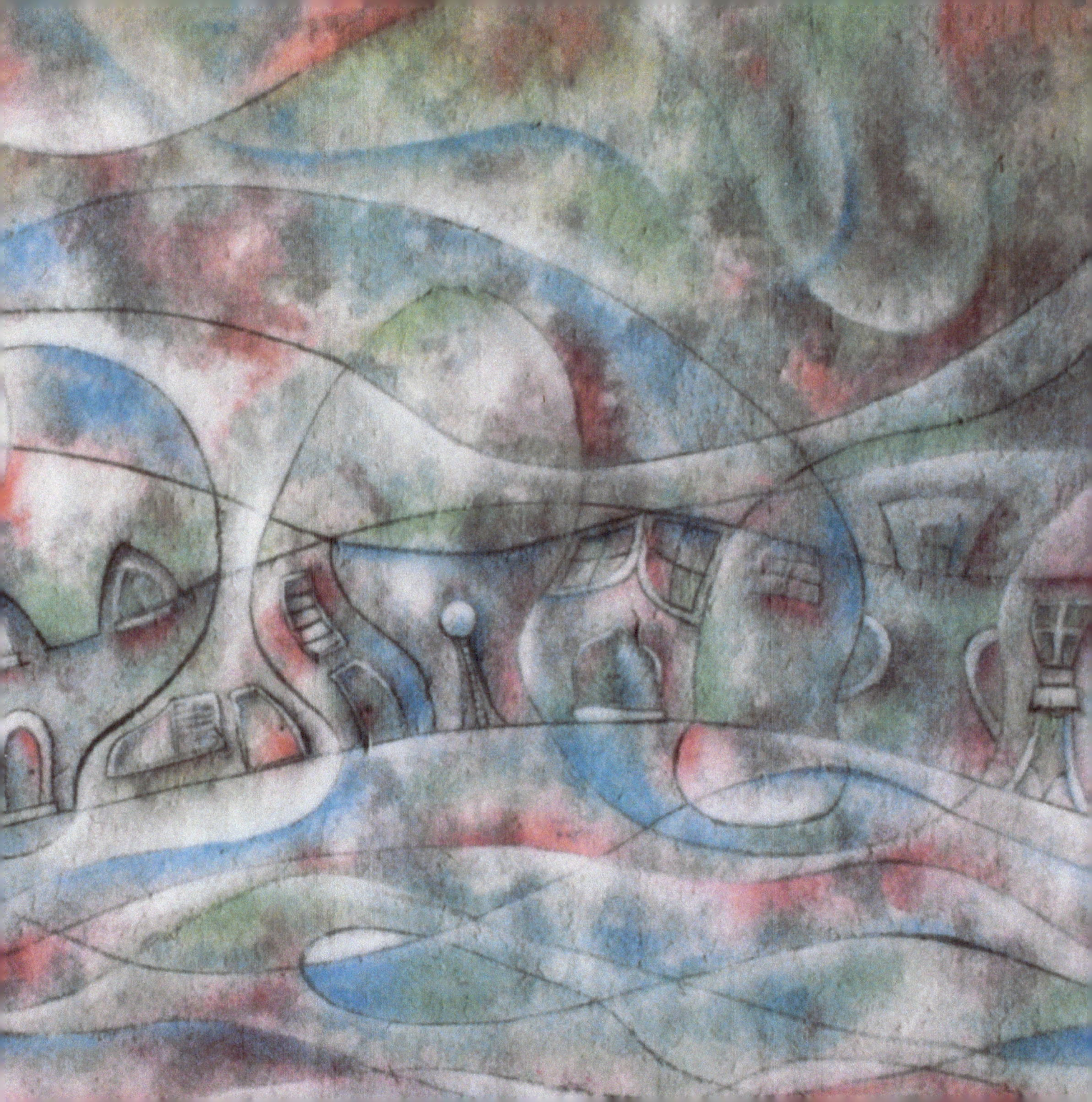

EROS

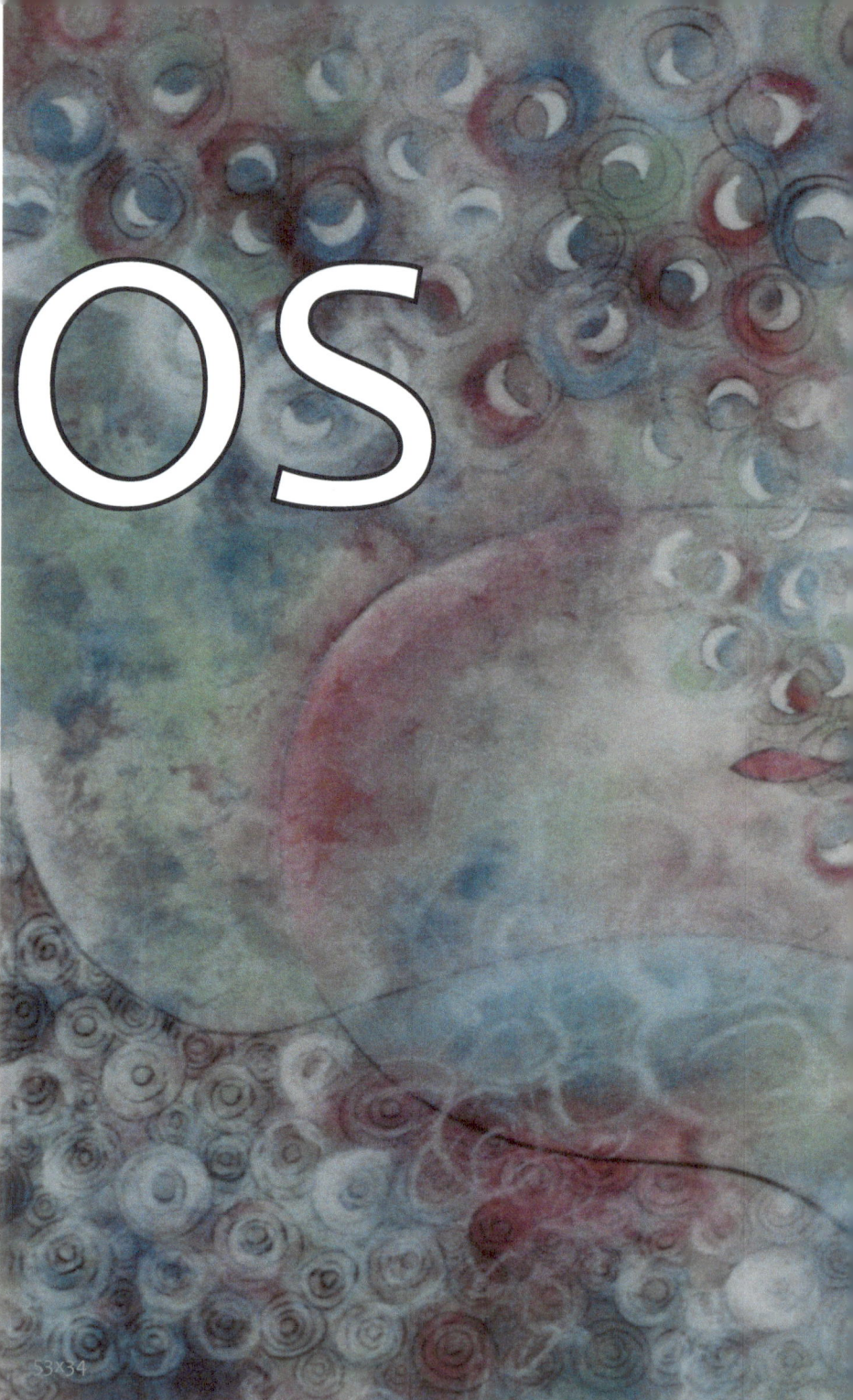

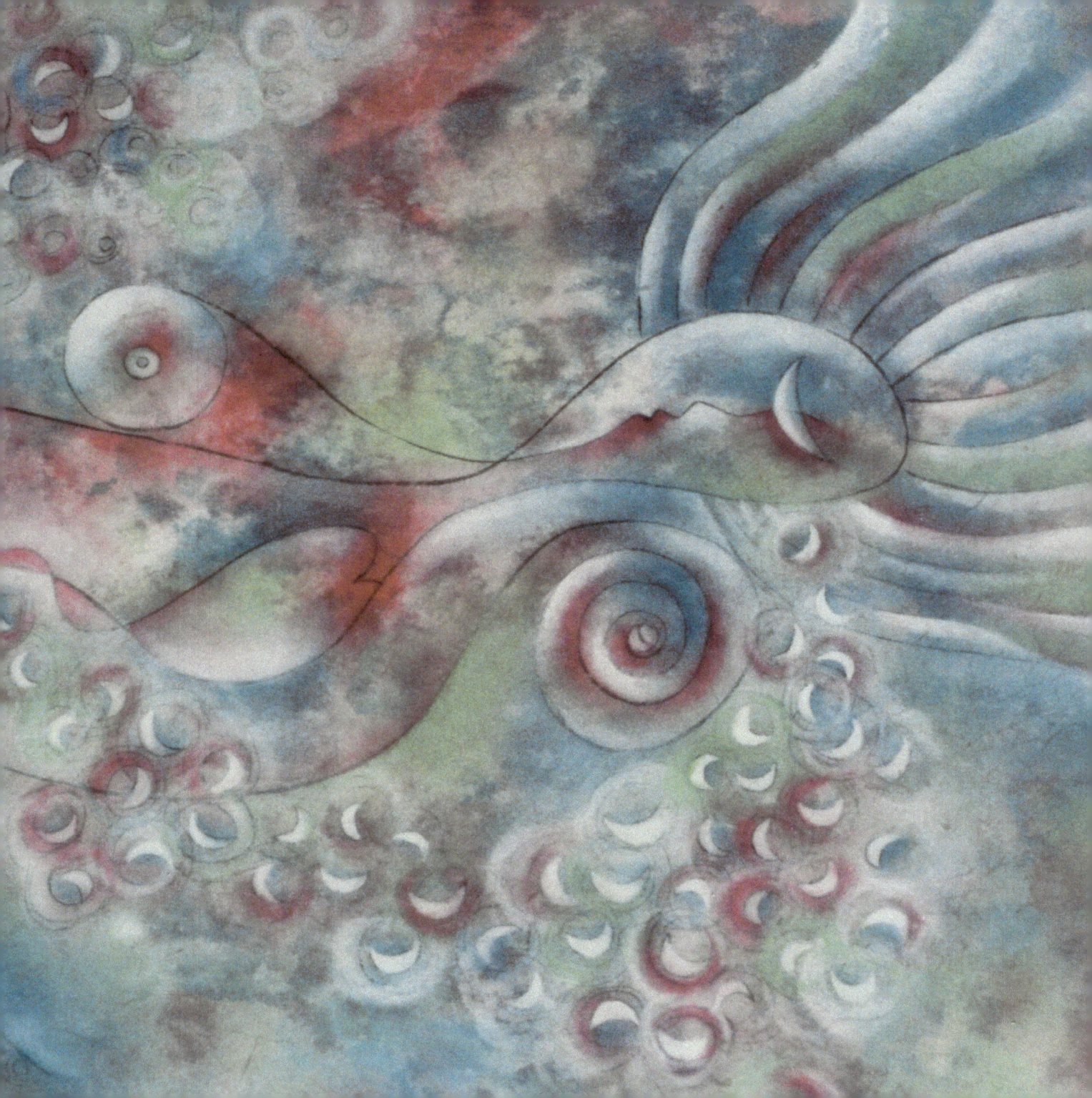

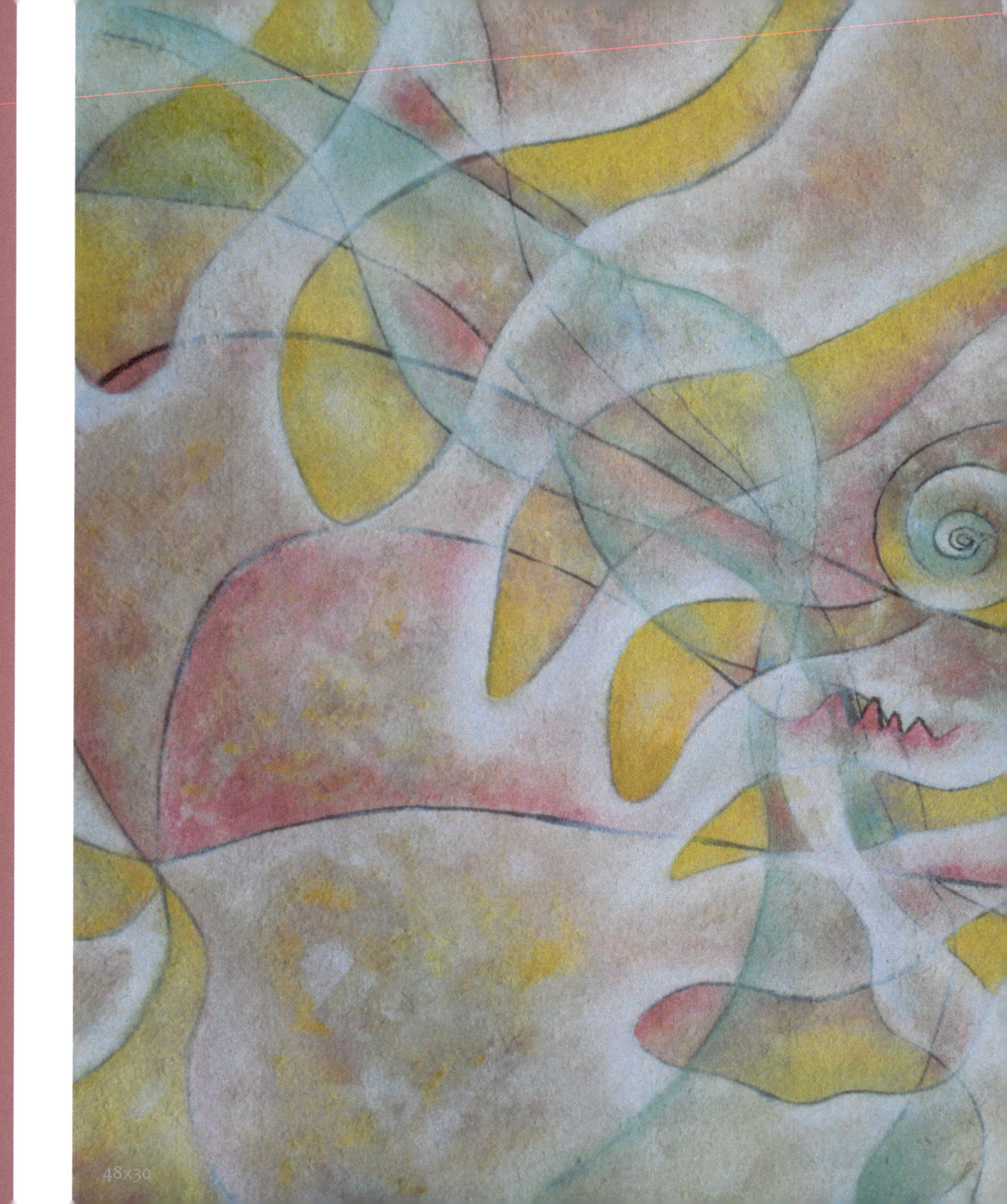
48x30

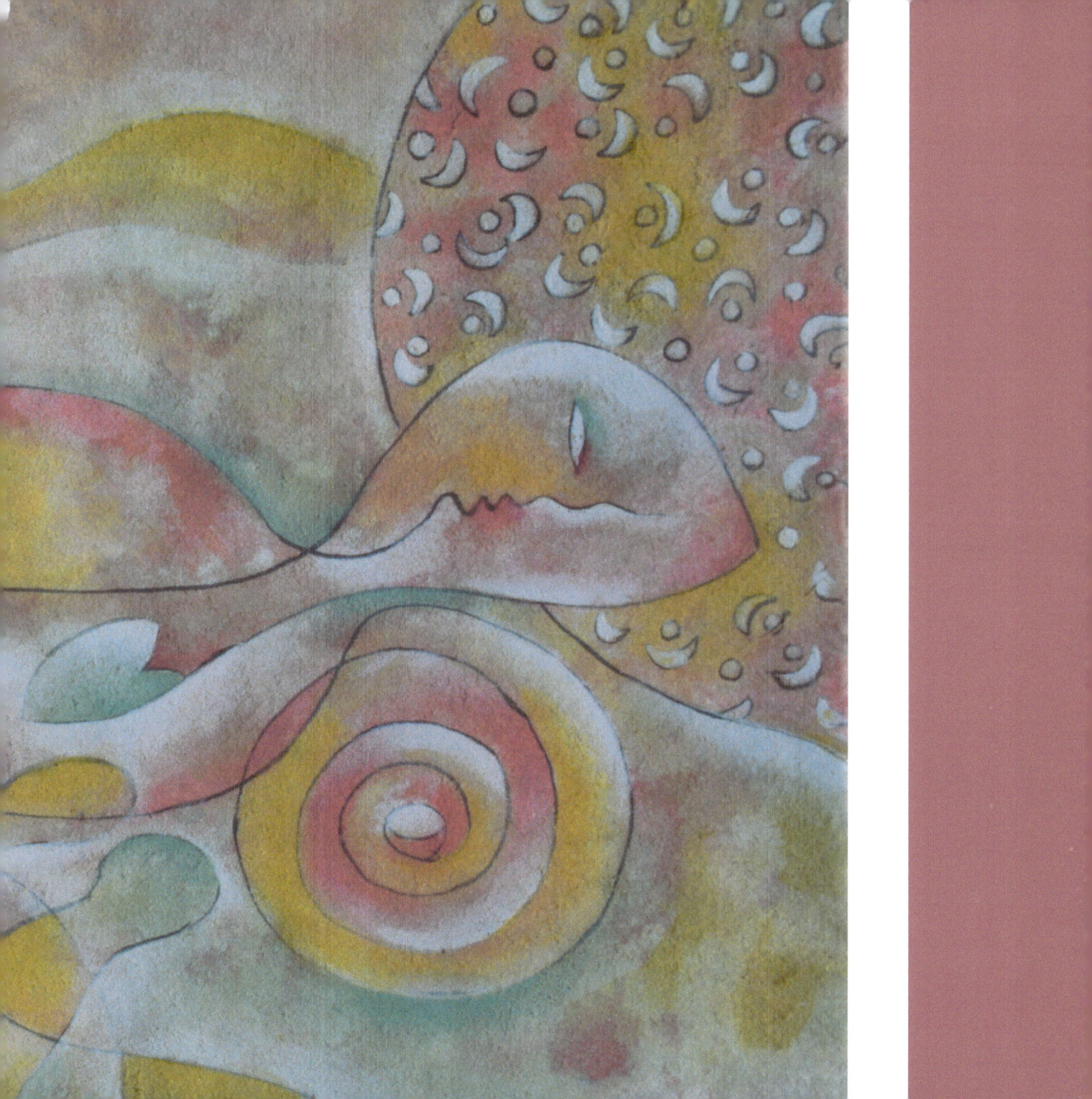

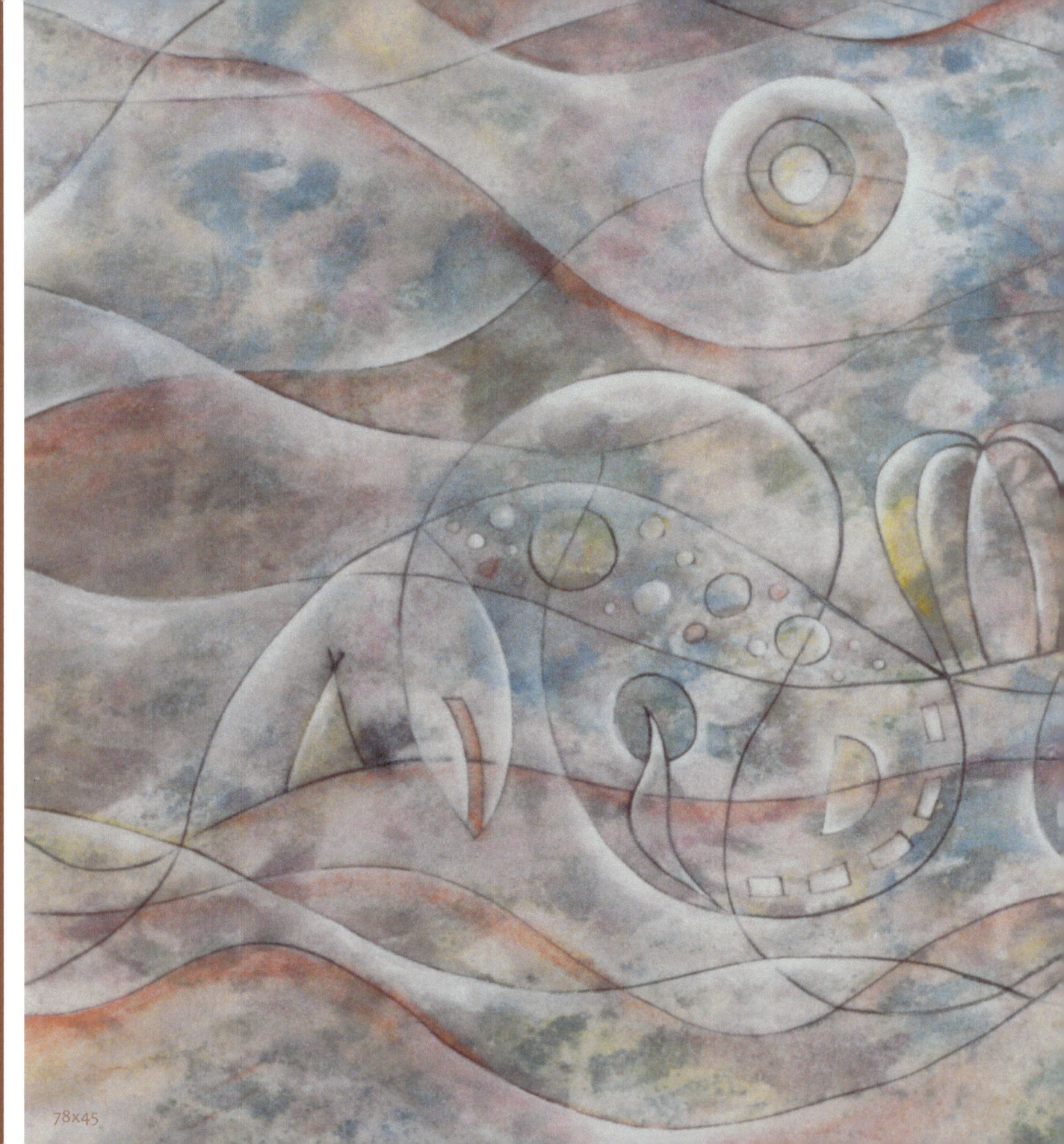

78x45

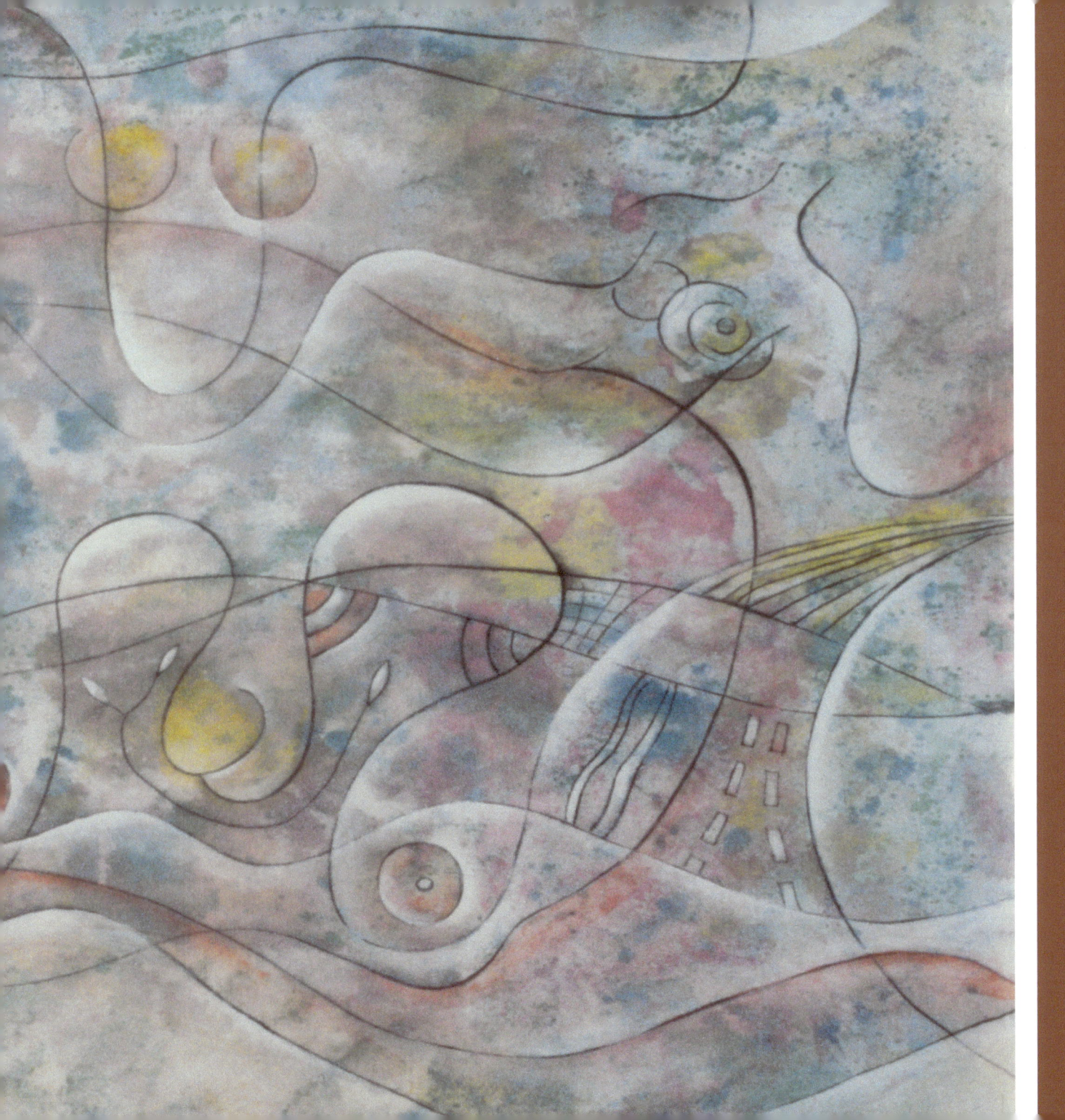

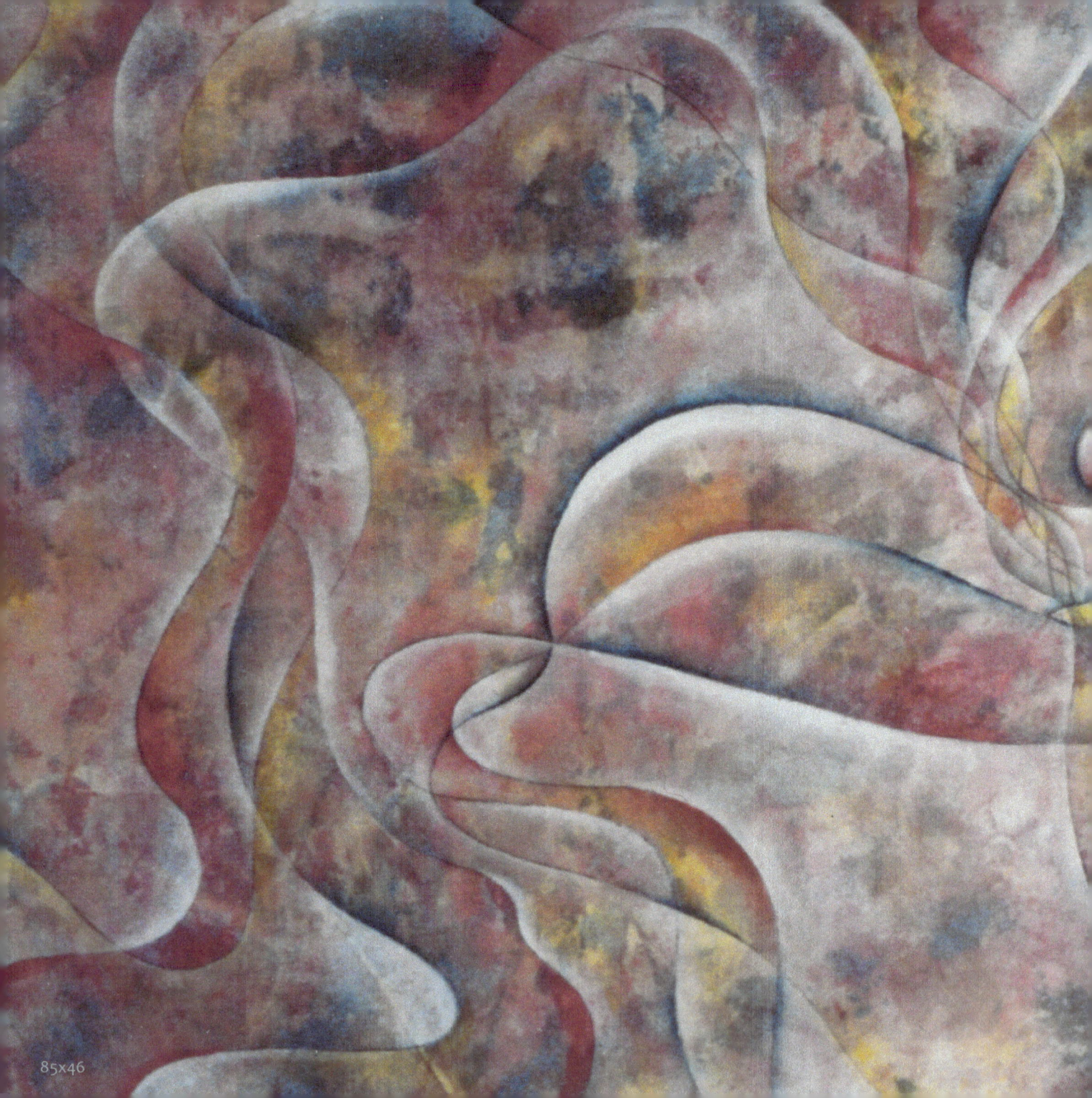

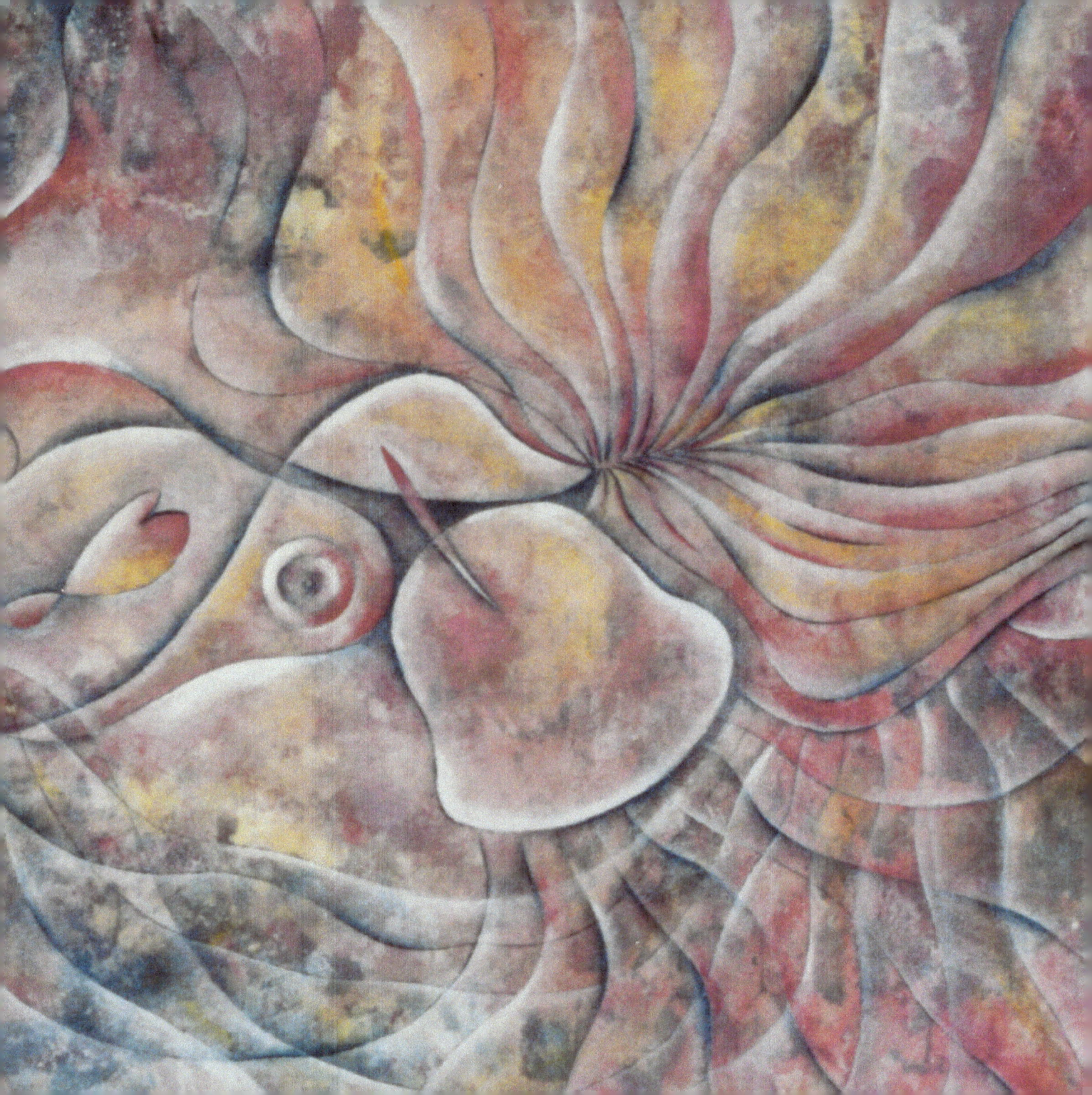

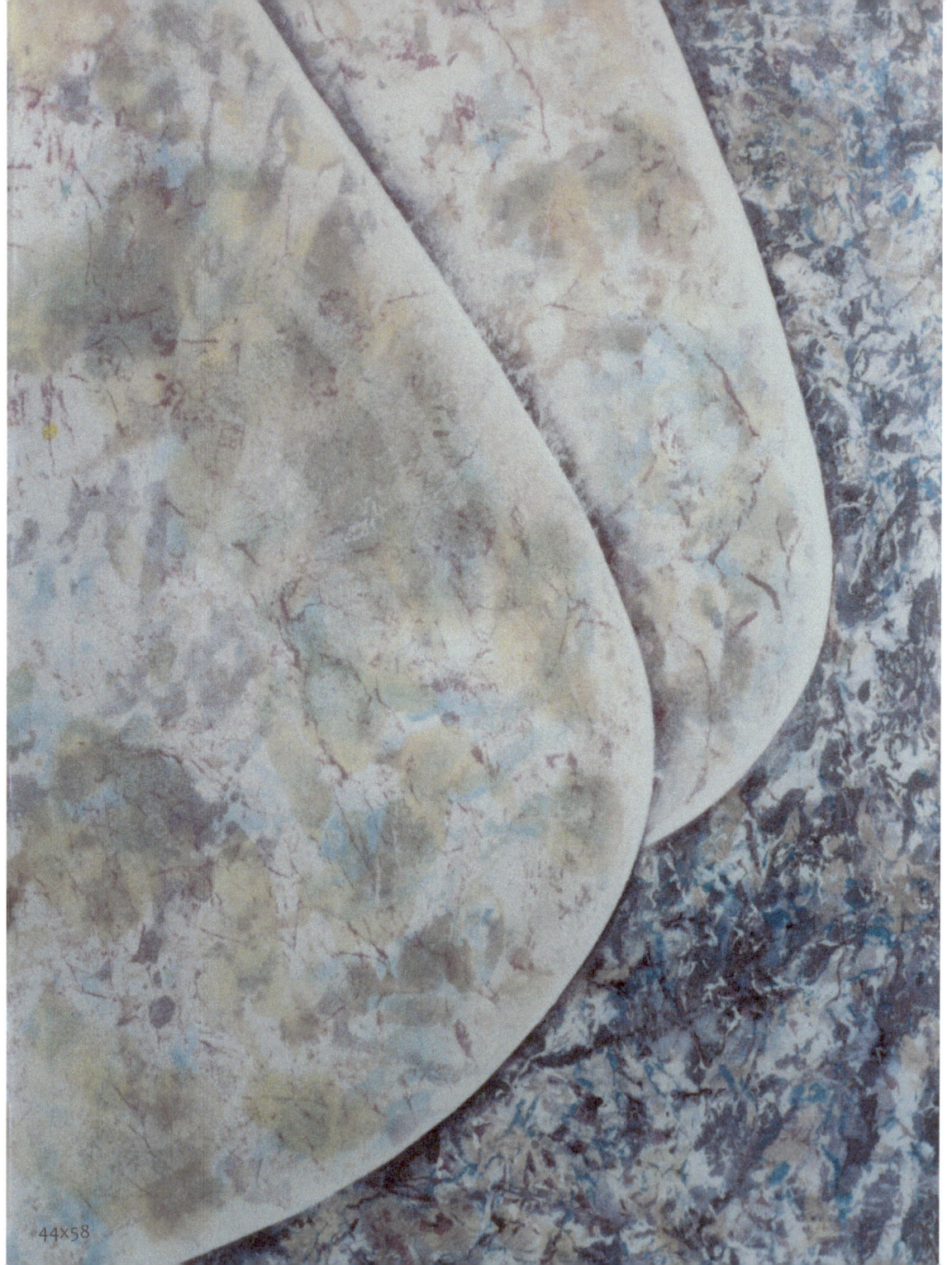

44x58

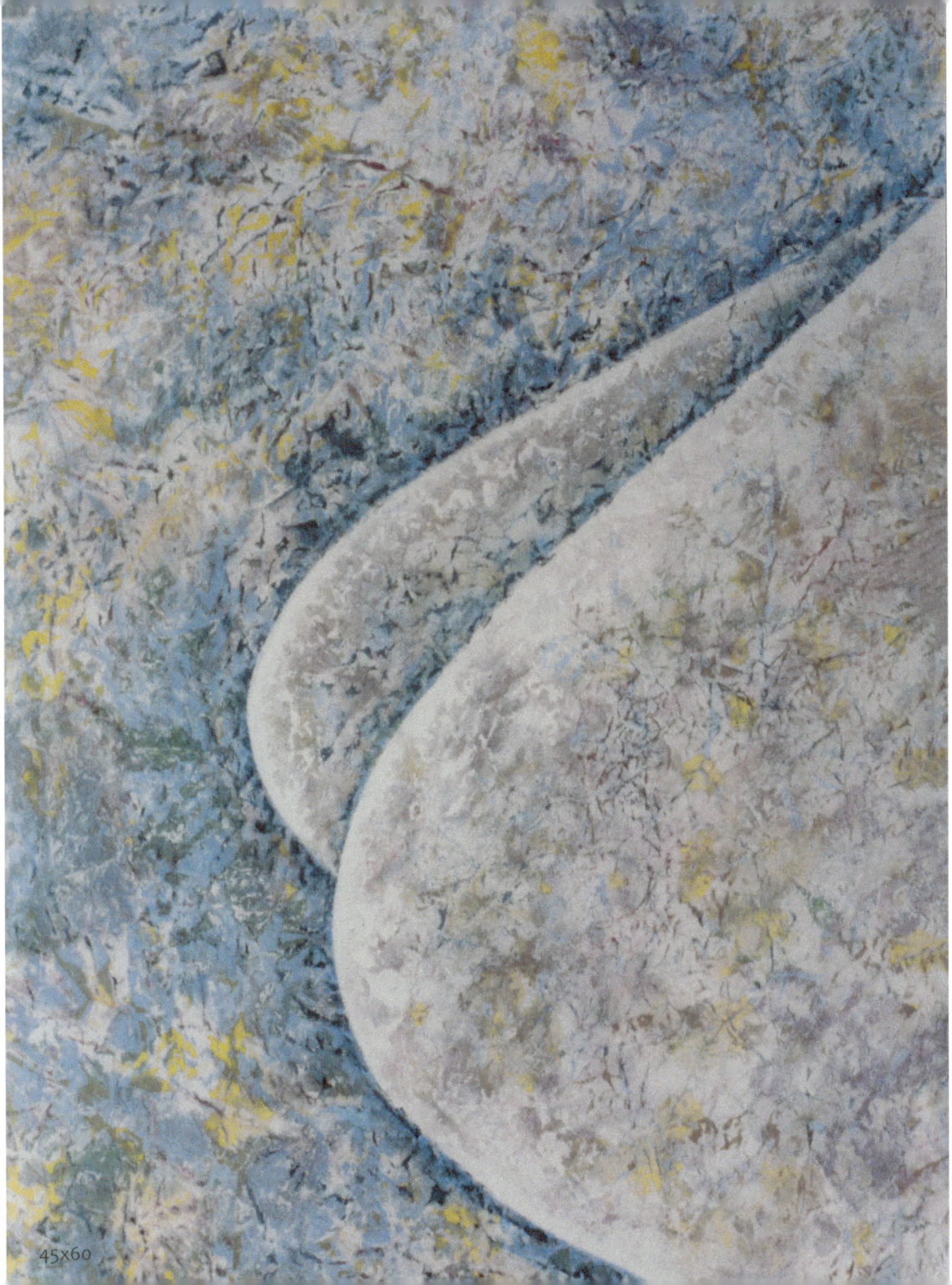

45x60

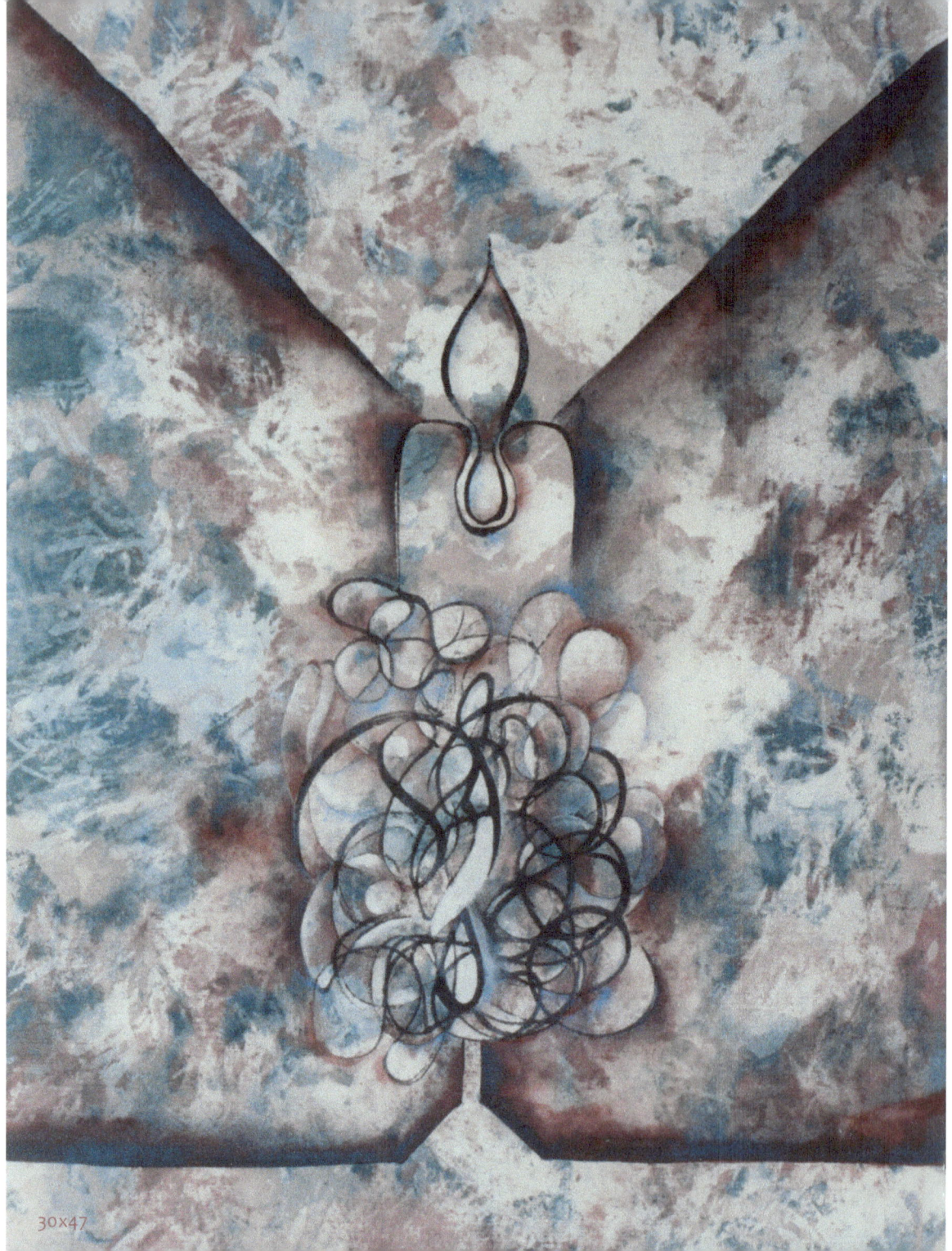

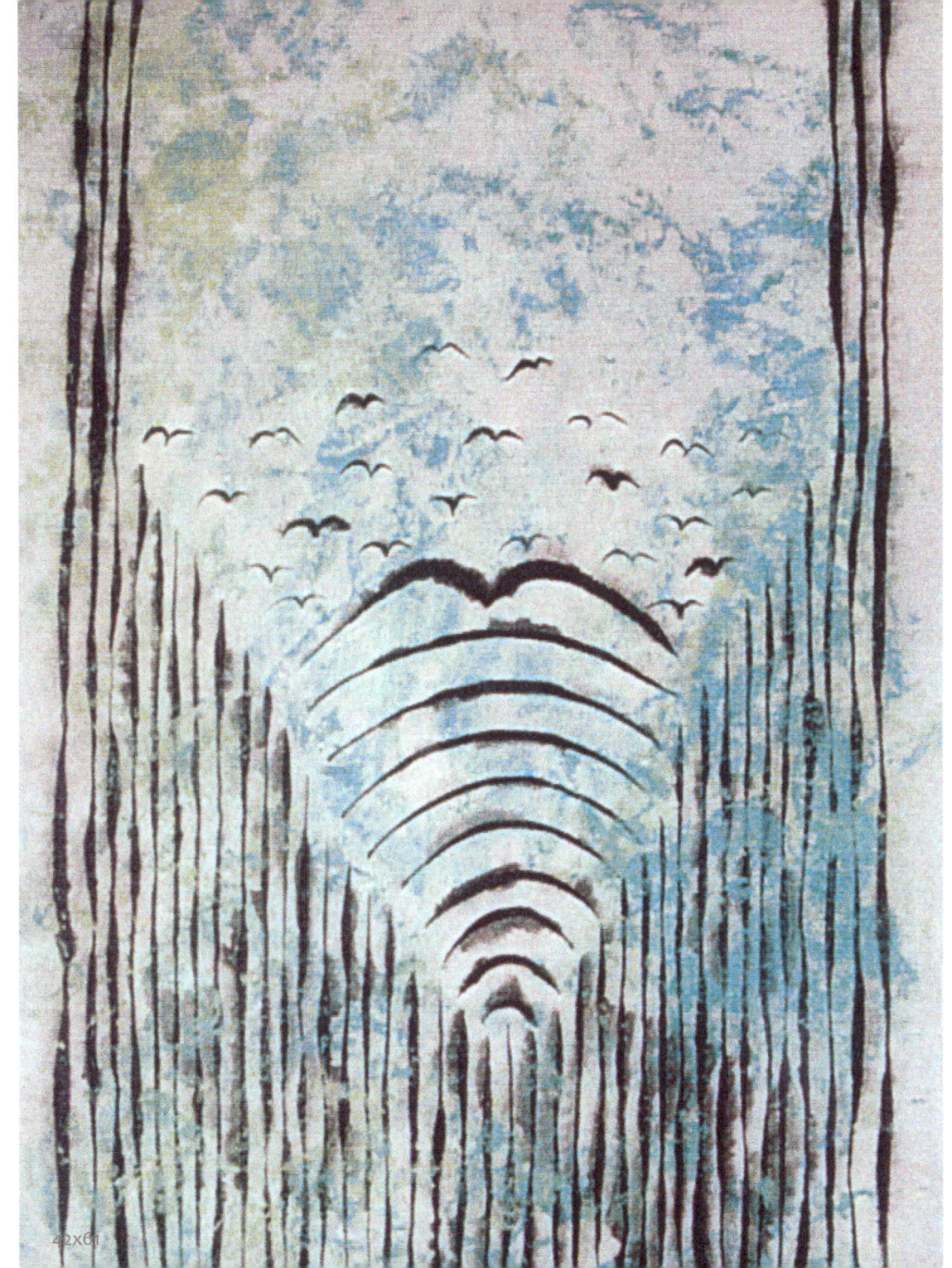

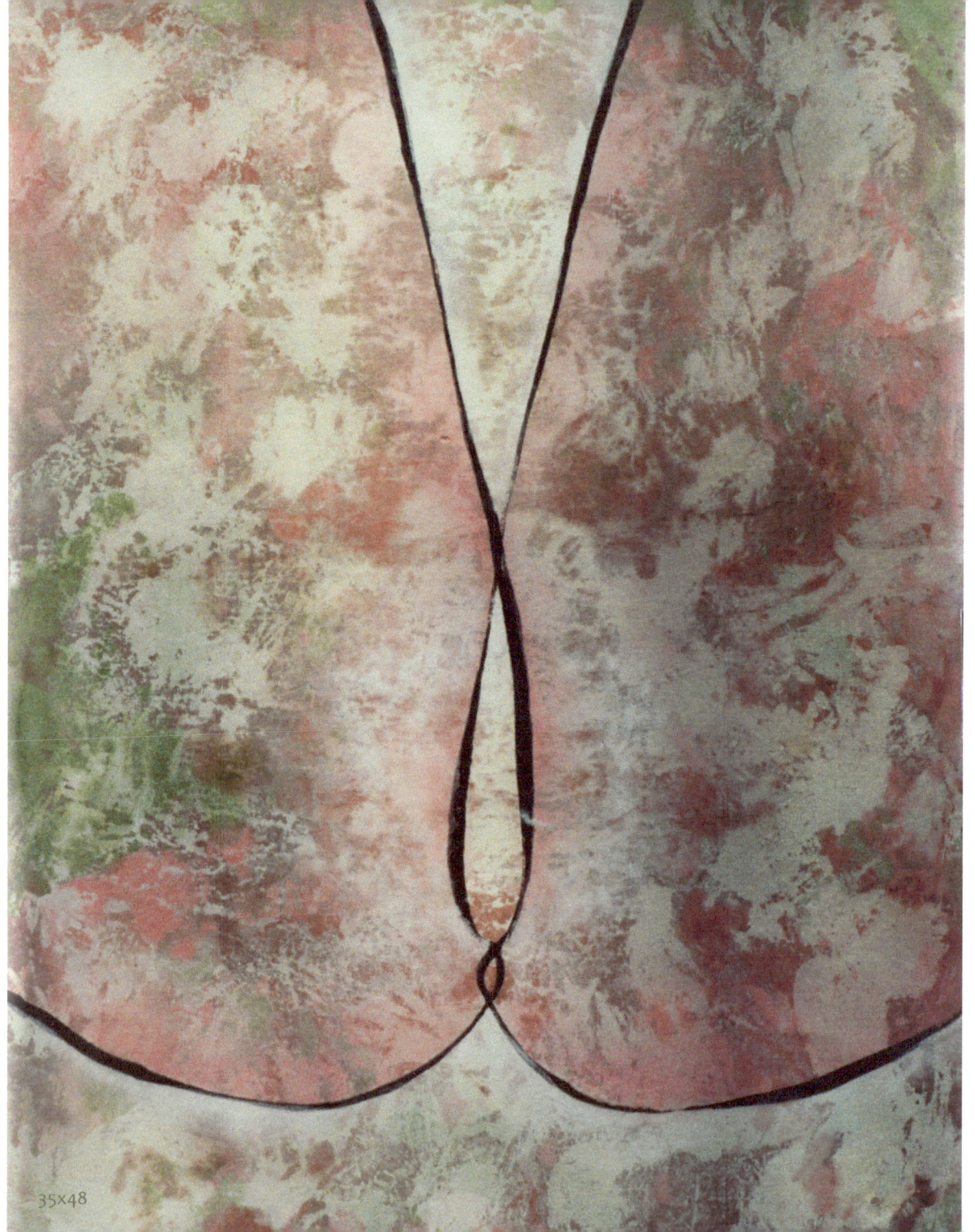

35x48

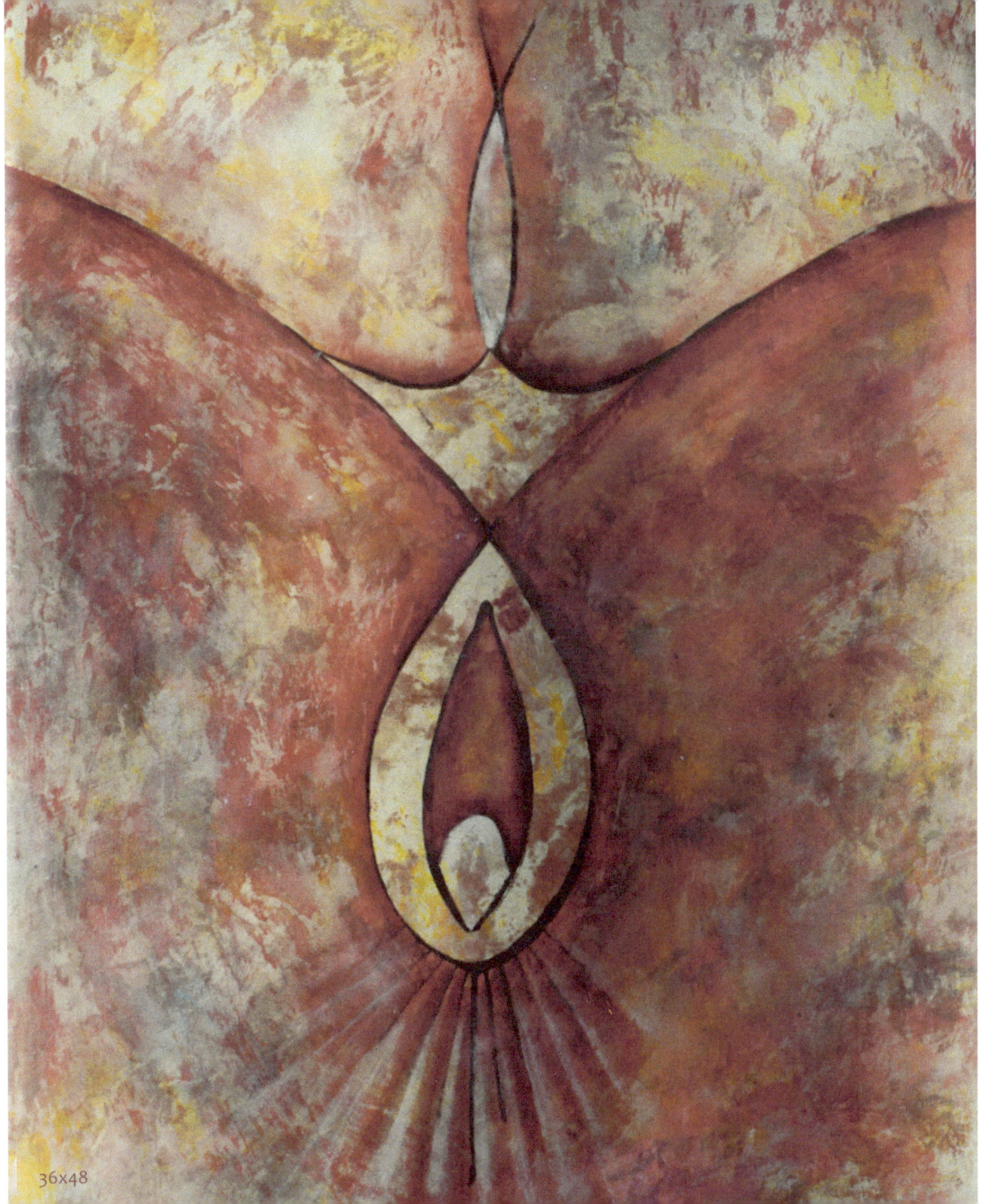

36x48

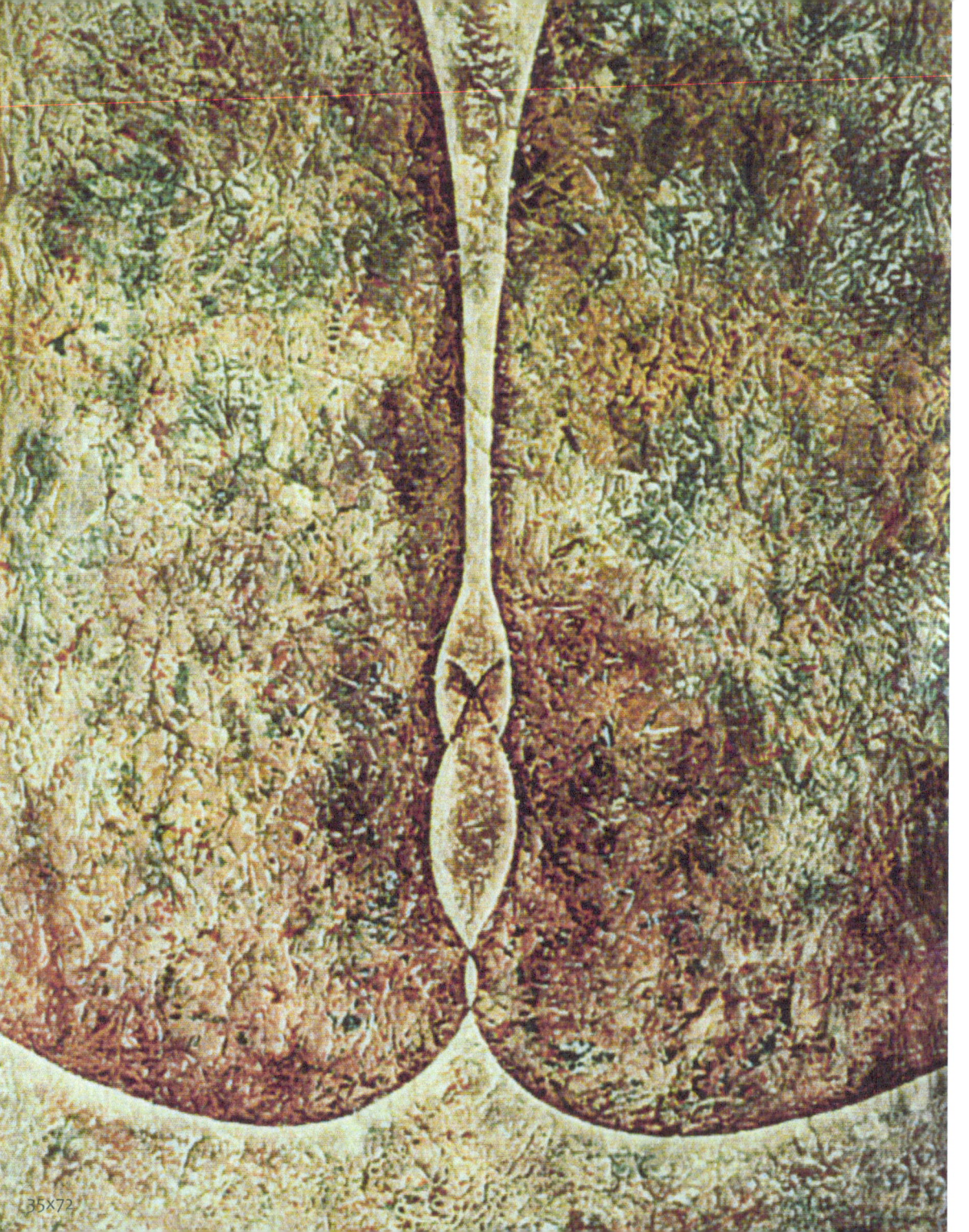

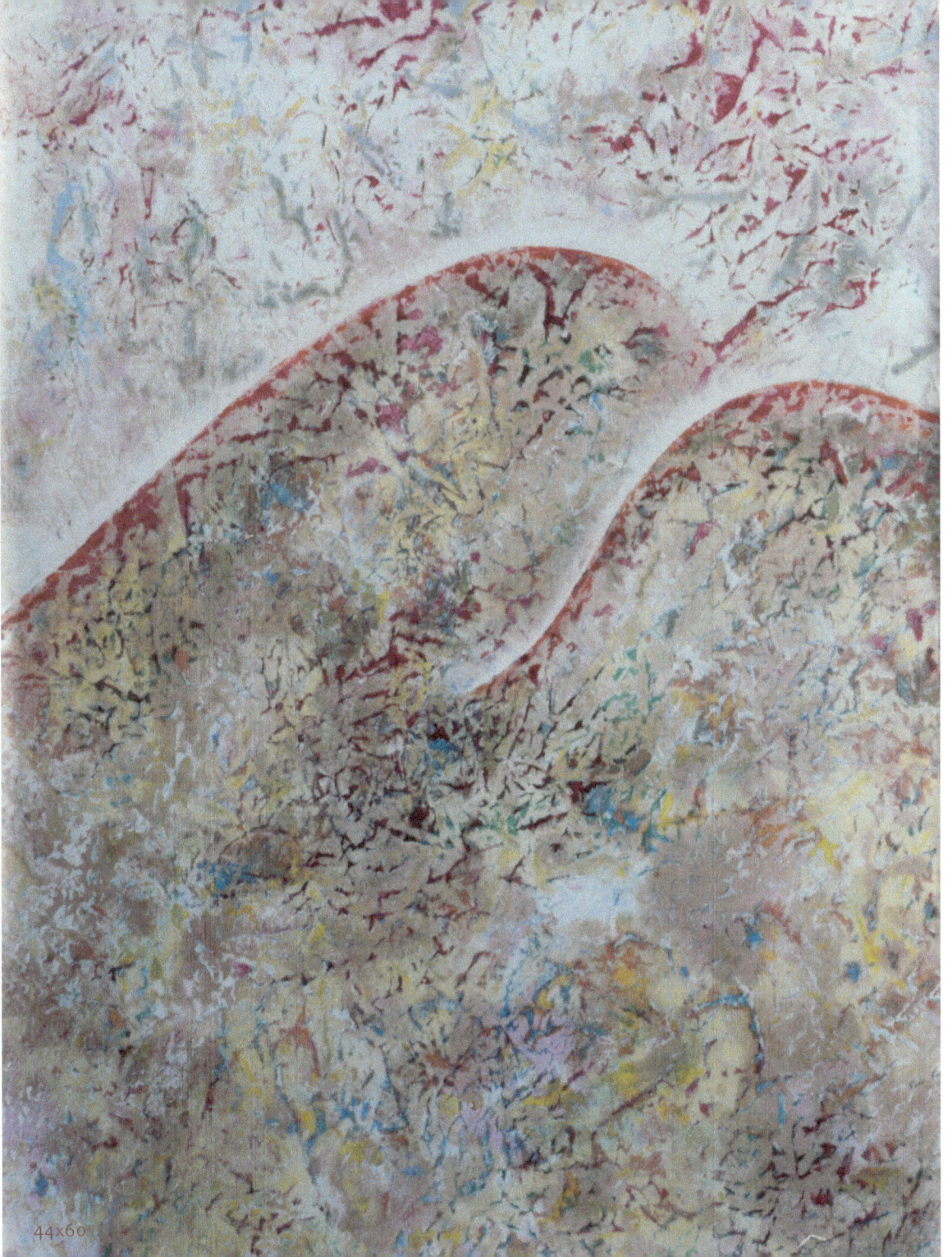

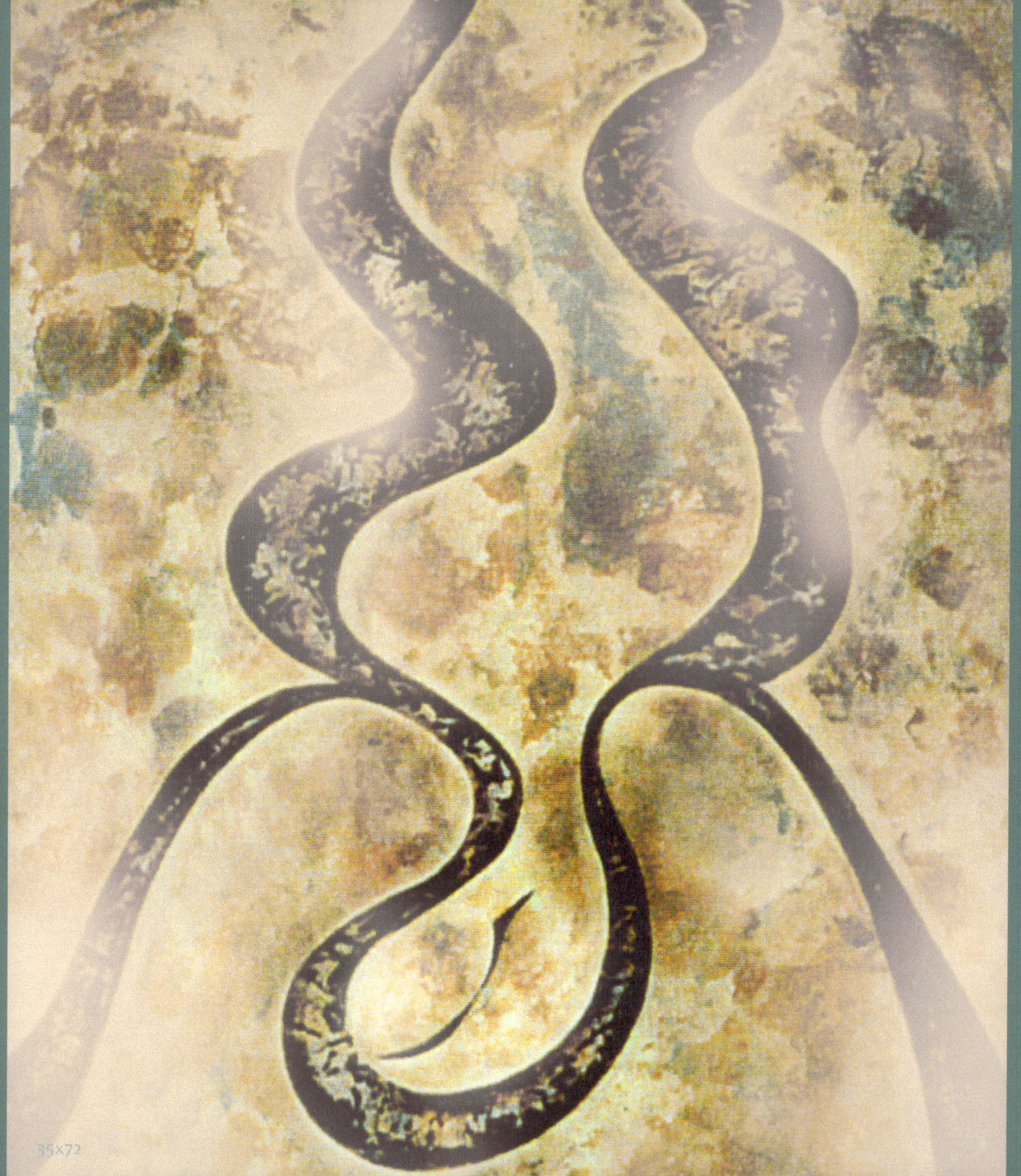

35x72

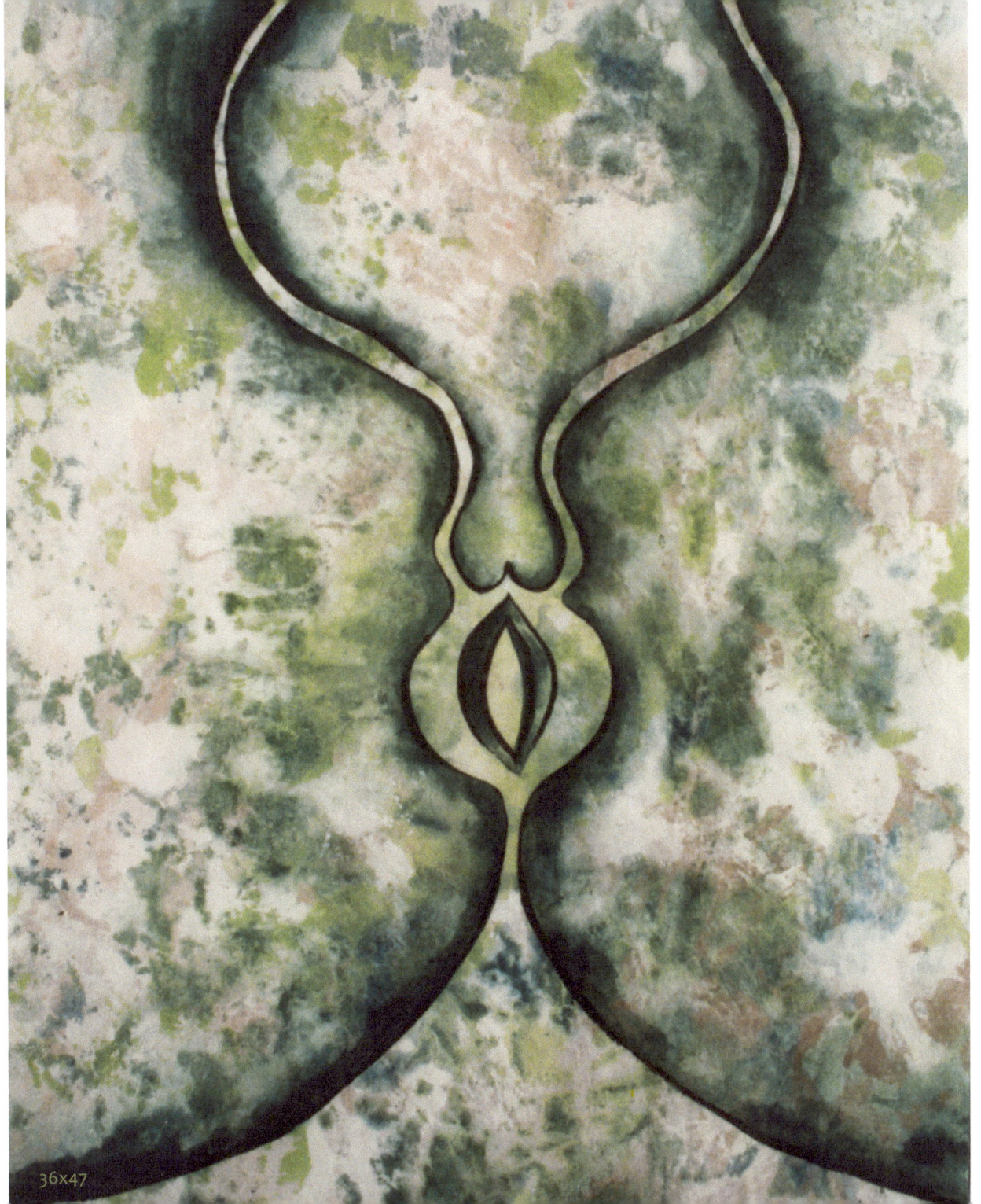

36x47

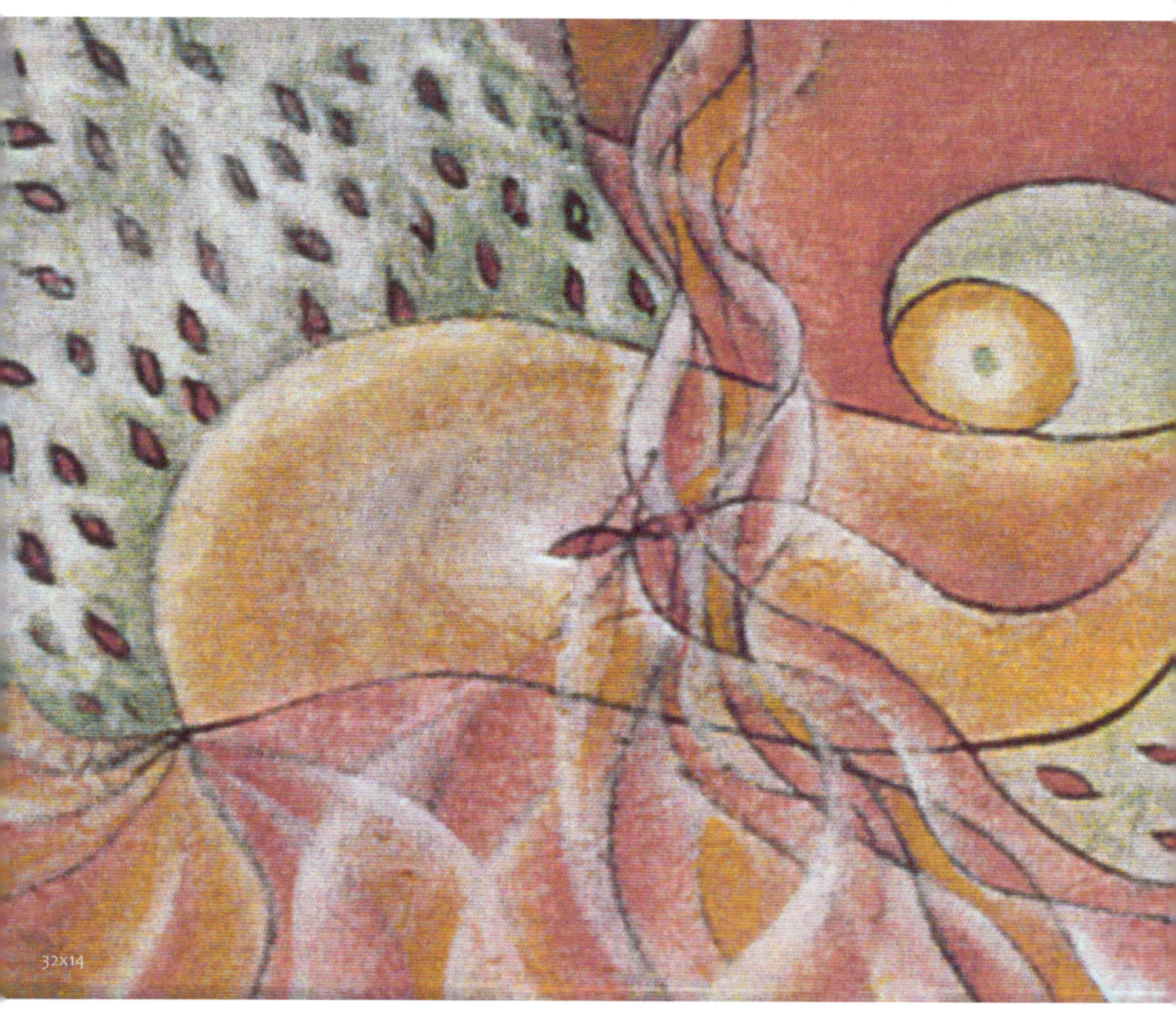

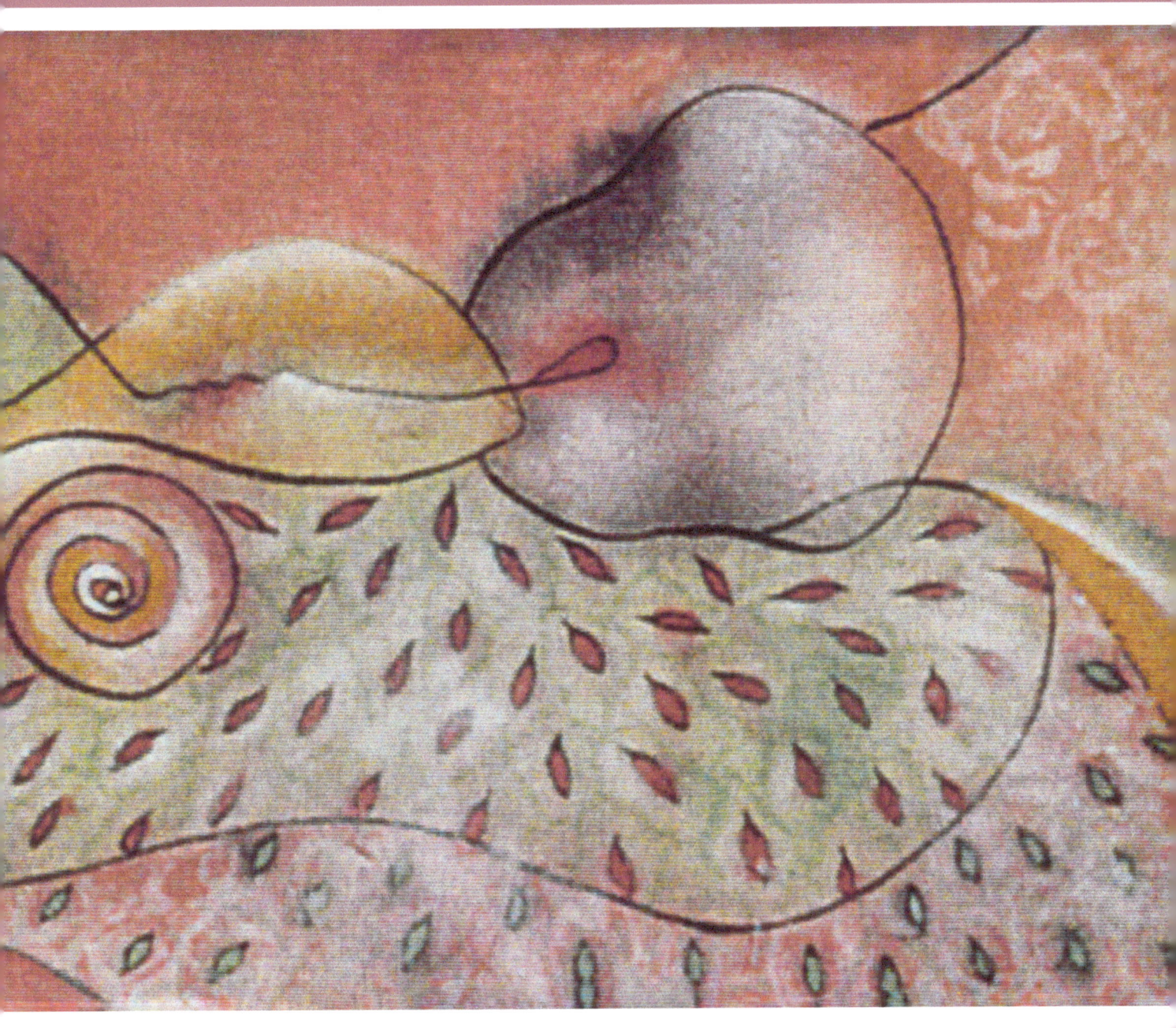

WATER COLOUR PAINTINGS

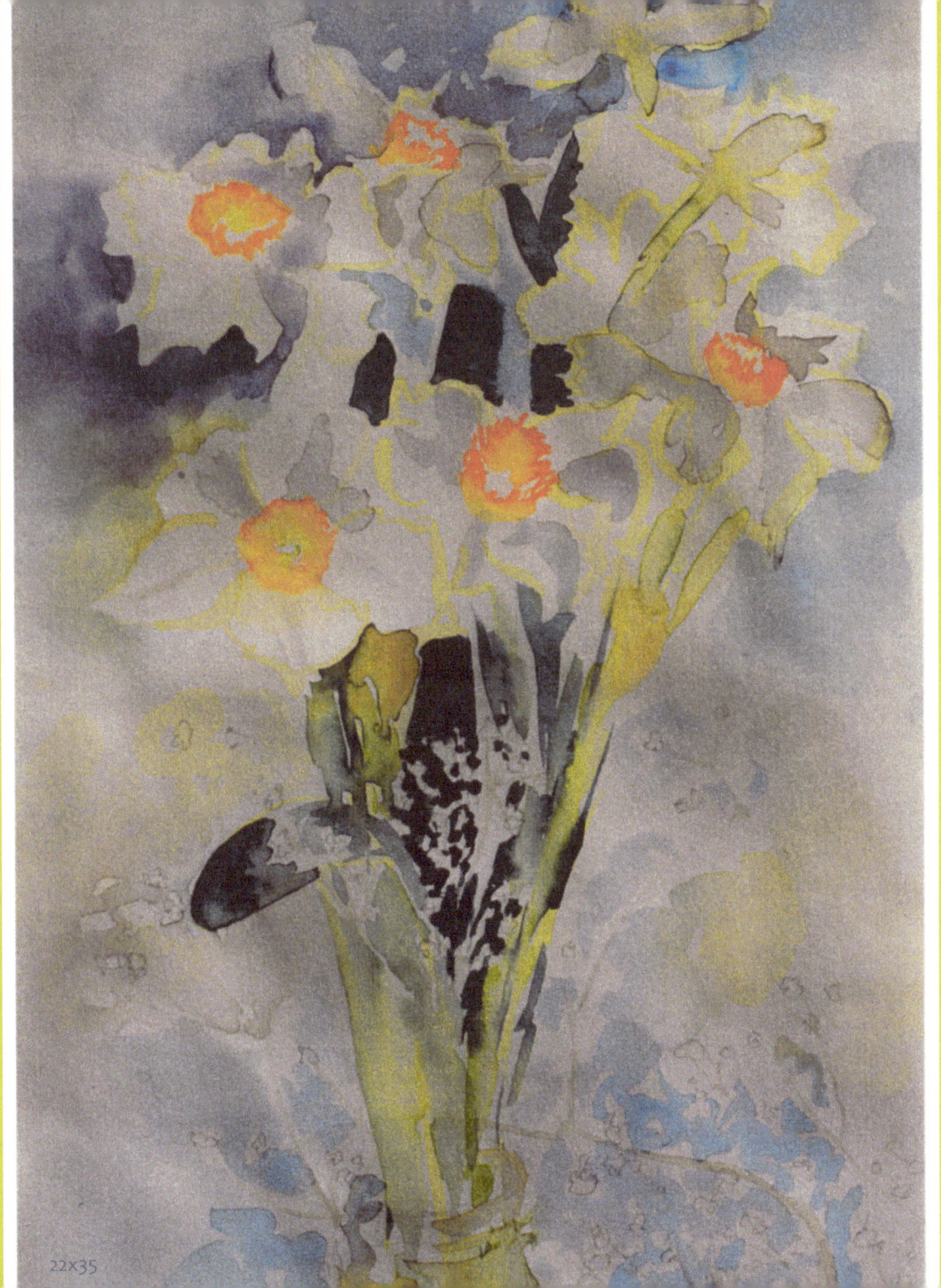

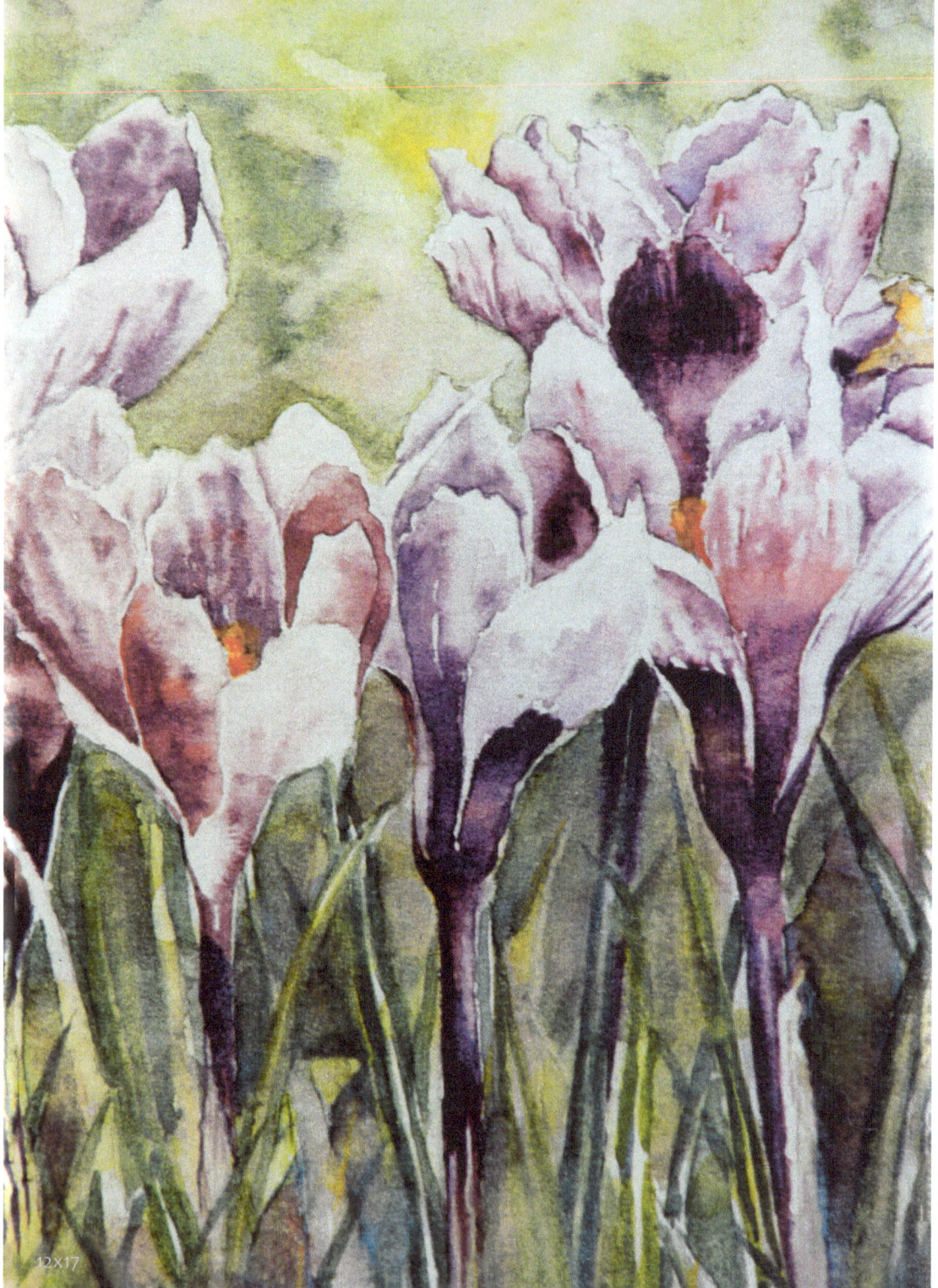

FLORA

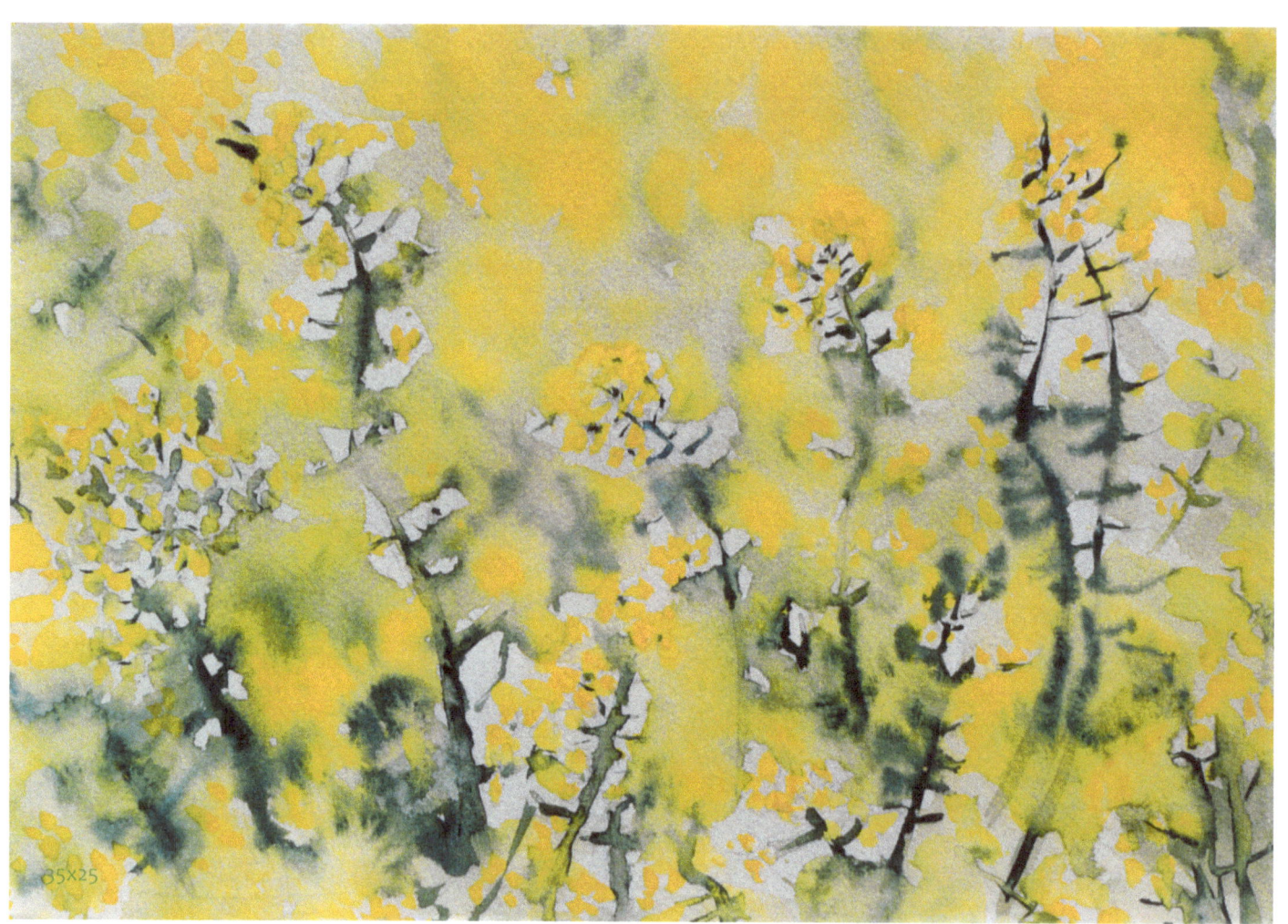

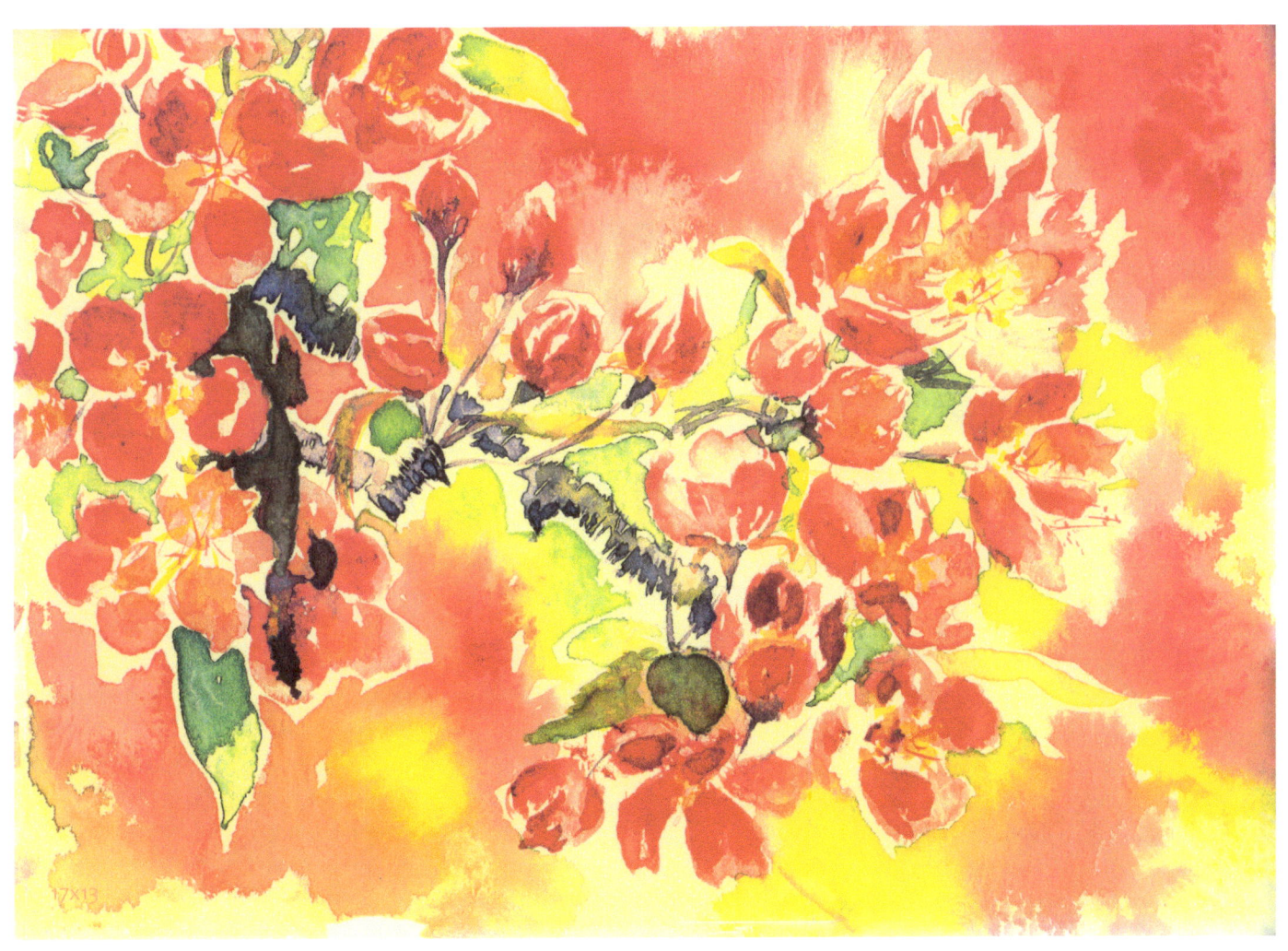

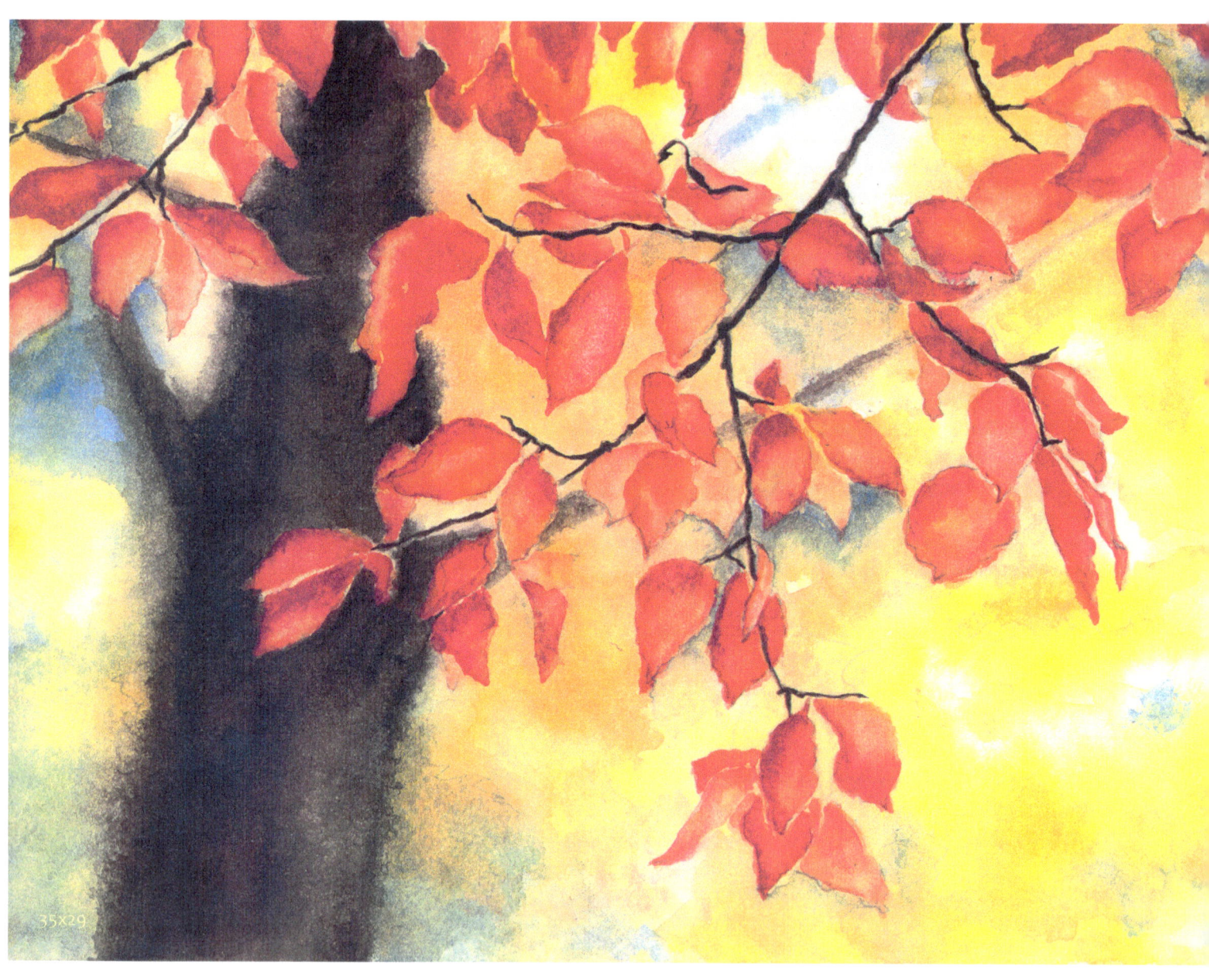

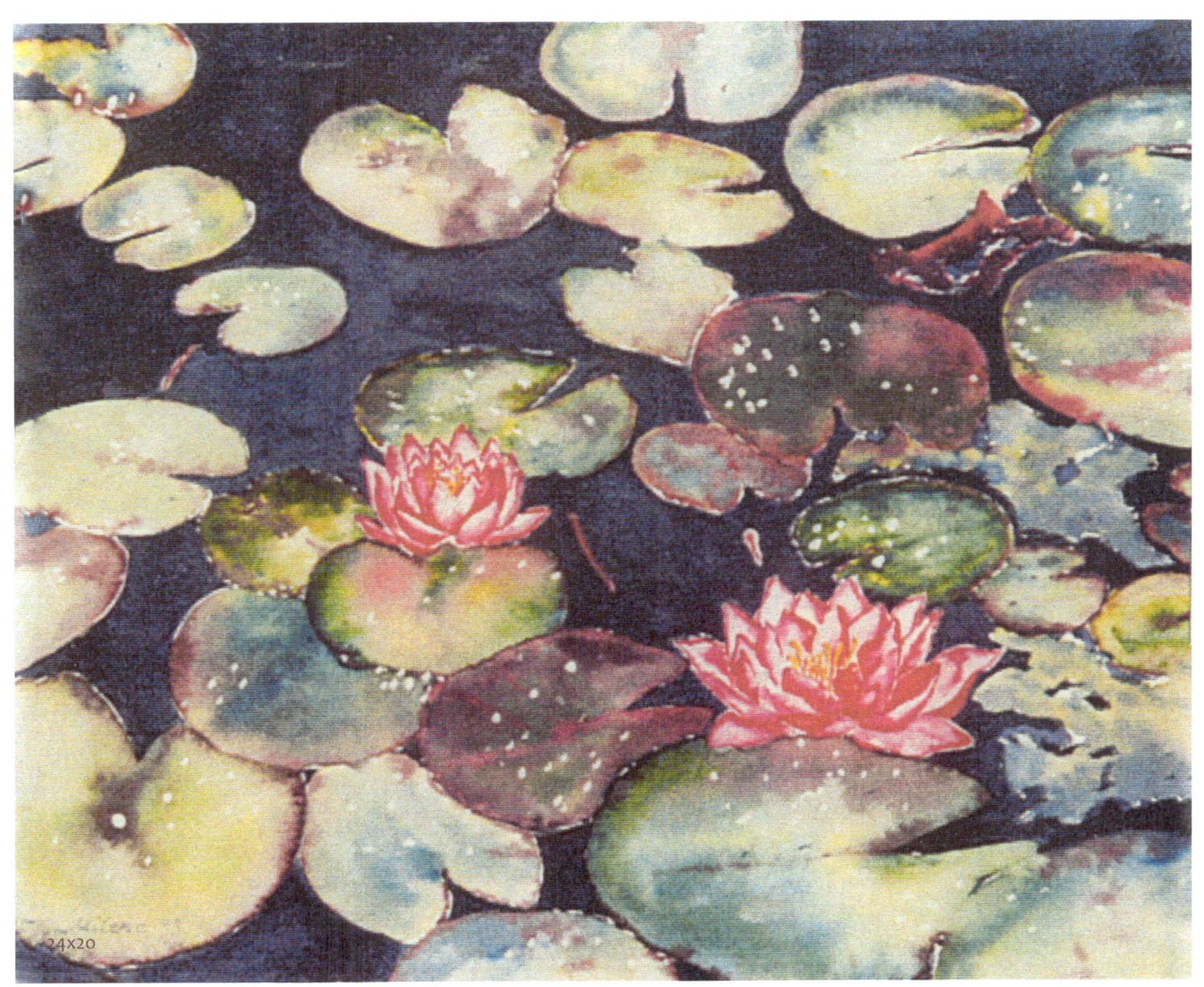

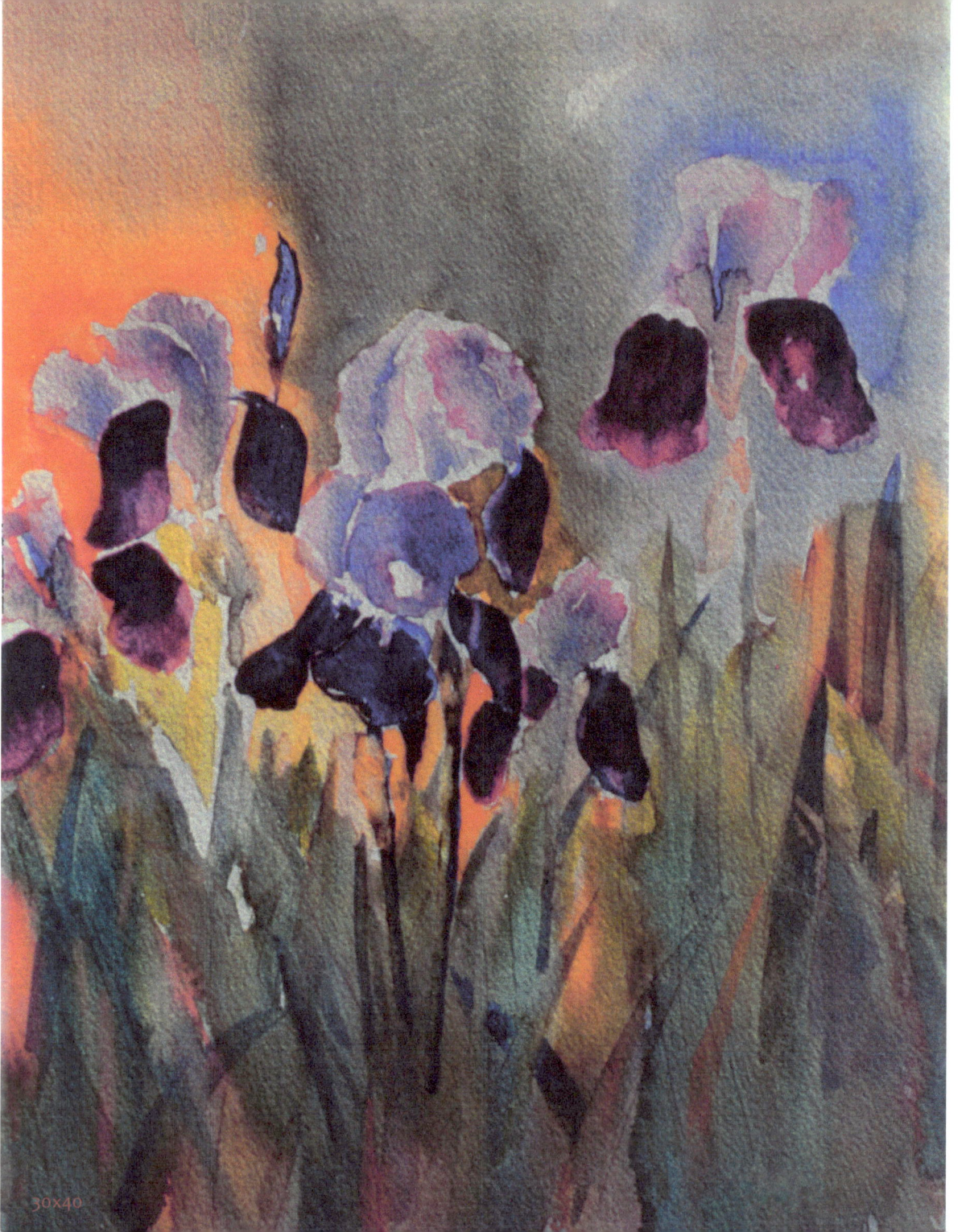

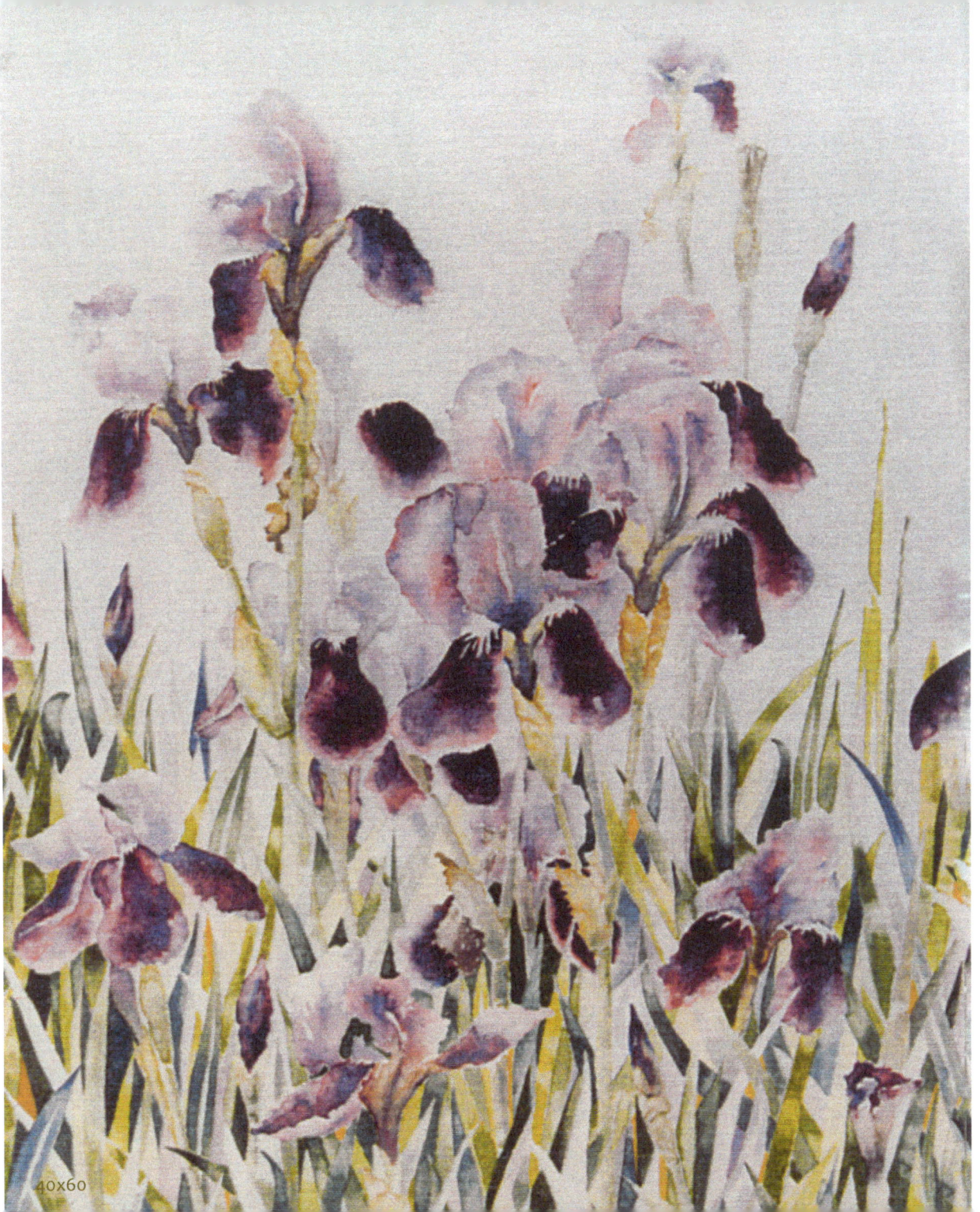

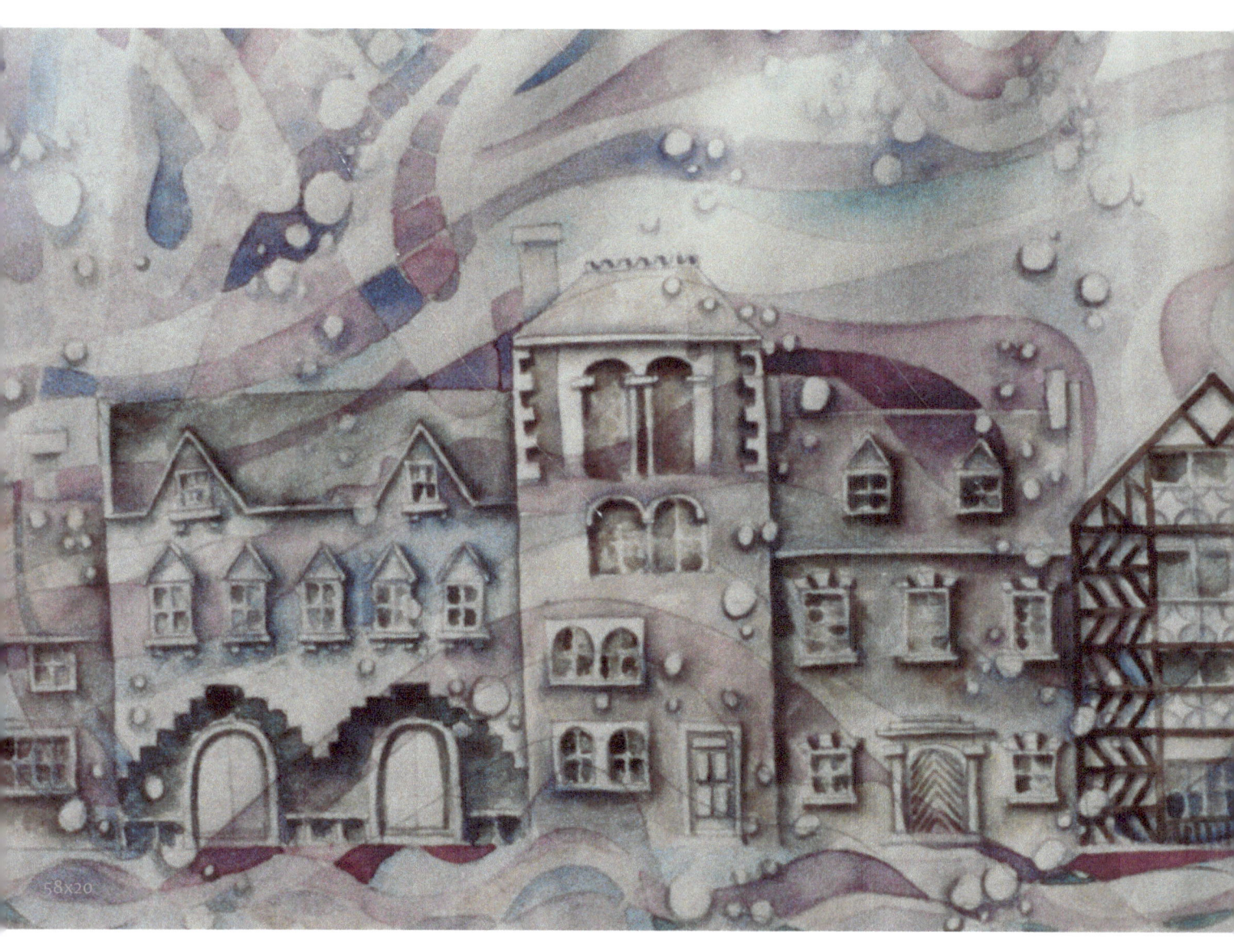

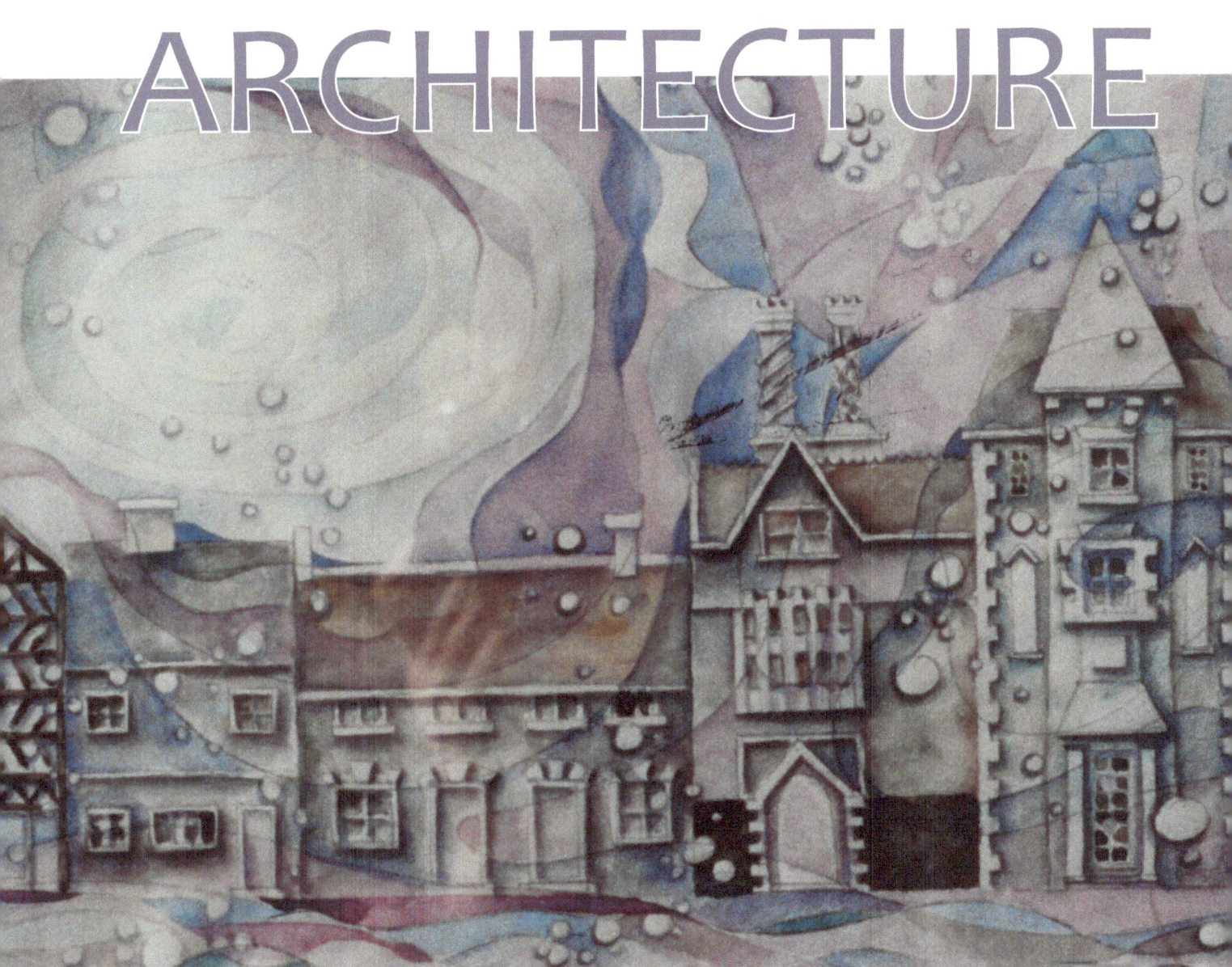

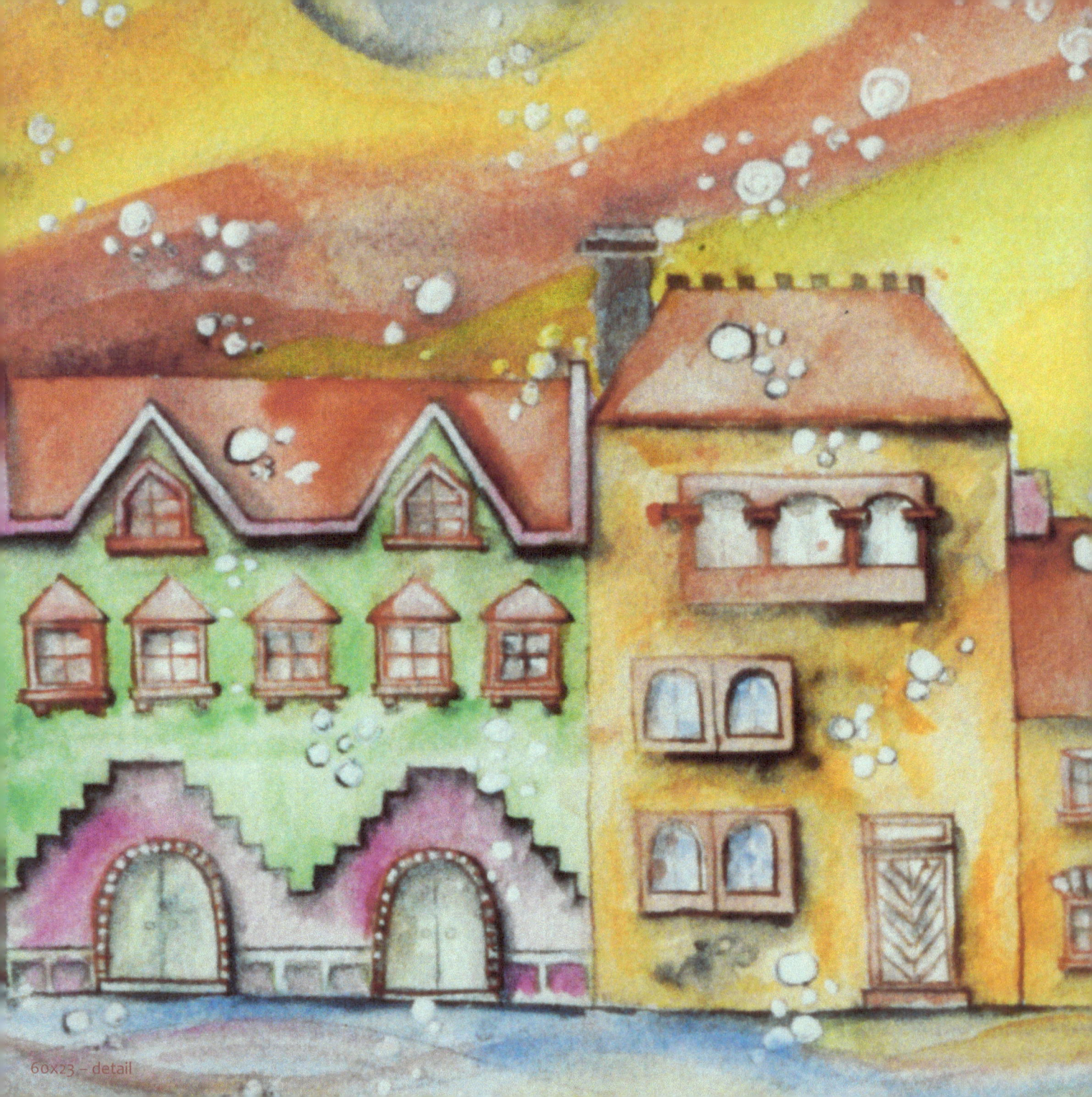

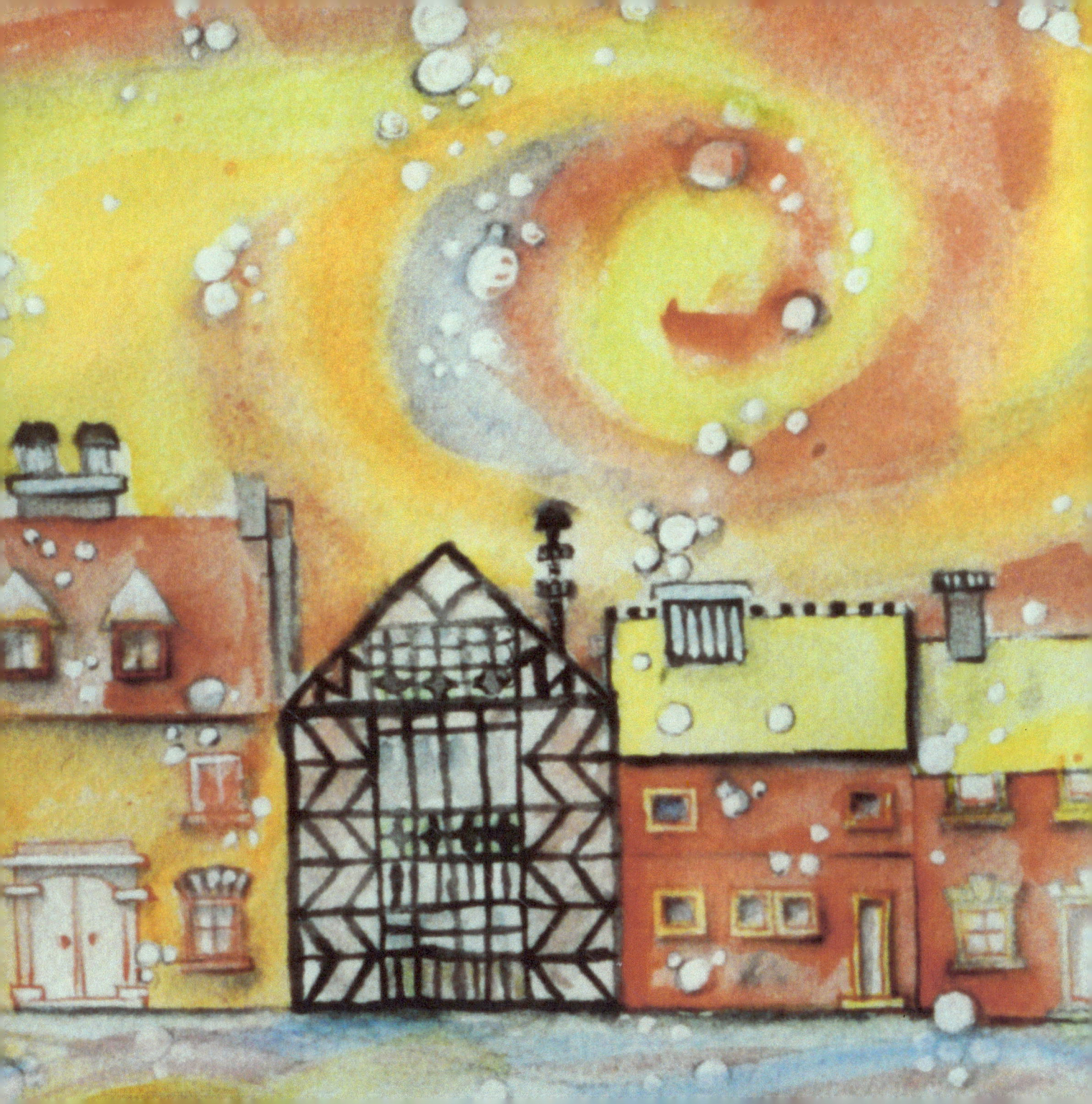

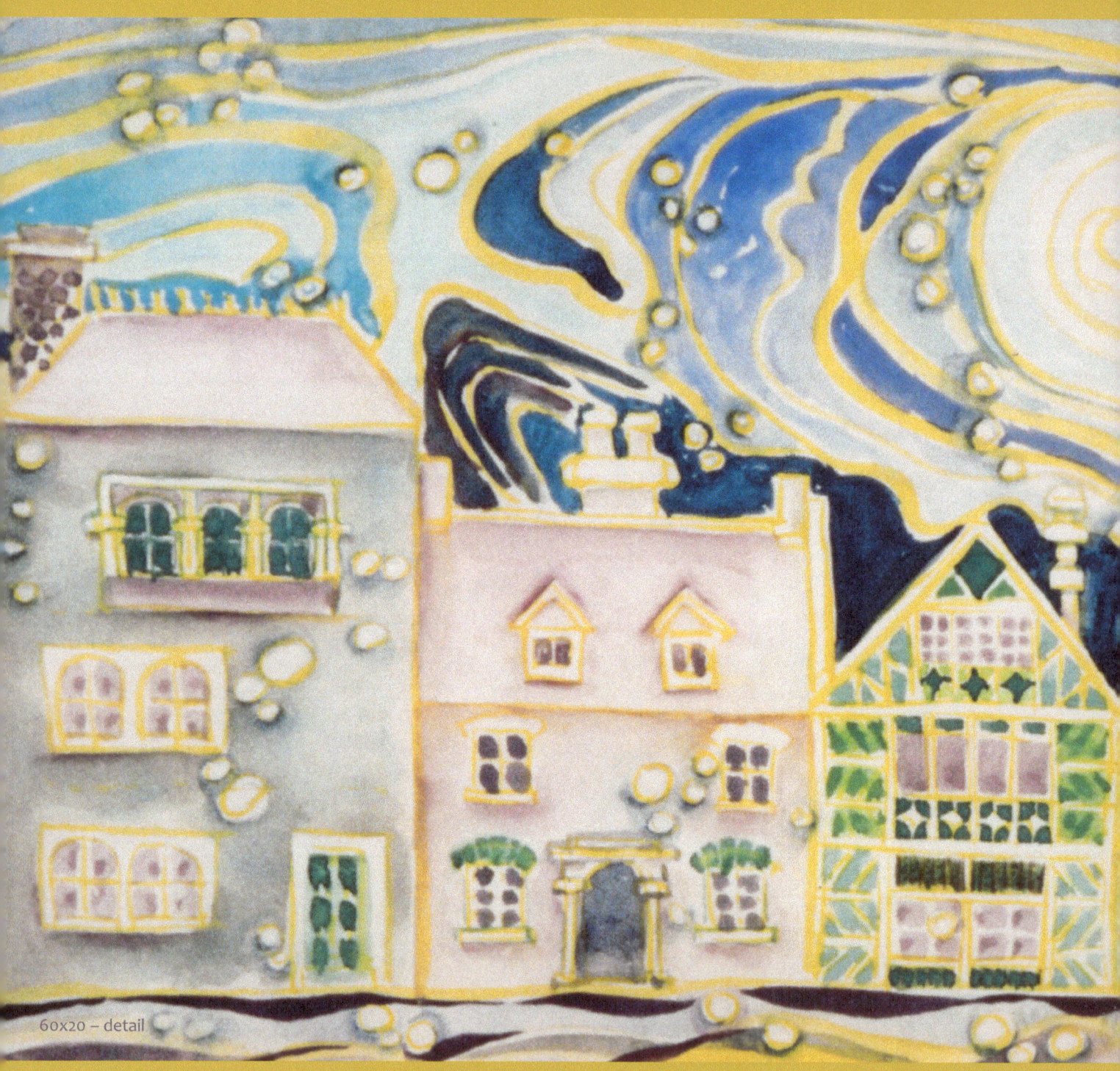

60x20 – detail

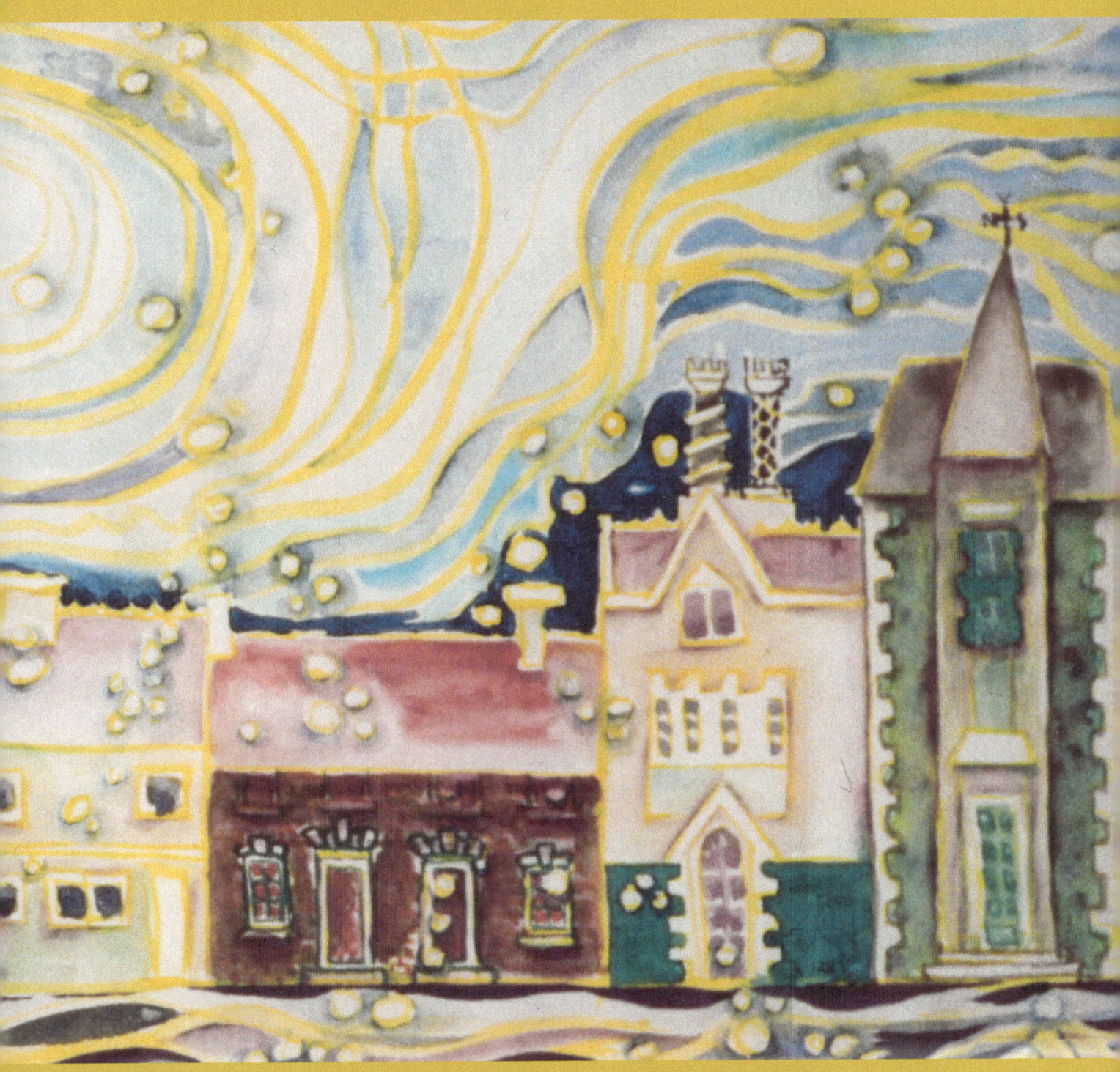

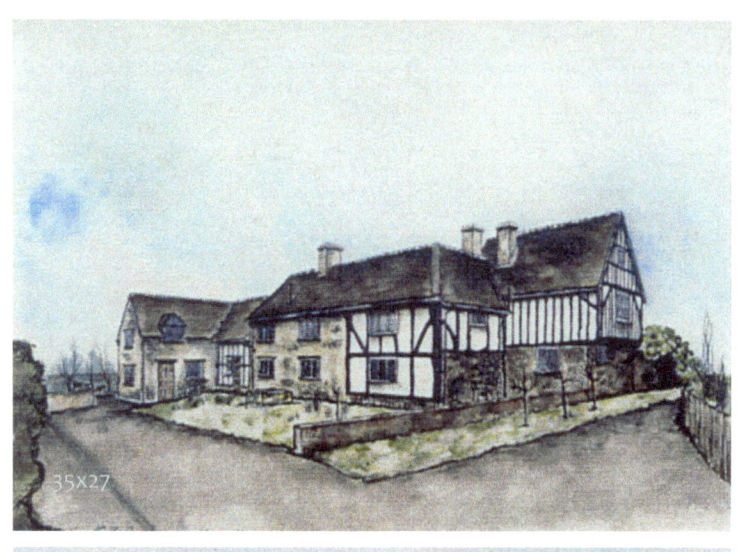

35x27

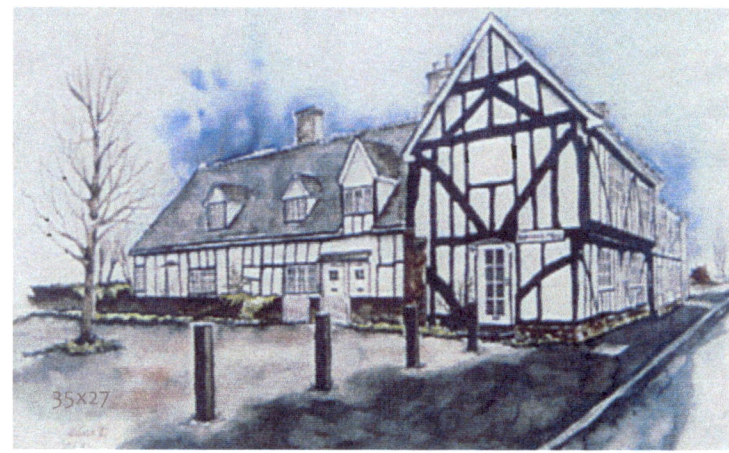

35x27

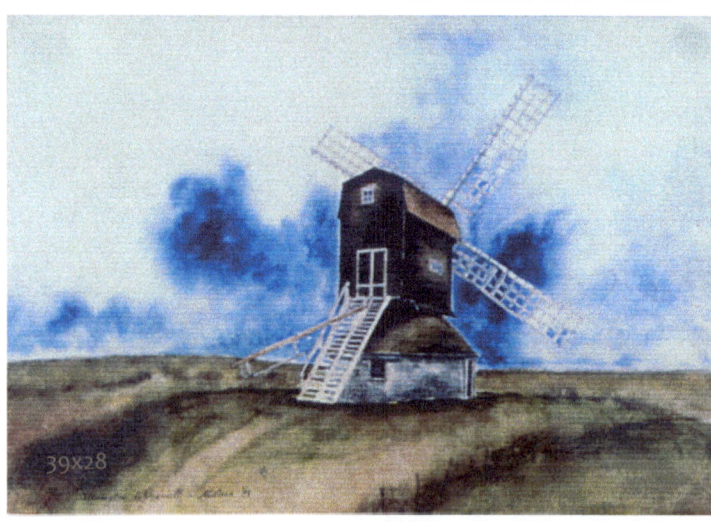

39x28

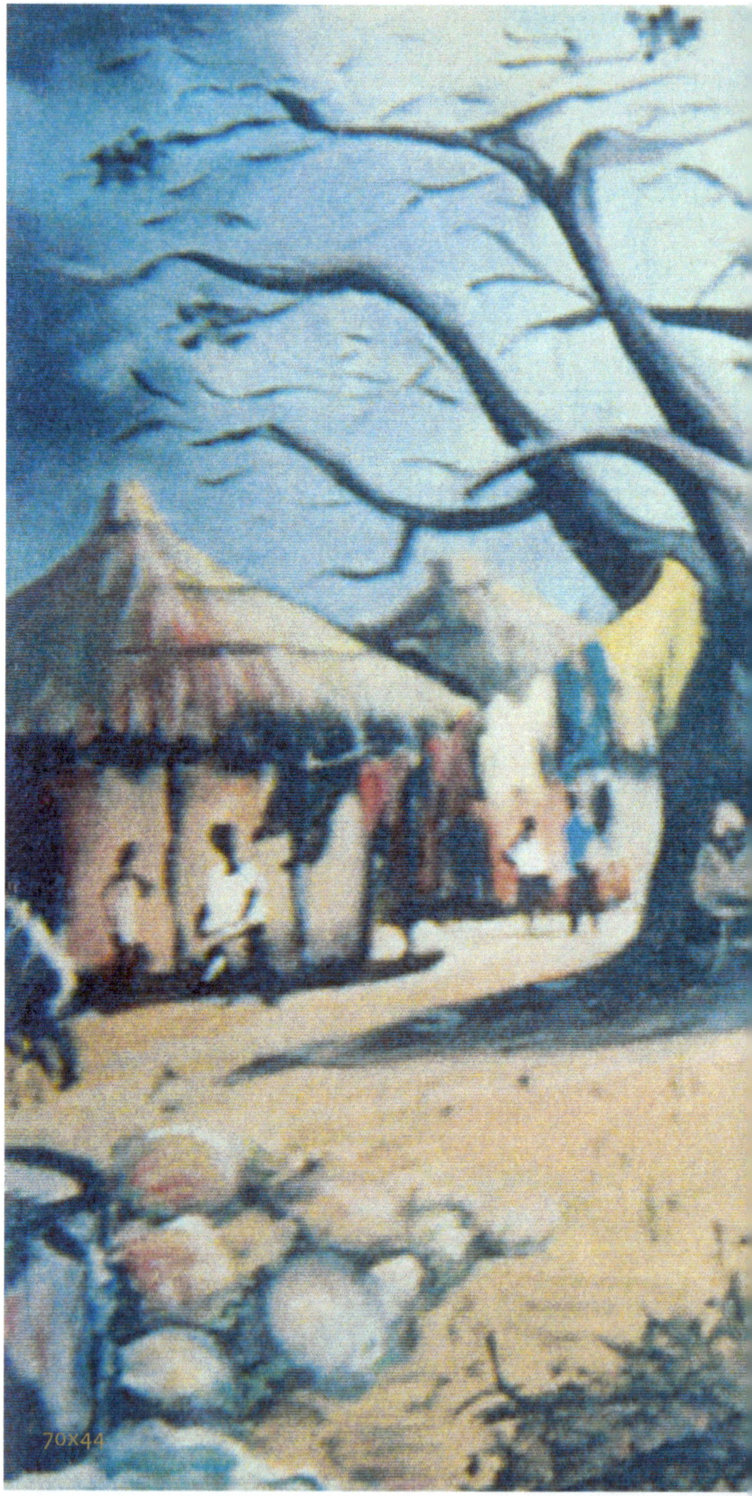

70x44

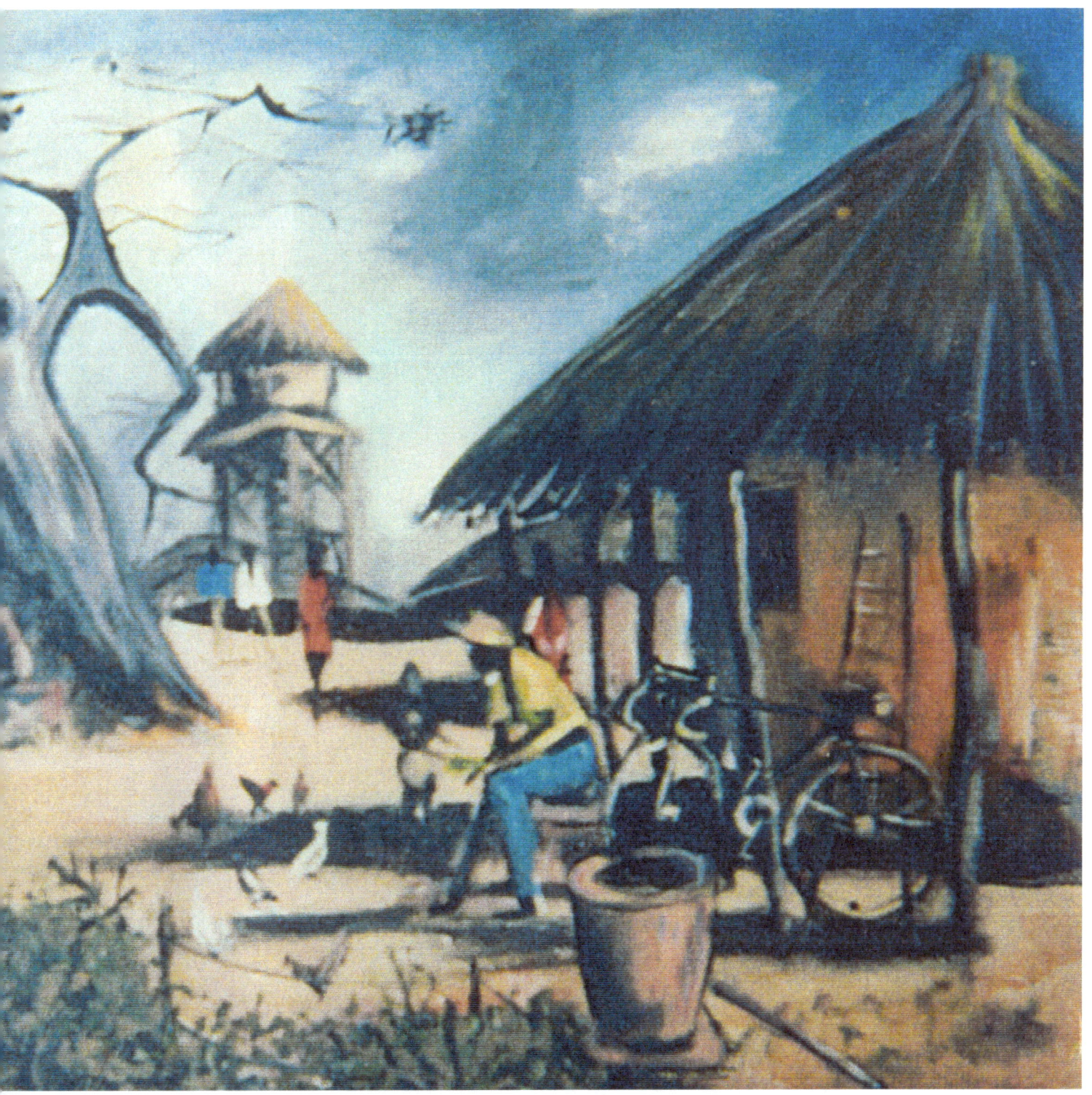

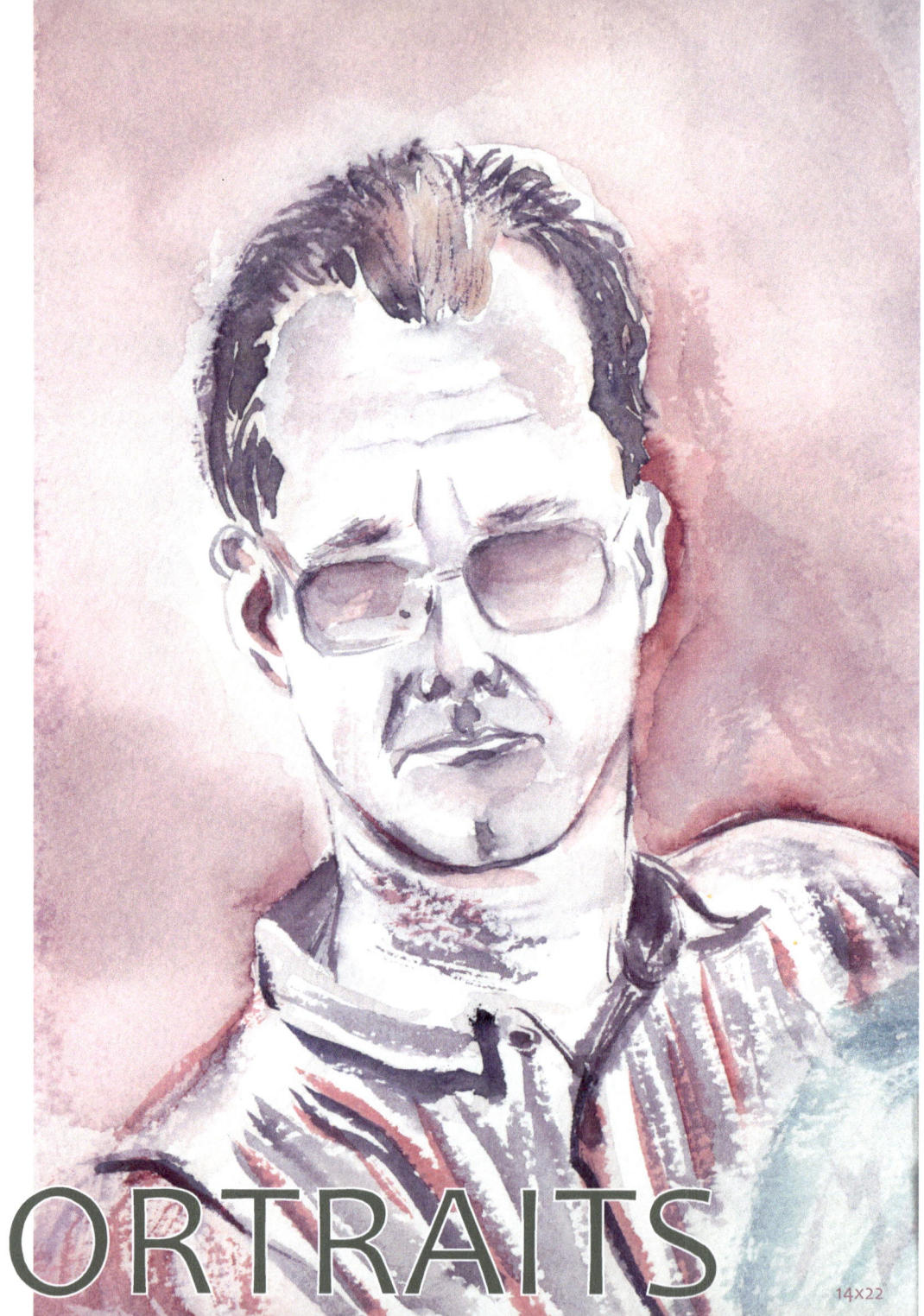

PORTRAITS

14x22

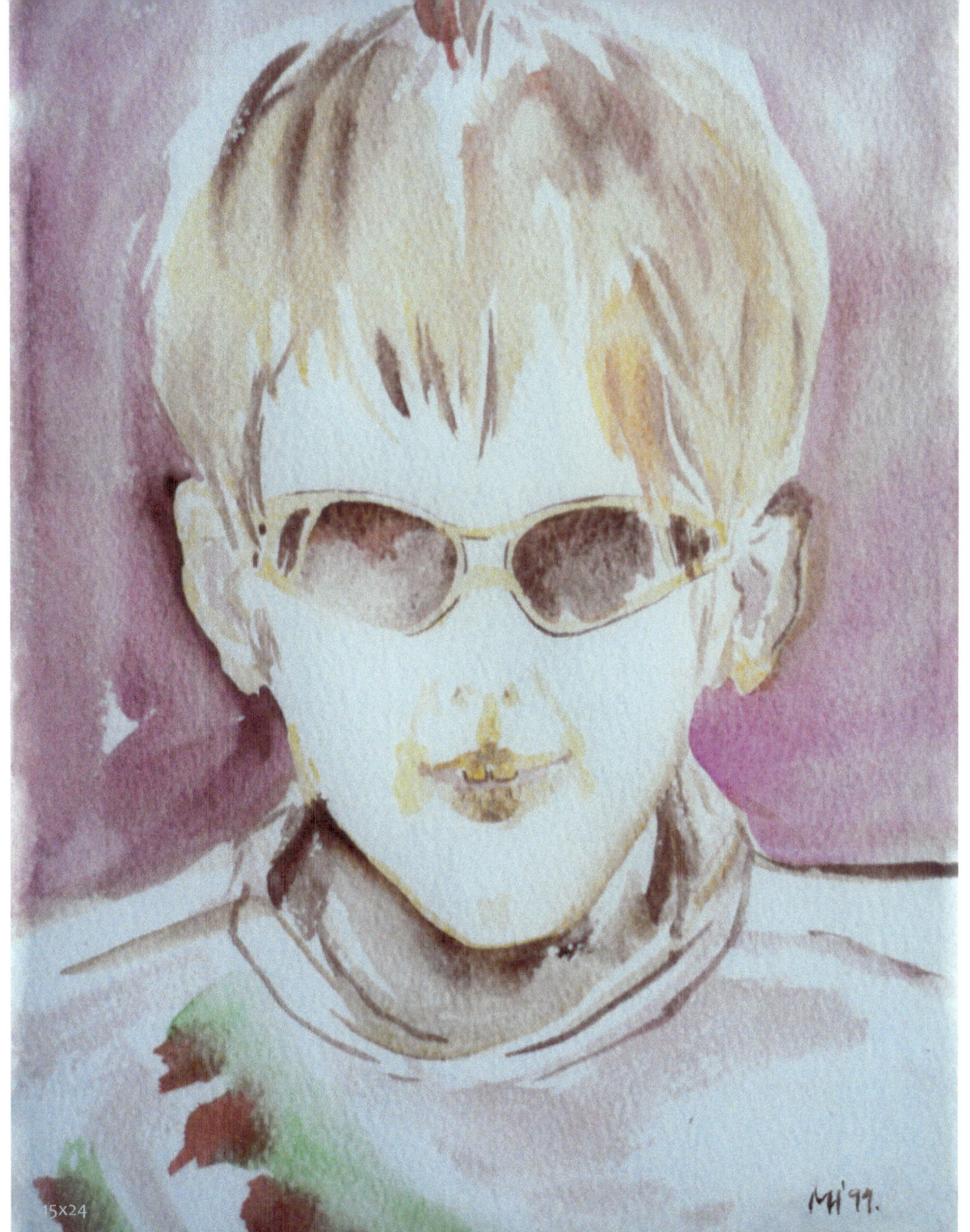

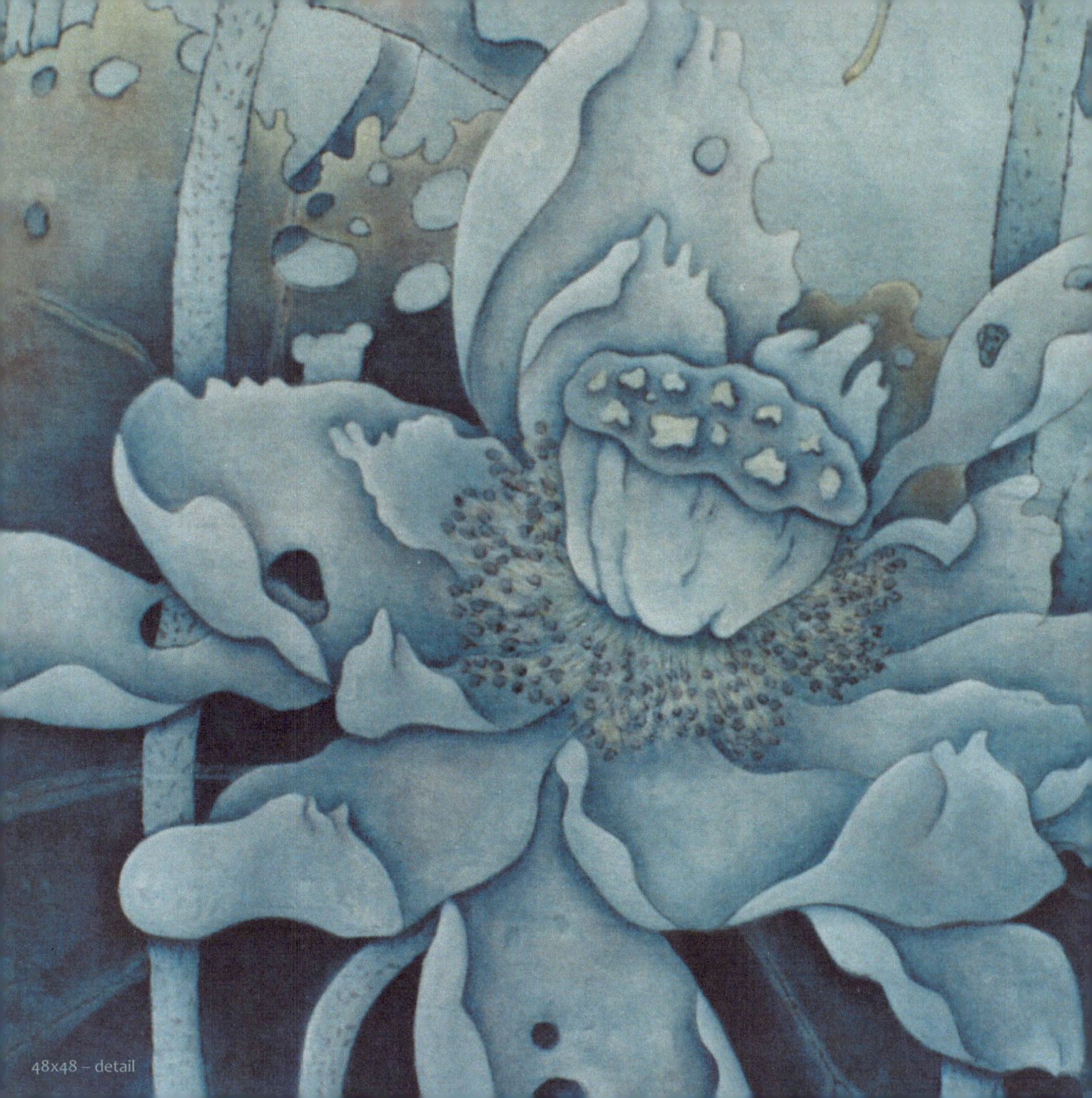
48x48 – detail

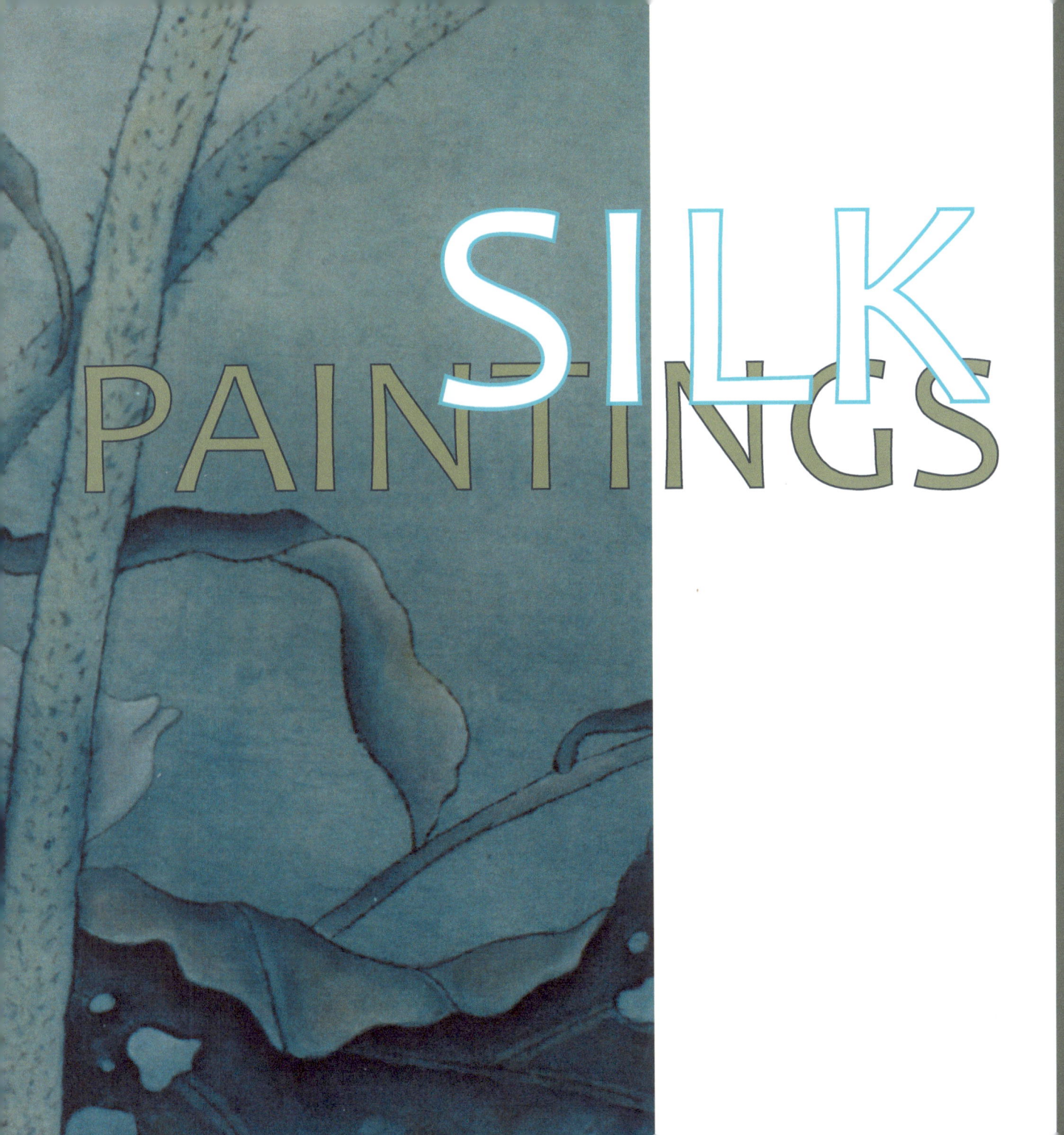

SILK PAINTINGS

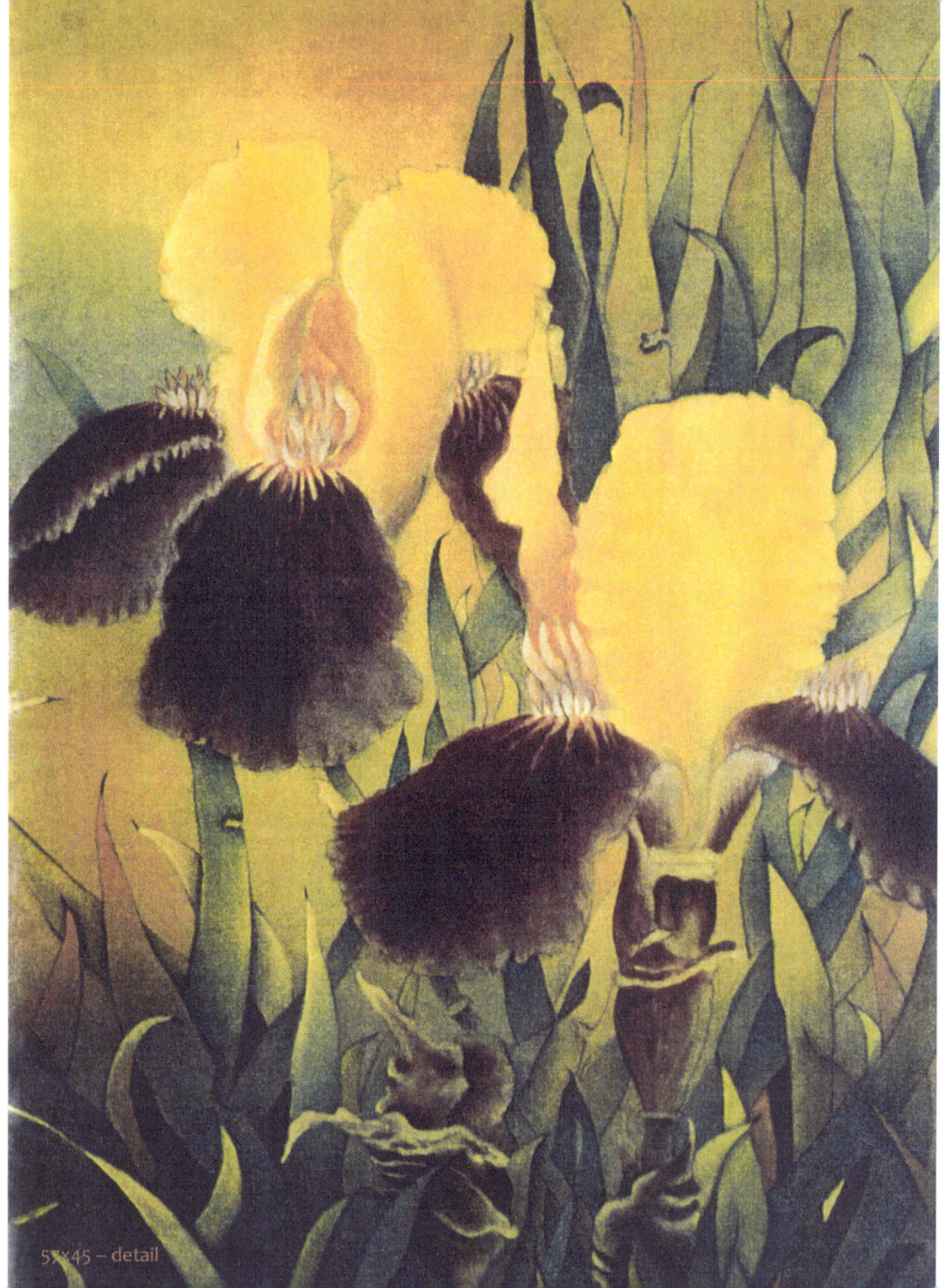

55x45 – detail

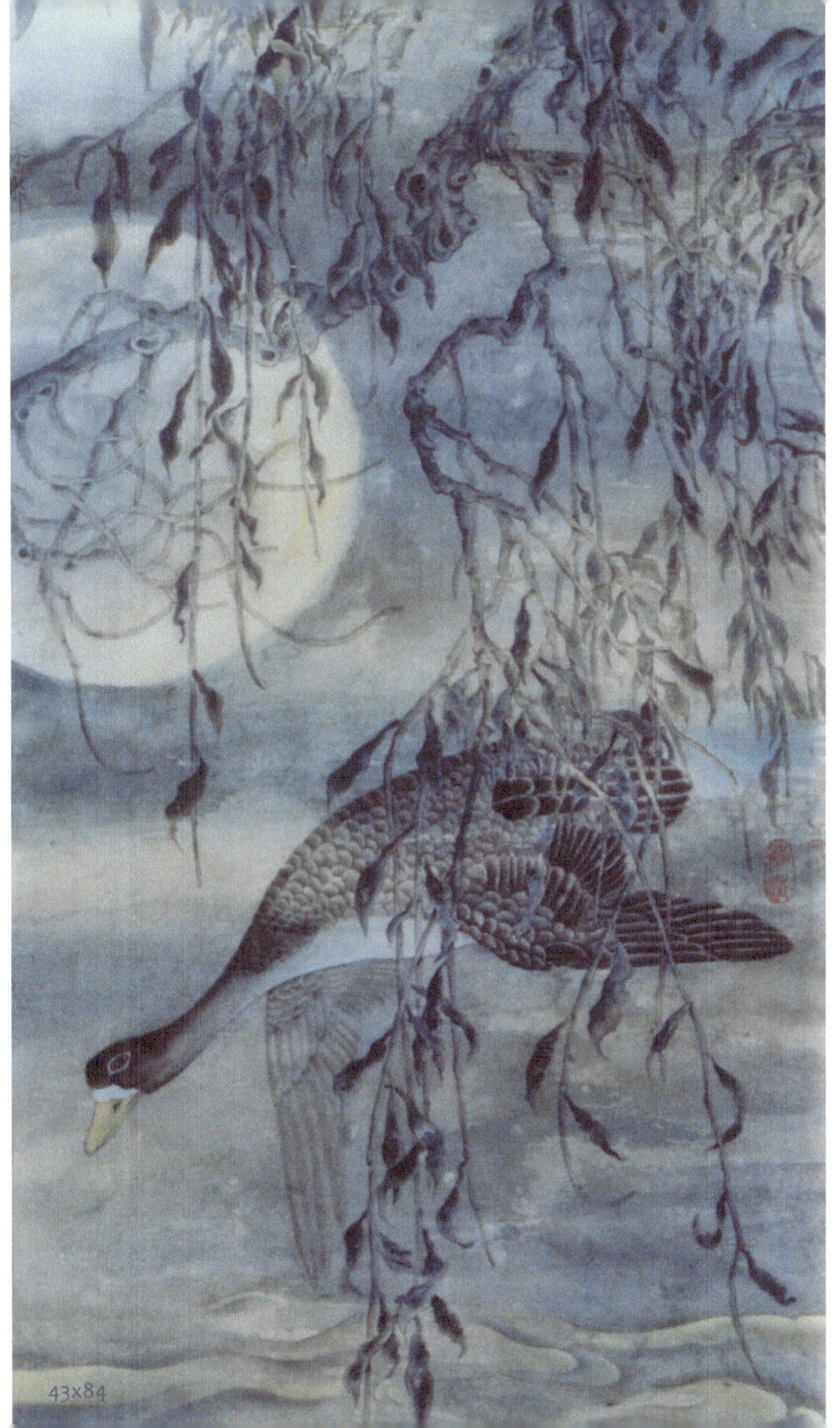